W9-BZD-042

Son
of the Living
God

GROWING IN RELATIONSHIP WITH CHRIST
AND WHO HE CALLS YOU TO BE

COURSE II
Who Is **Jesus Christ**?

Our Sunday Visitor

Curriculum Division

hs.osvcurriculum.com

The Subcommittee on the Catechism, United States Conference of Catholic Bishops, has found this catechetical text, *Son of the Living God*, copyright 2011, to be in conformity with the *Catechism of the Catholic Church*.

Nihil Obstat
Rev. Dr. S.R. Olds, S.Th.D.
Censor Librorum

Imprimatur
✠ Most Rev. John Noonan
Bishop of Orlando
December 23, 2010

The Imprimatur is an official declaration that a book or pamphlet is free of doctrinal or moral error. No implication is contained therein that anyone who granted the Imprimatur agrees with the contents, opinions, or statements expressed.

Copyright © 2011 by Our Sunday Visitor Curriculum Division, Our Sunday Visitor, Inc.

All rights reserved. No part of this publication may be reproduced or transmitted in any form or by any means, electronic or mechanical, including photocopy, recording, or any information storage and retrieval system, without permission in writing from the publisher.

Write:
Our Sunday Visitor Curriculum Division
Our Sunday Visitor, Inc.
200 Noll Plaza
Huntington, Indiana 46750

Our Sunday Visitor High School Series is a registered trademark of Our Sunday Visitor Curriculum Division, Our Sunday Visitor, 200 Noll Plaza, Huntington, Indiana 46750.

For permission to reprint copyrighted materials, grateful acknowledgement is made to the following sources:

Our Sunday Visitor Curriculum Division gratefully acknowledges the contributions of students from Saint Elizabeth Academy in St. Louis, Missouri; Archbishop Chapelle High School in Metairie, Louisiana; and Saint Pius X High School in Houston, Texas.

The Scripture quotations contained herein are from the *New Revised Standard Version Bible: Catholic Edition* copyright © 1993 and 1989 by the Division of Christian Education of the National Council of the Churches of Christ in the U.S.A. Used by permission. All rights reserved.

Excerpts from Vatican Council II documents are from "Vatican Council II: Constitutions, Decrees, Declarations" edited by Austin Flannery, O.P., copyright © 1996, Costello Publishing Company Inc., Northport, NY, and are used by permission of the publisher. All rights reserved.

Catechism excerpts are taken from the *Catechism of the Catholic Church*, second edition, for use in the United States of America, copyright © 1994 and 1997, United States Catholic Conference – Libreria Editrice Vaticana.

Prayer for the Virtue of Faith, Prayer to be Faithful in Serving God, Consecration to the Trinity, and the adaptation of the *Dialogued Prayer on the Beatitudes* were reprinted with permission of Catholic Online www.catholic.org

Excerpt from the song, *God Is* by Danielle Rose, copyright © 2001, Danielle Rose Skorich, published by World Library Publications, Franklin Park, IL. www.wlpmusic.com 800-566-6150. All rights reserved. Used by permission.

Excerpt from the English translation of Easter Preface II from *The Roman Missal* © 1973, International Committee on English in the Liturgy, Inc. (ICEL); excerpt from the English translation of "General Norms for the Liturgical Year and Calendar" from *Documents on the Liturgy, 1963-1979: Conciliar, Papal, and Curial Texts* © 1982, ICEL; excerpt from the English translation of *Rite of Christian Initiation of Adults* © 1985, ICEL; excerpt from the English translation of *Book of Blessings* © 1988, ICEL; excerpts from the English translation of *General Instruction of the Roman Missal* from *The Roman Missal* © 2010, ICEL. All rights reserved.

Excerpt from *Behold the Beauty of the Lord* by Henri J.M. Nouwen. Copyright © 1987, 2007 by Ave Maria Press, P.O. Box 248, Notre Dame, IN 46556, www.avemariapress.com. Used with permission of the publisher.

"The Red Bishop," by Flavio Rocha (January 30, 2009). © 2009 Commonweal Foundation, reprinted with permission. For subscriptions, www.commonwealmagazine.org

Son of the Living God Student Edition
Item Number: CU1513
ISBN: 978-0-15-902418-8

1 2 3 4 5 6 7 8 9 10   015016   15 14 13 12 11
Webcrafters, Inc., Madison, WI, USA; July 2011; Job# 92347

CONTENTS

CHAPTER 1
Having Faith .2

CHAPTER 2
God Comes to Save His People 30

CHAPTER 3
Understanding the Trinity 58

CHAPTER 4
Knowing Jesus 84

CHAPTER 5
Understanding Ourselves 112

CHAPTER 6
Following His Way 140

CHAPTER 7
Jesus Continues His Mission 166

CHAPTER 8
Jesus with Us Always 196

REFERENCE SECTION 224
Glossary 244
Index 247

Scripture vi
Primary Sources vii
Features x

CHAPTER 1

Having Faith 2

SECTION **1** Believing and Trusting 5
SECTION **2** Jesus Sees Our Faith 10
SECTION **3** Faith Is a Relationship 16
SECTION **4** Faith More than Conviction 20
Chapter Review 28

CHAPTER 2

God Comes to Save His People 30

SECTION **1** The Turning Point 33
SECTION **2** Mystery of the Incarnation 39
SECTION **3** Jesus Shows Us the Way 44
SECTION **4** The Trinity Is Revealed 50
Chapter Review 56

CHAPTER 3

Understanding the Trinity 58

SECTION **1** God the Father 61
SECTION **2** God the Son 67
SECTION **3** God the Holy Spirit 71
SECTION **4** The Trinity's Response to Evil 76
Chapter Review 82

CHAPTER 4

Knowing Jesus 84

SECTION **1** Jesus of Nazareth 87
SECTION **2** A Lifetime of Revelation 94
SECTION **3** True God and True Man 99
SECTION **4** Called to Follow 104
Chapter Review 110

CHAPTER 5

Understanding Ourselves 112

SECTION **1** Created in God's Image 115
SECTION **2** Redeemed in Christ 122
SECTION **3** Visions of the Human Person 126
SECTION **4** The New Life of Baptism 133
Chapter Review 138

CHAPTER 6

Following His Way 140

SECTION **1** A World Without Road Signs. 143

SECTION **2** Jesus Proclaims the Law of Love 147

SECTION **3** How to Enter the Kingdom 153

SECTION **4** The Good Shepherd. 157

Chapter Review 164

CHAPTER 7

Jesus Continues His Mission 166

SECTION **1** The Church of Jesus 169

SECTION **2** Handing on Christ's Message 174

SECTION **3** The Communion of Saints. 181

SECTION **4** The Unique Role of Mary 188

Chapter Review 194

CHAPTER 8

Jesus with Us Always 196

SECTION **1** I Will Be There. 199

SECTION **2** Jesus: Example and Teacher of Prayer 202

SECTION **3** Prayer In the Era of the Church 208

SECTION **4** Death Is Transformed. 213

Chapter Review 222

REFERENCE SECTION

The Body of Christ 224

Ecumenical Councils 228

Catholic Prayers and Practices 231

Voices of Tradition 237

Glossary 244

Index 247

End Notes 251

Photo Credits 252

SCRIPTURE

OLD TESTAMENT

Genesis 1:2 71
Genesis 1:16 61
Genesis 1:26 128
Genesis 1:27 12
Genesis 1:28 127
Genesis 1:31 52
Genesis 2:23 12

Exodus 3:14 199

Leviticus 19:18. 150

Deuteronomy 30:15-16, 19 145

Job 12:7-10 62

Psalm 8:4. 62
Psalm 68:5. 62
Psalm 68:6. 62
Psalm 23:1. 157

Sirach 6:14-17 8

Isaiah 49:15 66
Isaiah 61:1. 45

NEW TESTAMENT

Matthew 1:22-23 35
Matthew 5:16. 64
Matthew 5:3. . . . . .6, 179
Matthew 6:5. 202
Matthew 6:7. 211
Matthew 6:33 156
Matthew 7:2. 152
Matthew 7:12. . . . . .68, 146
Matthew 7:13. 152
Matthew 8:16. 11
Matthew 11:25-26 48
Matthew 13:58. 88
Matthew 16:13-17 42
Matthew 18:1. 44
Matthew 19:22. 153
Matthew 20:28. 91
Matthew 21:31-32 20
Matthew 23:27 203

Matthew 25:35-36 97
Matthew 27:46 134
Matthew 28:10 134
Matthew 28:19-20a 169
Matthew 28:19-20 45
Matthew 28:20 37

Mark 5:30 10
Mark 5:34 . . . . .5, 10, 23
Mark 9:22 14
Mark 9:23-24 14
Mark 9:24 24
Mark 10:47 14
Mark 10:52 14
Mark 12:29-31 147

Luke 1:35. 51
Luke 1:46-48 191
Luke 4:18 174
Luke 5:32 49
Luke 7:50 15
Luke 9:23 159
Luke 9:24 159
Luke 9:35 51
Luke 9:58 155
Luke 11:4-5 204
Luke 11:9 203
Luke 12:20-21 213
Luke 17:21 204
Luke 18:18 92
Luke 23:34 134
Luke 23:43 134
Luke 23:46 134
Luke 24:36 134

John 1:1-3a 33
John 1:18. 7
John 1:20. 200
John 2:5. 191
John 3:8. 74
John 4:26. 200
John 6:48. 200
John 6:51. 200
John 8:58. 200
John 11:25. 215

John 13:35. . . . . .89, 150, 185
John 14:6. 19
John 14:9. 7
John 15:9-11 159
John 15:12. . . . . .146, 147
John 17:20-21 187
John 18:17. 200
John 18:18-25 200
John 18:35. 200
John 20:19. 134

Acts 1:8 169
Acts 1:11 170
Acts 1:14 . . . . .190, 210
Acts 2:1 190
Acts 8:39 107
Acts 17:27-28 107

Romans 8:35, 37 80

1 Corinthians 2:9 216
1 Corinthians 6:19-20 . . . . .12, 52,
184, 206
1 Corinthians 12:3 7
1 Corinthians 13:12 134

2 Corinthians 4:5, 7 24
2 Corinthians 5:17-18 116

Ephesians 4:5. 64

Philippians 2:7-8 90
Philippians 3:8-9 155
Philippians 4:4-7 159

Colossians 1:13-14 70

1 Thessalonians 5:17 212

1 Timothy 2:3-4 64

Hebrews 11:1 5
Hebrews 11:39 7
Hebrews 12:1-2 26

1 John 1:1-2. 17

Revelation 1:8. . . . . .38, 206
Revelation 5:13 217
Revelation 21:1–2, 5. 116

PRIMARY SOURCES

CHAPTER 1

Catechism of the Catholic Church, 150 6

Dorothy Day 8

Pope John Paul II, *Theology of the Body*, 9.3 12

Catechism of the Catholic Church, 1878 13

Catechism of the Catholic Church, 2840 13

Sacrosanctum Concilium, "Constitution on the Sacred
   Liturgy," December 4, 1963, 10. 17

Encyclopedia of Catholicism 17

Sacrosanctum Concilium, "Constitution on the Sacred
   Liturgy," December 4, 1963. 18

Pope Paul VI, *Evangelii Nuntiandi*, "On the Evangelization in
   the Modern World," December 8, 1975, paragraph 21 . . . 18

Catechism of the Catholic Church, 787 19

Father Walter Ciszek, SJ. 20

Pope Benedict XVI, World Youth Day Message, 2008 21

Father Walter Ciszek, SJ, *With God in Russia* 22, 23

Catechism of the Catholic Church, 180 24

Catechism of the Catholic Church, 181 26

CHAPTER 2

African American Spiritual 33

Catechism of the Catholic Church, Glossary 34

Catechism of the Catholic Church, 2709 37

Catechism of the Catholic Church, 732 38

Maria Boulding 39

Catechism of the Catholic Church, 460 40

Catechism of the Catholic Church, 459 40

Vatican II, *Gaudium et Spes*, "Joy and Hope,"
   December 7, 1965, Article 22 41

Catholic Campaign Against Global Poverty 45

Mary Ann Holtz. 46, 47

Father Alfred McBride, O. Praem, *Truth for Your Mind
   Love for Your Heart* 48

Danielle Rose, "God Is" 50

Catechism of the Catholic Church, 237 50

Saint Thomas Aquinas, *Summa Theologica*, Vol. 1 51

Nicene Creed 51

Welcome and Justice for Persons with Disabilities,
   http://www.usccb.org/doctrine/disabilities.shtml 52

Catechism of the Catholic Church, 222 53

CHAPTER 3

Catechism of the Catholic Church, 320 61

Catechism of the Catholic Church, 292 61

Chris Muglia, "Our God Is Here" 61

Catechism of the Catholic Church, 316 62

Henri J.M. Nouwen, "The Icon of the Holy Trinity: Living
   in the House of Love," *Behold the Beauty of the Lord:
   Praying with Icons*. 63

Pope Benedict XVI, *Angelus*, 2005 65

Catechism of the Catholic Church, 242 67

Catechism of the Catholic Church, 253 67

U.S. Conference of Catholic Bishops (USCCB),
   Brothers and Sisters to Us 68

John Shea, Los Angeles Religious Education Congress,
   2007 71

Catechism of the Catholic Church, 689 72

C.S. Lewis 73

C.S. Lewis, *The Problem of Pain* 76

Catechism of the Catholic Church, 311 76

Catechism of the Catholic Church, 310 77

Trinity Benedictine website. .78

CHAPTER 4

Father Thomas à Kempis, *The Imitation of Christ*. 87

Father Raniero Cantalamessa. 90

Catechism of the Catholic Church, 561 94

Father Thomas à Kempis, *The Imitation of Christ*, Book 1,
    Chapter 1. 95

Father Thomas à Kempis, *The Imitation of Christ*, Book 2,
    Chapter 8. 95

Dr. Martin Luther King, Jr. 96

Catechism of the Catholic Church, 561 96

Catechism of the Catholic Church, Glossary 99

J. Michael Walker,
    All the Saints of the City of the Angels. 100, 101

Liturgy of the Hours, Antiphon I of Evening Prayer for
    January 1. 102

CHAPTER 5

Saint Irenaeus of Lyon, *Against Heresies* 115

Catechism of the Catholic Church, 36 118

Catechism of the Catholic Church, 37 118

Saint Augustine, *Confessions* 119

Thomas Merton, *The Seven Storey Mountain* 119

Catechism of the Catholic Church, 1987 122

General Norms for the Liturgical Year and the Calendar,
    1969, Article 18. 124

Anne Frank, *The Diary of a Young Girl*, July 15, 1944. . . .126

Pope John Paul II, *Crossing the Threshold of Hope*,
    1994. 126

Vatican II, *Gaudium et Spes*, "Joy and Hope,"
    December 7, 1965 126

John Donne, *Devotions Upon Emergent Occasions, XVII*,
    1624. 126

USCCB, *Global Climate Change: A Plea for Dialogue,
    Prudence, and the Common Good*, June 15, 2001 127

Pope Benedict XVI, *The Human Person, the Heart of
    Peace*, World Day of Peace, January 1, 2007, para. 8 . . .127

Pope John Paul II, August 2002 128

Pope John Paul II, Angelus, August 25, 2002 128

Catechism of the Catholic Church, 1703 128

Blaise Pascal, *Pensées*. 129

Flannery O'Connor, *Flannery O'Connor: The Complete
    Stories*, 1979. . . . . .130, 131

RCIA, 230 133

Easter Preface II 134

CHAPTER 6

Saint Teresa of Ávila 144

Catechism of the Catholic Church, Second Edition 145

Catechism of the Catholic Church, 1967 147

Jürgen Moltmann 148

"A Common Word Between Us and You," Open Letter
    from the Royal Aal al-Bayt Institute for Islamic
    Thought, October 13, 2007 154

Catholic Volunteers in Florida (CVIF) 158

Sofia Cavalletti, *The Religious Potential
    of the Child* 160, 161

CHAPTER 7

Catechism of the Catholic Church, 852 170

Pope Benedict XVI, *Deus Caritas Est*, "God Is Love,"
   December 25, 2005, 20 170

Pope John Paul II, *Redemptoris Missio*, "Mission of the
   Redeemer," December 7, 1990, 60 174

Vatican II, *Lumen Gentium*, the "Dogmatic Constitution
   on the Church," November 21, 1964, 13 175

Flavio Rocha, *Dom Hélder Câmara: Meditations for the
   Integrity of Creation*. 176

Cardinal Evaristo Arns of São Paulo. 177

Saint Joan of Arc. 178

USCCB, *Economic Justice for All*, 1986 179

USCCB, *A Place at the Table*, November 13, 2002, p. 6. . . .179

USCCB, *Global Climate Change: A Plea for Dialogue,
   Prudence, and the Common Good*,
   June 15, 2001, 15 179

Litany of the Saints, *The Catholic Source Book*, 2007. . . .182

Catechism of the Catholic Church, 823 183

Catechism of the Catholic Church, 830 183

Catechism of the Catholic Church, 866 183

Catechism of the Catholic Church, 1702 183

Pope John Paul II, *Theology of the Body*, 16:2 184

Catechism of the Catholic Church, 491 188

Saint Anselm, Discourse 52 188

Pope John Paul II 189

Catechism of the Catholic Church, 966 190

Catechism of the Catholic Church, 487 191

CHAPTER 8

Catechism of the Catholic Church, 2558 199

Henri J.M. Nouwen, *Out of Solitude* 202

Sister Janet Mead 204

Catechism of the Catholic Church, 2804 204

Pope John Paul II, *Theology of the Body*, 107:1 206

Catechism of the Catholic Church, 2854 206

Saint Thérèse of Lisieux. 208

Pope Leo XIII, May 4, 1897 210

Catechism of the Catholic Church, 2563 211

Saint Ignatius of Antioch, "I Am God's Wheat" 214

Catechism of the Catholic Church, 1025 216

Catechism of the Catholic Church, 1033 216

National Geographic 220

This is a private reflection that will give you a way to keep track of your spiritual journey, your discoveries along the way, your aspirations, truths, and goals.

Faith as a Journey 25
"Who do You Say That I Am?" 42
Presence of the Holy Spirit 74
Miracles and Me 96
The Care and Feeding of a Strong Soul 129
Relationship with God 162
With a Communion of Saints 186
Praying 209

GO TO THE SOURCE

Often the textbook will discuss Scripture, but sometimes we will send you directly to the Bible with this feature. You may be analyzing the passage, discussing it, breaking it open, and applying it to your life.

Embracing the Truth 20
Joseph (Genesis 37) 35
Wisdom Literature 38
The Disciples Discover Jesus 43
The Jews and Taxes (Matthew 9:9-13) 44
Who Is the Greatest? (Matthew 18:1-4) 45
Jesus Blessing Children 48
The Baptism and the Transfiguration of Jesus 53
Feminine Images Reveal God 64
The Sermon on the Mount 64
The Holy Spirit Revealed 71
Jesus' Promise of the Spirit 72
Reality of the Trinity 74
God's View of Evil 76
God Speaks to Job 80
Jesus' Early Years 88
The Parable of the Good Samaritan 89
Jesus' Attitude Toward Sinners 90
What Must I Do to Inherit Eternal Life? 92
Jesus' Human Emotions, Pain 102
Jesus' Promise 107
Saint Paul's Letters to the Corinthian Church 116
The Book of Genesis 119
Saint Paul Explains the Redemption
    (Romans 5:12-19) 122
God's Law (Psalm 19) 145
The Beatitudes 148
Judging Ourselves, Not Others (Matthew 7:3-5) . . . 150
Entering the Kingdom of Heaven (Matthew 7:21-23) . . 152
Which Commandment Is the Greatest? 153
The Good Shepherd (John 10:1-21) 157
The Risen Jesus 169
Mystical Body of Christ (1 Corinthians 12) 172
Peter as the Church's First Leader
    (Matthew 16:13-20) 174
Laying on of Hands (2 Timothy 1:3-14) 178
Unity (John 17) 183
Mary's Role in the Early Church 191
God Calls Moses 199
God the Son's "I Am" Statements 200
Jesus and Prayer 202
The Pharisee and the Tax Collector 203
Resurrection of the Dead (Mark 12:18-27) 213

PRIMARY SOURCES

This feature will take you directly to a source that is not the Bible such as Church documents, the Catechism, or historical writings, to help you process the information.

Evangelii Nuntiandi, "On the Evangelization
    in the Modern World" 18
Gaudium et Spes, "Joy and Hope" 41
Andrei Rublev's Icon: The Holy Trinity 63
The Imitation of Christ 95
Guidelines for the Liturgical Year 124
"A Common Word Between Us and You" 154
Lumen Gentium, "Dogmatic Constitution
    on the Church" 175
Saint Ignatius of Antioch's Letter to the Church
    in Rome 214

Catholic LIFE

Here you will find stories about people and organizations in the Catholic Church that have modeled discipleship.

Father Walter Ciszek, SJ 22
James McGinnis 46
Trinity Monastery, Fujimi, Japan 78
The Lives of Saints 100
Getting at the Painful Truth, Flannery
    O'Connor 130
Sofia Cavalletti and the Catechesis of the
    Good Shepherd 160
With the Poor in Brazil: Dom Hélder
    Pessoa Câmara 176
The Apocalypse Tapestry 218

THINKING THEOLOGICALLY

This feature will help you talk about your understanding of the nature of God using contemporary insights and experiences.

Truths about Faith 73

Paschal Mystery 134

Already, Not Yet! 148

Hypocrites 203

Spiritual Practices in the Life of DISCIPLESHIP

These are specific behaviors that when done over time, help open us up to God's grace and make us instruments of his grace.

Keeping Company 8

Solidarity 97

Second Chances 120

Making Changes 171

Faith & Culture

These historical, geographical, and cultural snapshots are designed to give you a better appreciation for a time, place, or culture that you have read about.

The Constitution on the Sacred Liturgy 17

The Jordan River 40

Wind Symbol of the Holy Spirit 71

Nazareth 88

Corinth 116

Saint Francis of Assisi 155

The Lord's Prayer 204

GLOBAL PERSPECTIVES

This feature includes statistics, connections, and other information to step outside your own world. The information will usually bring global awareness to a subject such as the environment and the use of resources.

Catholic Health Care Worldwide 14

Global Poverty .45

The Evil of Genocide 77

World Christian Population 91

Catholic Population Worldwide 126

The Ethic of Reciprocity 150

Patron Saints 187

How Old Is the Earth? 220

EXPRESSIONS OF FAITH

This feature focuses on symbols, rites, seasons, and devotions of the Catholic faith. It introduces or reacquaints you with the rich fabric, layers, and expressions of Catholicism and explains Catholic practices and involvement in the world.

World Youth Day 21

Stained Glass 36

National Migration Week 65

Catholic Charities 105

Paschal Candle 135

Catholic Volunteers in Florida 158

Litany of the Saints 182

Our Lady of Guadalupe 189

Novena 210

Going Moral

These are designed to involve you in the process of making moral decisions by presenting real-life moral dilemma based on something in the chapter.

A Break from the Ordinary 106

Grace Helps Us Respond to God 117

Taking Shortcuts 151

Inappropriate Dress 205

JUSTICE AND DISCIPLESHIP

These features will delve into Catholic Social Teaching and will serve as a reminder that those who accept Jesus' message to follow him are called his disciples.

Health Care 11

Racism 68

Caring for Creation 127

Poverty 179

HONORING THE BODY

These features explore body-related topics based on a series of talks by Pope John Paul II called Theology of the Body. The topics include sexuality and health-related issues for all of us made in the image and likeness of God.

Somebody 12

Everybody 52

Whole Body 184

Language of the Body 206

What expressions of faith does this photo evoke? In what ways are the people in this picture about to encounter God?

CHAPTER **1**

Having Faith

Go to the student site at
hs.osvcurriculum.com

DO

- Identify expressions of faith in today's culture.
- Study the meaning of faith.
- Reflect on a time when your faith was challenged.
- Imagine an encounter with Jesus from the Gospel according to Mark.
- Reflect on the connections between friends and faith.

DEFINE

faith
mediator
disciple
Constitution on the Sacred Liturgy
Christian disciples
human dignity
religion

Catholic high school students were asked:

Who has taught you the most about God?
And what were you taught?

From a senior: My dad taught me the most about God. When he was young his mother died. His dad was a drunk, abused him and his sisters, stole all his money, and made fun of him. My dad met my mom, got a great job, and adopted my brother and me. Over the past two years, my dad has been out of work. It was a devastating loss for him, as he has always loved working and supports eight people, which includes my son. My dad was lost and had no clue what to do. He still does not have a job and is still depressed, but he has prayed more than others, tries to keep a positive attitude, still has faith, and has attended church more frequently. He has taught me to still have faith and believe in God, no matter what is thrown at you.

From a senior: My mother taught me the most about God. She has a firm understanding of theology. She encourages me to learn about our faith and to trust in God's presence. I'm still looking for a full understanding, but I know it'll come in time.

WHAT ABOUT YOU?

Where Are You?

Choose the response that best reflects where you are right now.

My faith affects my daily life.	☐ Quite a bit	☐ Somewhat	☐ A little	☐ Not at all
My life would be different if I did not have faith.	☐ Quite a bit	☐ Somewhat	☐ A little	☐ Not at all
I'm able to get spiritual insights from music, TV, and movies.	☐ Quite a bit	☐ Somewhat	☐ A little	☐ Not at all
My faith has changed since I was in second grade.	☐ Quite a bit	☐ Somewhat	☐ A little	☐ Not at all
I see a lived faith in the people I have in my life.	☐ Quite a bit	☐ Somewhat	☐ A little	☐ Not at all

Believing and Trusting

From what do we want to be saved?

Who or what remains worthy of our belief, even when others fail?

What is the object of our faith?

Is belief in one's self enough?   *Isn't it better to seek and trust God's infinite will and wisdom?*

Everyone has some kind of faith. It comes with being human. In fact, we could not get through a single day without it. Faith—belief—is at work every time we flip a light switch, cross the street, text a friend, or put money in the bank. Faith and trust go hand in hand. We usually have to believe in someone or something in order to trust. It's true that trust can be broken. Beliefs can crumble. But no one can survive for long without believing in someone or something.

> Faith is the assurance of things hoped for, the conviction of things not seen.
>
> —Hebrews 11:1

Some people put their faith in science and progress. They believe in the human capacity to build up knowledge and skill. But is this enough? For all the progress the human race has made in science and medicine, people still die. New problems come with changes in technology. Knowledge and skill have limits.

People once believed that science could be used to end all wars. Now that nuclear weapons threaten our existence, many people realize that the solutions to our problems lie beyond the reach of science and technology.

Some people put their faith in political leaders and systems of government, in markets and economic forces. But is this enough? There is a dark side to every political or economic system. When political leaders turn out to be corrupt and systems come crashing down, people look back in amazement, asking, "How did we ever believe in this?"

Some people believe in themselves. They trust in their physical strength or beauty or will to succeed. But strength, health, and beauty fade. Worldly success is no guarantee of happiness.

Most people now realize that war, hunger, crime, terrorist attacks, many diseases, and loneliness are symptoms of deeper human weaknesses. Are we looking in the right place? Here is an answer from the Gospel according to Mark: "Your faith has made you well" (Mark 5:34).

The earlier quotation from the Letter to the Hebrews couples trust and hope as well as offers a definition of **faith**. It is a God-given virtue that allows us to believe in everything God has told us about himself. A person of faith accepts God's Revelation and submits his or her whole self—mind and will—to God (see *Catechism of the Catholic Church,*

faith a theological virtue through which we believe in God and all that he has revealed

176). The chapter from Hebrews also refers to people who have done this and believed in God's promises, such as Noah, Abraham, and Moses. These people made heroic sacrifices because of their faith in God. They believed in God despite persecution and obstacles. Why? The writer of Hebrews points to something essential when he says that Abraham believed that God's promise could be trusted.

Sometimes it's hard to know whom to believe. If someone betrays our trust, we may lower the level of trust in that person the next time. Or we may not trust him or her again. We never have to worry about the trustworthiness of God. As the *Catechism* points out, "It is right and just to entrust oneself wholly to God and to believe absolutely what he says. It would be futile and false to place such faith in a creature" (CCC, 150). Believing in God absolutely, as Abraham did, is made possible through God's grace and only by the Holy Spirit working in us. Nevertheless, faith is a genuinely human act in which our minds and our hearts cooperate to say "yes" to God and to what he has revealed (see CCC, 154).

We are invited to freely align our spirit and will with God. This is what the Beatitudes mean by "Blessed are the poor in spirit . . ." (Matthew 5:3). It is God who truly fills our deepest needs and inner poverty—not science, political or economic systems, material possessions, and not our own personal strength, health, and beauty. While all are important to our lives, their benefit will only come about if they are truly rooted in the wisdom of God. By definition, our human will and wisdom are limited.

List What are the two qualities or characteristics of any sort of faith?

Elaborate What makes it possible for us to believe in God absolutely?

Compose
Popular songs frequently make reference to faith and encourage people to have faith.

○ Find several songs and compare what they say about faith.

○ What does each song urge the listener to believe in: a person, an ideal, God? What difference does faith make, according to the songwriter? How does the music convey the songwriter's beliefs?

○ Write your own song lyrics about your experience of faith.

Faith Chart

Examine several definitions of the word "faith" in one or more dictionaries or on language websites. If you know the word for faith in other languages, look those up too. Using the chart below, list the words and as many meanings for them as you can find. What do they all have in common?

Languages	Words	Definitions
Hebrew	āman	
Biblical Greek	pistis	
Latin	fides	
English	faith	

Believing in Jesus

The Letter to the Hebrews notes that our ancestors in faith were looking forward to something they never saw. "Yet all these, though they were commended for their faith, did not receive what was promised" (Hebrews 11:39). What they did not live long enough to see, we have seen: Jesus the Christ. Jesus fulfills the promises of God, whose very being is truth and love. Jesus is the gift, sent from the Father, who opens the way for a new and intimate relationship with God. Jesus told his disciples: "Whoever has seen me has seen the Father" (John 14:9).

The gift of Jesus surpasses all other divine gifts. Because Jesus is the ultimate Revelation of God, our belief in him can be as deep and lasting as our faith in God, his Father. To believe in Jesus, to have faith in him, is to have found the One on whom we can depend—all our life long, even beyond death.

It is the Holy Spirit, working in us, who enables us to believe in Jesus. Saint Paul knew this. He wrote: "No one can say 'Jesus is Lord' except by the Holy Spirit" (1 Corinthians 12:3). The title "Lord" signifies Christ's divine reign. We affirm that Jesus is God when we call him Lord. Mary knew this as well. Her "yes" allowed the Holy Spirit to complete in her the preparations for the arrival of Christ among God's People.

We build a stronger relationship with God every time we place our faith in Jesus. Out of love for us, God revealed himself most fully in his Son, Jesus, and established through Jesus his everlasting covenant. We can know God intimately and trust him completely because Jesus is truly God, truly man, and the only **mediator** between God and humans. "No one has ever seen God," the Gospel according to John tells us. "It is God the only Son, who is close to the Father's heart, who has made him known" (John 1:18).

Growing in Faith

The religious faith that many experienced in childhood was simple and unquestioning, especially for those who grew up in a religious family and a community of believers.

The Annunciation, by Henry Ossawa Tanner

Faith may be something taken for granted. When we grow to adulthood, however, new horizons of faith emerge. Life events, such as experiences of injustice, suffering, and loss, may cause us to question our beliefs *or* to want to hold onto them more firmly. We may begin to seek deeper wisdom from religion. We face choices about our priorities, and faith enters into the mix in new ways.

We become disciples. The word "disciple" comes from the Latin word *discere*, which means to learn. As the root of the word suggests, a **disciple** is someone who studies and follows the teachings of a master.

Our faith is strengthened by such challenges. Faith is a theological virtue, which means it is a gift from God. Faith makes it possible for us to act as children of God and merit eternal life. Faith is the promised presence of the Holy Spirit in our very person. Faith in God is a matter of:

1. Beliefs—intellectual conviction of believing in all that God has revealed and all that the Church offers for our belief.

2. Trust—spirituality and relationship with God as we seek to know and do his will. Trust is part of the virtue of hope, another theological virtue.

3. Discipleship—actively living faith out in our lives, professing faith by words and actions, making choices based on it.

disciple someone who studies and follows the teachings of a master

mediator one who serves as intermediary, to intercede and/or reconcile differences

Keeping COMPANY

A spiritual practice for the life of discipleship

> The very word *practice* brings with it the idea of learning. And any practice is awkward and difficult at first. But it is necessary to attain any kind of proficiency in the spiritual life.
>
> —Dorothy Day

Jesus called his disciples to follow and believe in him. Together they formed a group of fellow followers and good friends. Before he left this Earth, Jesus reminded them to travel the path of discipleship together. We are not meant to take the path of discipleship by ourselves.

Keeping company involves deliberately choosing the people you want to travel with on the path of discipleship. Keeping company requires that you invest in those relationships. It requires that you reach out to stay in contact with these friends and intentionally set aside time to be with them.

The most important part of the practice of keeping company is the people you choose to be near. Everyone has good friends. But *spiritual strength* comes from keeping company with friends who are good. There's a difference. Keeping company is about establishing a group of people who seek to live the right way, who get it when things go wrong, and who have a way of reminding you why it is worth it to stay on the right spiritual path.

And the people who make up the company you keep don't even have to know each other. You can form a group that includes a friend from a place you used to live, someone from back in junior high, an adult relative, a grandparent, a teacher, a coach, one or two BFFs, even someone who has passed on.

It's not important that you keep company with people who know each other. It's only important that you keep company with people who understand the value of

trying to walk with God and who remind you how to do it and why it's worth the effort.

Faithful friends are a sturdy shelter:
* whoever finds one has found a treasure.*
Faithful friends are beyond price;
* no amount can balance their worth.*
Faithful friends are life-saving medicine;
* and those who fear the Lord will find them.*
Those who fear the Lord direct their friendship aright,
* for as they are, so are their neighbors also.*

—Sirach 6:14-17

>> Write the initials of five to seven people with whom you want to practice keeping company.

What do you need to do specifically or deliberately to improve your practice of keeping company with these people?

With whom do you need to quit keeping company?

A person can be strong in one area, but weak in another. We exercise our God-given faith by attending to all three of these dimensions: head (beliefs), heart (trust), and hands (discipleship). We do this when we are thinking, praying, and living as disciples. We can respond to the gift of faith and grow as disciples:

- by nurturing our gift of faith in prayer and through receiving God's grace in the Sacraments;

- by being open to the Holy Spirit's direction and presence in our lives;

- by attempting to express our faith to others;

- by trying to better understand our faith for ourselves; and

- by striving to live by our faith more wholeheartedly and in new ways.

Changing circumstances may lead to a greater faith than we ever thought we had. Our faith in Jesus remains rooted in the faith we've always had, yet becomes stronger and more resilient when we practice it with the help of the Holy Spirit.

Recall What did Jesus tell his disciples about having a relationship with God the Father?

Explain What are some of the challenges to your faith that you have faced as you approach adulthood?

Share
Write a short paragraph about each of the three people who have had the most influence on your faith life or who have helped you become a better person. Be prepared to share what you wrote for one of the people you have named.

REFLECT

Think about a time when something or someone caused you to "give your faith a workout" by challenging your faith, sharing it, asking questions about it, stretching it, having it influence something you did, or having an experience that caused you to doubt.

>> **Describe the situation. What did you do? What was the outcome?**

Write about your experience. Be sure to include the reactions you had at the time and how you think about the experience now.

SECTION 1 REVIEW

QUICK REVIEW

1a. Explain What is the problem with having faith in material possessions or manmade institutions?

b. Examine Interpret the meaning of the *Catechism* quotation, "It is right and just to entrust oneself wholly to God and to believe absolutely what he says" (CCC, 150).

c. Synthesize How is Jesus the fulfillment of God's promise?

2a. Analyze What is a child's faith based on?

b. Apply What sorts of experiences deepen a person's faith?

c. Apply What sorts of events challenge a person's faith?

Listen and Discuss With a partner, discuss the following statements and questions.

○ Nothing and no one deserves our complete and unconditional love as God does.

○ Why can it be difficult to believe in God?

○ How can we help others learn to profess and spread their belief in God?

Pray Compose a short prayer asking for help in learning to trust God.

SELF-ASSESS

Which statement best reflects where you are now?

☐ I'm confident enough about the material in this section to be able to explain it to someone else.

☐ I have a good grasp of the material in this section, but I could use more review.

☐ I'm lost. I need help catching up before moving on.

Jesus Sees Our Faith

In the Gospels, we learn much about faith from the people Jesus encountered. Jesus did not tell us about the great faith of priests, teachers, and religious leaders. Instead he taught us about faith in surprising and unexpected places. Consider the following three stories from the Gospel according to Mark.

The woman with a hemorrhage (Mark 5:21-34). This woman was suffering from constant bleeding. She must have been severely weakened by this illness that had lasted for twelve years. Not only was she seriously ill, she also had no resources to take care of herself. She had gone to all sorts of doctors. No one succeeded in helping her. She had spent all her money, and now her life savings were gone. When Jesus passed by, she recognized him. The encounter perhaps gave her new hope. She did not ask him to look at her or talk to her or interact with her. She thought if she could only touch his clothes, she would be healed.

She took a big risk in approaching him. Women in that society did not have equal standing with men, and Jesus was an important man, a famous rabbi. Moreover, there was a strict religious taboo against touching someone who was contaminated with blood. If she touched and contaminated him, he would have had to undergo purification

Connect

In recent decades, the public has become interested in studying the impact of faith on healing and recovery. Some research suggests that people who have a faith community recover more quickly from major illnesses and live longer.

○ If faith communities could be shown statistically to have a beneficial effect on health, what implications could this have when government and health officials make health care decisions?

○ If such a connection could not be proven, would that have an impact on faith? Why or why not?

○ How seriously do you take the effect of faith on health and healing? Explain.

according to the Jewish law of the time. In her condition, she shouldn't have gone near him, especially if she had respect for him.

But the woman believed, and she took a great risk. Imagine her anxiety when the famous rabbi caught her at it. "Who touched my clothes?" Jesus asked (Mark 5:30). This was an unusual question because Jesus was in a large crowd and many people were pressing him on every side, but he knew.

Fearfully, she came forward trembling. The story has a surprise ending, one that would have surprised anyone who heard it in Jesus' day. Not only did Jesus heal the woman, he gave her credit for her faith. "Daughter, your faith has made you well; go in peace, and be healed of your disease" (Mark 5:34).

JUSTICE AND DISCIPLESHIP

Jesus tells us that discipleship involves praying to the Father, studying his teachings and following his example, participating in the Eucharist, and living the virtues. He also calls us to act for justice.

WHAT DO YOU DO WHEN YOU ARE REALLY SICK OR badly injured? What if you (or your parents) couldn't afford to pay for the treatment?

In many miracle stories, Jesus relieved suffering and "cured all who were sick" (Matthew 8:16). According to the U.S. Catholic Bishops, the biblical perspective sees health as physical, spiritual, and psychological wholeness[1]. Today, health care refers to the prevention, treatment, and management of illness and disease.

Our country primarily relies on employers to provide insurance that covers the bulk of the cost to care for one's health. But not everyone has health insurance, and with the high cost of health care, that means less preventative care and more postponing treatment of illnesses and diseases. Although medical professionals have an obligation to treat people with life-threatening conditions, unless it is a matter of life and death, people who cannot pay for treatment are often turned away.

The Church teaches that the human person should be the focus of every social organization, including health care. It also encourages society in general to accept the same idea. Health care is a basic human right, explained Pope John XXIII in his encyclical *Pacem in Terris,* or "Peace on Earth." Moreover, respect for life and human dignity demand that medical professionals treat the whole person, not just life-threatening conditions.

As a matter of justice, you have the choice to act.

Visit the sick and vulnerable—become a hospital volunteer or visit a local nursing or retirement home.

Educate yourself and others about Catholic Social Teaching and the issues surrounding health care. Visit the student site for links to websites with information about the state of health care in the United States and proposals to reform the health care system. If there is a Catholic health care ministry in your area, find out what challenges they face in serving the poor.

Advocate improvements in the health care system. Contact your elected officials and ask what they are doing to address the issue of health care in the U.S. Adapted from the U.S. Conference of Catholic Bishops *Health Care for All* brochure.

Go to the student site at
hs.osvcurriculum.com

EMERGENCY ROOM

EMERGENCY ROOM

You can be for justice without being a disciple, but you cannot be a disciple without being for justice.

"Do you not know that your body is a temple of the Holy Spirit within you, which you have from God, and that you are not your own? ... Therefore glorify God in your body."

—(1 Corinthians 6:19-20)

Somebody

WE KNOW THE creation account from the Book of Genesis. "So God created humankind in his image, in the image of God he created them; male and female he created them" (Genesis 1:27). As individuals we reflect the God who created us, but our connections with other humans also show how we are made in the image and likeness of God.

In his Theology of the Body, Blessed Pope John Paul II discusses the second creation story where Adam meets Eve for the first time. Adam states, "This at last is bone of my bones and flesh of my flesh" (Genesis 2:23). He says this because he can see from the way she is made that he and she are made for one another. Adam's own body makes sense when he sees Eve's body. He can see that they are made to be in relationship with one another. The body reveals this, but the compatibility of Adam and Eve is not just physical. They are made to be companions to one another physically, emotionally, and spiritually.

Adam's reaction to Eve demonstrates the value of individual humans, but there is an even deeper value because man and woman were made for each other.

> Man became the image of God not only through his own humanity, but also through the communion of persons ... from the very beginning.
> —Pope John Paul II, *Theology of the Body* 9:3

We are created to be a communion of persons—equal to each other as humans and complementary to each other as male and female. This compatibility of the sexes impacts everything about the human person through the unity of body and soul. It allows us the capacity to love in two ways—to love and procreate as married spouses and the other, in a more general way, to love those around us and in society.

According to Blessed Pope John Paul II, the physical compatibility of woman and man tells us something. The way woman and man are made speaks to us about God's plan. In this way, the body, by its very design, speaks a language. In the Sacrament of Marriage, the man and woman become one and express their gifts of masculinity and femininity to each other. By giving themselves to one another, they also speak a language with their bodies. The language of the body reflects our creation and our relationship with God from the beginning. It is the essential sign of the couple's covenant with God. Pope John Paul II makes the point that language describing the giving of self between married persons was also used in the time of the prophets to describe God's relationship with his People. God's People were sometimes faithful to him, and other times, they were described as an unfaithful spouse. This spousal relationship between God and his People is an ancient concept that helps us encounter the great mystery of God's Redemption.

On the night before he died, Jesus gave his disciples a new commandment, to "love one another" as he had loved them. Jesus wasn't simply talking about "loving your neighbor" because that wouldn't have been a new commandment at all. Loving one another as Jesus loves us means giving of ourselves to someone else and also receiving their gift of self. This is called having "communion" with one another. This happens most completely in the relationship with married persons, but it also happens at some level with many other significant people in our lives.

This communion of persons gives us a deeper human identity. It's part of who we are and how we are created. We all need people in our lives—family, friends, and community. It's great to have people to hang out and have fun with, but there's something more going on at the core of our humanity. The communion of persons is about real connections—involving deep, honest, and open communication, which we need to live in society. These connections are in our nature. Society enables us to experience each other through service and dialogue. In this way, we develop and respond to each person's vocation (see CCC, 1879).

Quality relationships based on truth and love with family, friends, and others nourish our bodies and souls. These same connections reflect God's love for us. The *Catechism* says such relationships have some resemblance to the unity of God the Father, Son, and Holy Spirit. The origin and source of all true human love and the communion of persons we experience comes from God.

Our absolute need for communion aids our ability to love God. "Love of neighbor is inseparable from love for God" (CCC, 1878). In other words, "We cannot love the God we cannot see if we do not love the brother or sister we do see,"[136] (CCC, 2840). Since we're all made in the image and likeness of God, it makes sense that we can know and love God through others.

We need a community of believers, a parish or church, to hear God's voice more completely. What does this tell us about the importance of practicing one's faith in a community (for example, a prayer group or youth group)?

Think about your parents, siblings, and friends and how you communicate with them. When are you really present to people?

Sometimes we are only with people "superficially." Although we may be physically present, we may often tune out. When we don't pay attention, it's hard to connect with others. And without that connection, it's more difficult to hear the voice of God as reflected in that person.

Sometimes we can be with another person in no other way than "virtually." The ability to instantaneously connect with people globally is incredible. Texting and posting on social networks is convenient, easy, and fun, but they are starting a conversation. We can be "in-touch" with everyone, but not actually let them into our lives in a significant way. Chatting, texting, and email can either help the communion of persons that reflects our Creator, or it can keep us distanced from each other and therefore, from God.

Cultivating that deeper relationship with someone else through technology is definitely hard, but *how* we are present counts because it impacts the level at which *we are* present for others. With genuine communication—someone can be an instrument of God's voice.

And then the question becomes: how open are we to hearing God's voice through the deeper human communication that often comes from our communion of persons? The thing is, we need to really listen.

>> Are we open to hearing the voice of God speaking through someone else?

With whom are you able to be communicate deeply?

What is the voice of God telling you through a trusted friend or parent?

With whom do you find yourself struggling with being just "superficially" present?

Are there limits to the degree that we can be really present? How deeply can we communicate with someone through the Internet?

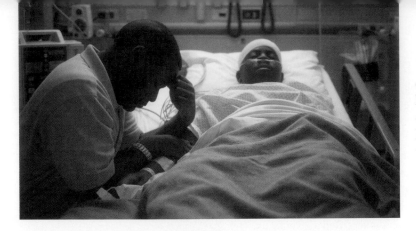

cried out more strongly, "Jesus, Son of David, have mercy on me!" (Mark 10:47). Jesus called Bartimaeus forward and asked what he wanted. Jesus said to him the same words that he spoke to the woman with the hemorrhage: "Your faith has made you well" (Mark 10:52). Immediately, the man was healed. Then, Mark tells us, he followed Jesus on the road.

The boy with a spirit (Mark 9:14-29). In Chapter 9 of the Gospel according to Mark, we find a different kind of story. In one sense, we could call it a "growing faith" story. A father, distraught over his son's inability to speak and his suffering from convulsions, first brought the boy to Jesus' disciples. He wanted them to cast out a spirit from his son, but they could not do so. When Jesus came on the scene, the spirit convulsed the boy. The father explained to Jesus that the boy had been suffering since childhood. The father pleaded with Jesus: "If you are able to do anything, have pity on us and help us" (Mark 9:22).

The reply of Jesus called for faith on the part of the father. "Jesus said to him, 'If you are able!—All things can be done for the one who believes.' Immediately the father of the child cried out, 'I believe; help my unbelief!'" (Mark 9:23-24). Jesus then freed the afflicted youth from the spirit. Did this help the father's unbelief? The Gospel writer doesn't say. What the story does make clear is that the man had faith enough to ask for help from the One who could actually help him. His faith wasn't perfect, but he put it in the right place—in Jesus.

Evaluate

In these accounts, the subjects of the stories were considered outcasts by the general public, and they were treated as such. Though the people always had their attention on Jesus, he put his attention on those in need. Evaluate your own school's student body.

○ Is anyone at your school often picked on or made fun of?

○ How compassionate and helpful is the student body toward students with disabilities?

○ What are ways your student body could do a better job at imitating Christ by giving more attention to those in need or on the fringes?

○ What can you do to better imitate Christ in this regard?

Blind Bartimaeus (Mark 10:46-52). This man, sitting by the roadside, was called Bartimaeus, or son of Timaeus. He went blind at some point in his life and was reduced to the humiliating position of begging for his daily food. When Bartimaeus heard that Jesus was coming down the road with a crowd leaving Jericho, he called out to Jesus to have mercy on him.

The crowd with Jesus was not pleased with this disruption. But despite their best efforts to make this blind beggar keep quiet, he

GLOBAL PERSPECTIVES

Catholic health care continues the healing ministry of Jesus around the world. In the United States alone, there are 614 Catholic hospitals. In 2006, these hospitals admitted more than 5.5 million people, according to the Catholic Health Association of the United States. In that same year, these hospitals logged more than 16.6 million emergency room visits. In 2007, Catholic hospitals employed more than a half-million full-time and 237,000 part-time workers. The Catholic Health Association says its ministry is rooted in the belief that every person is a treasure, every life a sacred gift, and every human being is a union of body, mind, and spirit.

○ Research the Catholic health care facility nearest to your school.

○ Write a paragraph about what you find out.

○ How do you think Catholic health care continues Jesus' ministry of healing people?

↗ Go to the student site at **hs.osvcurriculum.com**

Too often when we read these stories, we focus on the miracle of healing. However, that is not actually Jesus' own focus. In all these stories, Jesus recognizes faith. He encounters people who put their faith in him, despite many obstacles, uncertainties, and risks. He sees the person, not his or her socially unacceptable condition. He sees the person's faith. "Your faith has saved you," Jesus says (Luke 7:50).

In each of these accounts, faith pays big dividends. In fact, it makes a huge difference to the people who believe: the difference between debilitating illness and healing, the difference between being "left by the roadside" and being able to get up and follow Jesus, the difference between danger and safety. The Gospel stories inspire the question that must finally be answered by each believer: What difference does faith in Jesus make to *me*?

Recall What did faith do for the woman with a hemorrhage?

Explain In the account of the boy with a spirit, how did the father's faith grow?

Create

Imagine that you are one of the people whose interactions with Jesus are recounted in these stories from the Gospel according to Mark.

○ Create an imaginary conversation expressing your feelings about that event as well as your friends' comments and questions.

○ If Jesus healed your faith, what part of your faith would he heal: belief, trust, or discipleship?

REFLECT

The three Jesus encounters that we looked at in the Gospel according to Mark focused on people needing healing

>> Which of the following do you need most from God these days?

physical or emotional healing

better ability to see what's right or wrong, true or false

spiritual cleansing

Take some time now to write a prayer to God or write a letter to yourself.

SECTION 2 REVIEW

QUICK REVIEW

1a. Summarize Retell the story of the woman with a hemorrhage.

b. Recall How did Bartimaeus get Jesus' attention?

c. Recall How did Jesus help the boy suffering from convulsions?

2a. Contrast How is the story of the boy with a spirit different from the other stories?

b. Synthesize How are the three Scripture stories—the woman with a hemorrhage, Bartimaeus, and the boy with a spirit—alike?

c. Assess How does Jesus appear to feel about being asked to help people?

Listen and Discuss On your own, complete the statements below, and then share your answers with a classmate. If a meaning is not clear to you, ask clarifying questions.

○ I think it would be hard/easy to ask Jesus for help with faith because . . .

○ The thing that has helped me most to grow in faith is . . .

SELF-ASSESS

Which statement best reflects where you are now?

☐ I'm confident enough about the material in this section to be able to explain it to someone else.

☐ I have a good grasp of the material in this section, but I could use more review.

☐ I'm lost. I need help catching up before moving on.

Faith Is a Relationship

The people in the Gospel stories from Section 2 connected with Jesus directly and in a vivid way. He came to their villages. They listened to him preach. He saw them, touched them, and listened to their needs.

Can we even come close to having such a vital and living relationship with Jesus today? It's one thing to believe in an idea or an abstraction that exists in our minds and is as close to us as our own thoughts. But Jesus is not an idea or an abstraction. He lived on this Earth two millennia ago. It is easy for us to believe in a contemporary person, someone we can see and talk to. We can interact with him or her face-to-face and decide for ourselves what we think. But Jesus is not available for direct inspection. He does not give interviews or appear at photo shoots. He doesn't have a social network profile. We cannot come to know who he is in the same way we come to know our friends or our next-door neighbors. So, how do we get to know Jesus today?

The answer is simple. We come to know him through the Gospels and the Church, through regular prayer, participation in Mass, and devotion to the Blessed Sacrament. From the very first communities of disciples, this was the case. Not everyone had the privilege of seeing Jesus in the flesh. Even in the time of the Apostles, many people believed in Jesus without ever seeing him. Like us, they believed because of what others told them. They recognized the change within those who believed. They understood that what they were hearing was the truth. And they entered into a relationship of faith with Jesus.

This message about Jesus—his life, his words, deeds, identity, mission, and especially his death and Resurrection—continues to be passed on today. It is the living witness of the Church. The Church, founded by Jesus Christ, continually passes on the Good News, and invites people to faith. The writer of the First Letter of John puts it this way: "We declare to you what was from the

The *Constitution on the Sacred Liturgy* was the first major official document of the Second Vatican Council. It changed the way we worship in the Church by adapting parts of culture, such as language, music, and art, into the liturgy.

○ It also provided general principles to renew and restore the liturgy.

○ One principle stated that "liturgy is the summit toward which the

Faith & Culture

activity of the Church is directed; it is also the fountain from which all its power flows" (10).

○ Another principle said Catholics should come to Mass ready to tune their minds and voices to God and cooperate with God's grace or risk wasting it (see 11).

These were important, according to the *Encyclopedia of Catholicism*, "because God desires to meet people in and through the sacraments and other liturgical rites of the Church, the Church must not hinder, even as it must regulate, the circumstances of that

meeting." There is a wider use of vernacular language in readings and prayers. Sacred music and sacred art make prayer more pleasing, encourage unity, and make sacred rites more solemn.

↗ Go to the student site at **hs.osvcurriculum.com**

---

beginning, what we have heard, what we have seen with our eyes, what we have looked at and touched with our hands, concerning the word of life—this life was revealed, and we have seen it and testify to it" (1 John 1:1-2).

Believing in Jesus is not like believing in Socrates or Caesar. Jesus is still with us. By faith, we believe that he is present and that we can have an ongoing relationship with him. He remains alive in us and in the world through the Holy Spirit. Faith is about strengthening our spiritual relationship with him, a real relationship. That is why the work of the early Church continues today. That's why musicians still write songs about Jesus. Through the work of the Church, we are able to build on our relationship with Jesus in the witness of good people, the liturgy—especially the Eucharist and the Sacraments—in service to the community, and in prayer.

When reading Jesus' words in Scripture, we hear him speak. As the Second Vatican Council affirmed in the **Constitution on the Sacred Liturgy**, Christ is still proclaiming his Gospel when the Church gathers to listen to his word. When we pray, we share with him our needs, hopes, and fears. And when

we act as his disciples, following his teachings and example with sincerity, we do our part as members of the Church.

Retell How do we come to know Jesus even though he isn't among us as a man?

Explain How is believing in Jesus different from believing in historic people such as Socrates and Caesar?

Faith and Discipleship

We are all "on the way" somewhere in life. The journey is often used to describe life itself. Perhaps this influenced why the early Christian community called the Christian faith and lifestyle "the Way." For them, this image of the right road meant not only the journey of life, but also a way of being in relationship with Christ. Like Bartimaeus, the blind man mentioned earlier, our faith gives us the opportunity to get up off the side of the road and walk with him.

The *Catechism* explains that from the start Jesus connected his disciples to his own life and told them about the mystery of God's Kingdom. **Christian disciples** would share Jesus' mission, joys, and sufferings. "Jesus spoke of a still more intimate communion between him and those who would follow

Constitution on the Sacred Liturgy first major official document of the Second Vatican Council, which set principles for liturgical reform

Christian disciples those who hear the Gospel message of Jesus, accept it, and live their lives according to it

PRIMARY SOURCES

In 1974, Pope Paul VI described this initial act of evangelization, which means sharing the Gospel message by telling and living it. Pope Paul VI's apostolic exhortation on spreading the Gospel identifies various ways the Church gives witness to her faith. His document is called *Evangelii Nuntiandi*, or "On the Evangelization in the Modern World."

➤ Go to the student site at
hs.osvcurriculum.com

Take a Christian or a handful of Christians who, in the midst of their own community, show their capacity for understanding and acceptance, their sharing of life and destiny with other people, their solidarity with the efforts of all for whatever is noble and good. Let us suppose that, in addition, they radiate in an altogether simple and unaffected way their faith in values that go beyond current values, and their hope in something that is not seen and that one would not dare to imagine. Through this wordless witness these Christians stir up irresistible questions in the hearts of those who see how they live: Why are they like this? Why do they live in this way? What or who is it that inspires them? Why are they in our midst? Such a witness is already a silent proclamation of the Good News and a very powerful and effective one.

—Pope Paul VI, *Evangelii Nuntiandi*, paragraph 21

>> Read the rest of *Evangelii Nuntiandi* paragraph 21 as well as paragraphs 22, 29, and 31.

Explain in your own words the connections between "wordless example," explicit proclamation, and work for the betterment of society.

him: 'Abide in me, and I in you . . . I am the vine, you are the branches'" (CCC, 787).

Jesus also describes the response of a true disciple in the Parable of the Sower. The good disciple will hear the Gospel message, accept it, and bring it to the part of his or her life that the Holy Spirit wishes. The true disciple will not abandon the message when trouble erupts because of his faith. The true disciple will not allow the cares of the world, the lure of wealth, and the desire for things to deter him or her. A disciple of Jesus accepts his message, grows from this relationship, and lives it (see Mark 4:13-20).

We are called to study the ways of Jesus and travel with him on the road of life, as people who share his values and mission. We are called to be the voice, the hands, and the feet of Jesus in order to be his presence, his "body" on Earth. The path may not always be clear, but by living as disciples of Jesus, we trust that he will lead us. "I am the way," Jesus said (John 14:6).

Identify What did early Christians call the Christian faith and lifestyle?

Elaborate How does the image of the "right road" help explain the idea that Jesus is "the Way"?

SECTION 3 REVIEW

QUICK REVIEW

1a. Compare How is your relationship with Jesus like his relationship with people of his time?

b. Contrast How is your relationship with Jesus different from his relationship with people of his time?

c. Recall How do we come to know Jesus today?

2a. Name What are people who accept Jesus' message called?

b. Interpret What does the term "the Way" tell us about the early Christian community?

c. Evaluate How are you a disciple of Jesus?

ACT

Part of this section develops the metaphor of faith as a journey. Work with some classmates on developing a metaphor for living in faith.

○ Write a paragraph explaining your metaphor.

○ Make a poster or another type of visual aid to illustrate your metaphor.

Pray Compose a short prayer asking for help in your faith journey.

SELF-ASSESS

Which statement best reflects where you are now?

☐ I'm confident enough about the material in this section to be able to explain it to someone else.

☐ I have a good grasp of the material in this section, but I could use more review.

☐ I'm lost. I need help catching up before moving on.

Faith More than Conviction

Remember that faith is more than just conviction or belief in Jesus. It also involves trust and discipleship, both of which are made possible and strengthened by the virtue of hope. We know from surveys that approximately 90 percent of Americans believe in God. But taking the next step to living as a disciple of Jesus is not an easy task. We may prefer a faith that allows us to be comfortable instead of challenged. We may choose to develop a faith that is more convenient than one that asks a lot from us. But discipleship calls us to embrace the truth. Jesus told us that the truth can be costly and difficult. There are passages in the Gospels that illustrate just such dynamics.

In the Gospel according to Matthew, Jesus tells a parable about two sons. Their father asks both sons to go out and work in the vineyard. The first says "no," but later goes out and works. The second says "yes," but never goes out to the vineyard. Jesus then

---

GO TO **THE SOURCE**

Two readings from the Gospel according to Luke also show how difficult it can be to "embrace the truth."

Read Luke 9:57-62 and Luke 18:18-25.

Luke 9:57-62

○ What is your reaction to Jesus' response to those who want to take care of a few things before they follow him?

○ If Jesus were with you in body right now and said, "Follow me," what would your response be?

Luke 18:18-25

○ Put yourself in the shoes of the rich ruler from this passage. Could you part with such a fortune?

---

asks the chief priests and elders who are listening which son did his father's will. Of course, the first son had done what the father had asked. It's a lot easier to make promises than it is to follow through and keep one's promise. Jesus adds, "Truly I tell you, the tax collectors and the prostitutes are going into the kingdom of God ahead of you. For John [the Baptist] came to you in the way of righteousness and you did not believe him, but the tax collectors and the prostitutes believed him; and even after you saw it, you did not change your minds and believe him" (Matthew 21:31-32).

Faith is like a dark tunnel: God gives us the Light to take one step at a time. The Light is not given to see the end of the tunnel.

—Father Walter Ciszek, SJ

World YOUTH Day

"**D**o not be afraid to say 'yes' to Jesus, to find your joy in doing his will, giving yourself completely to the pursuit of holiness, and using all your talents in the service of others," Pope Benedict XVI told more than 225,000 young people and their chaperones who attended World Youth Day 2008 in Sydney, Australia.

Blessed Pope John Paul II started World Youth Day in 1984 as a way to gather people between sixteen and thirty-five years old from across the world to celebrate their faith as one. World Youth Day is actually a week-long faith-sharing journey, which includes prayer, song, concerts, liturgy, catechesis, dramas, a vigil, and closing Mass with the Pope.

Although World Youth Day is celebrated every year, international World Youth Day celebrations happen every two to three years.

When it is not an international celebration, World Youth Day is celebrated in local parishes or dioceses across the world. In most places, it is celebrated on Palm Sunday. In the United States it is celebrated on the thirtieth Sunday in Ordinary Time.

One participant summed up the feelings of those who attended the 2008 World Youth Day: "It's hard to put into words how moving it is to worship with hundreds of thousands of other young Catholic people. You get to see the worldwide Catholic Church. It's diverse. It's full of young people who are excited and happy with their faith."

Host cities have included Buenos Aires, Argentina (1987); Santiago de Compostela, Spain (1989); Czestochowa, Poland (1991); Denver, Colorado, United States (1993); Manila, Philippines (1995); Paris, France (1997); Rome, Italy (2000); Toronto, Canada (2002); Cologne, Germany (2005); Sydney, Australia (2008); and Madrid, Spain (2011).

International World Youth Day takes place every two to three years.

>> Do you know anyone who has attended a World Youth Day?

What did they say about the experience?

What do you think World Youth Day expresses?

Look up the theme of the next international World Youth Day.

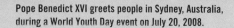

Pope Benedict XVI greets people in Sydney, Australia, during a World Youth Day event on July 20, 2008.

Father Walter Ciszek, SJ

(NOVEMBER 4, 1904–DECEMBER 8, 1984)

In October 1963, Father Walter Ciszek landed in New York City after spending twenty-three years in prisons and labor camps in the former Soviet Union. He had no idea he had officially been declared dead in 1947. Jesuit friends had celebrated memorial Masses for Ciszek. As he considered the turn his faith journey had taken in the labor camps, Ciszek offered thanksgiving to God. "I felt only a simple sense of gratitude to God for having sustained me through those years and, in his providence, bringing me home again at last," Ciszek said.

As a young man growing up in Shenandoah, Pennsylvania, Walter Ciszek felt the call to religious life and entered the Jesuit order of priests. He was on fire with the mission of going to the Soviet Union. He wanted to serve as a priest for the people whose religion was being suppressed by the Communist state. Almost as soon as he entered the country, however, he was arrested and accused of being a spy for the Vatican. He was kept in the infamous Lubyanka prison in Moscow in solitary confinement for five years, and interrogated daily before signing a false confession and being sentenced to hard labor in Siberia. There he suffered cold, hunger, violence, and many kinds of deprivation.

In his book, *With God in Russia*, Father Ciszek described the departure from the prison in Moscow en route to a Siberian labor camp:

❝ *There were last-minute farewells and hasty messages to other prisoners. We were off on a ride to nobody knew where, but we were certain it would be a long one. Many might never come back.* ❞

Crowded in hot railroad cars for the ride to the labor camps, Father Ciszek talked about the parasites that soon invaded the bodies of the prisoners:

❝ *After a few days on the road, everyone was continually scratching absentmindedly at some part of his anatomy. We also suffered from sores on our feet, backs, and buttocks, for there was no room for exercise and no opportunity to get out of the cars.* ❞

While some prisoners were harsh on others, kindness was not unheard of, as Father Ciszek found out upon reaching the end of their rail ride:

❝ As I sat there drinking in the fresh air, another prisoner crept up to me with my shoe. He winked at me and muttered, 'Tie it tighter next time,' then slipped back to his own group. He had braved a reprimand from the guards for this effort, and I was touched. ❞

Next, Father Ciszek and hundreds of other prisoners were stuffed into barges for a two-week river trip. Finally they arrived at the labor camp. Instead of the summer heat they had left behind, it was now snowing as they disembarked:

❝ On deck, in the full face of the wind, the air was so cold it took the breath right out of us. We were forced to gasp for air. Everyone immediately began to pile on anything left in his bundle of clothing . . . 'My God,' said a man next to me, 'it's winter! What'll we do?' ❞

Once in the labor camp, another priest who had been there for a year found Father Ciszek and asked him if he wanted to celebrate Mass. Father Ciszek was overwhelmed, for it had been five full years since he had presided at Mass.

❝ They made the Mass wine for him out of raisins they had stolen on the docks, the altar breads from flour 'appropriated' in the kitchen. My chalice that morning was a whiskey glass, the paten to hold the host was a gold disc from a pocket watch. But my joy at being able to celebrate Mass again cannot be described. ❞

What happened to Walter Ciszek, however, should not be measured by the list of hardships he endured. It ought to be measured instead by the way he believed God was present in every one of these circumstances. He saw humanity in his jailors, his interrogators, and the hardened and desperate fellow prisoners whose whole existence revolved around simply surviving. He learned humility, respect for the body, and the true meaning of freedom. He lived by the conviction that God was working through everything that happened to him, good and bad. He faced sickness and hunger. When most would have despaired, he found answers in the same Gospel message that we mentioned at the start of this chapter: "Your faith has made you well" (Mark 5:34).

Think About It How do you think Father Ciszek was able to see God in the hardships he endured?
How does Father Ciszek's story speak to you about your own suffering?

➤ Go to the student site at
hs.osvcurriculum.com

Distinguish

From believer to disciple:

○ How can someone be a believer but not yet a disciple? What's the difference between the two?

○ Make a chart with two columns. Write "Believer" over one column and "Disciple" over the other.

○ In the Believer column, list the characteristics of someone who simply but truly believes in God the Father, Son, and Holy Spirit.

○ Then in the Disciple column, list the characteristics of someone who is both a believer and a disciple.

Sometimes an additional obstacle arises. The Church can be weakened by individuals whose words and deeds are contrary to the Gospel. The record of the followers of Jesus through history has been mixed. It has included crimes and misdeeds as well as many good works. Sometimes people use the sins of others as an excuse to reject Jesus. Others say they believe in Jesus but they reject organized religion. Sometimes people of goodwill begin by believing, but become disillusioned and lose their faith.

The message of Jesus is entrusted to human beings who at times are weak and sinful, as well as strong and good. Some may wonder: Wouldn't it have been better if God spoke to people directly, without mediation? Then they would all believe, without question. Such questions have arisen many times in Church history. They are not new. They are questions that deserve a serious response.

Recall Why did Jesus tell the priests and elders that the tax collectors and prostitutes would go into Heaven ahead of them?

Infer How do words and misdeeds that are contrary to the Gospel weaken the Church?

Faith and Freedom

Simply because we were created by God, in his image and likeness (Genesis 1:26-27), each person has a specialness or integrity that is often referred to as **human dignity**. The *Catechism* makes clear, "'Believing' is a human act, conscious and free, corresponding to the dignity of the human person" (CCC, 180). We have the gift of a free will. If God had arranged matters so that irrefutable

proof made it impossible for anyone to doubt, where would faith come in? That is not God's way. Faith must be freely given, or it's not faith. The best part is that everything about faith does not rest on our shoulders. We have help from the Holy Spirit and the Church when we respond to the faith God has given us.

If the Church did not include sinners as well as saints, she would be untrue to her mission. Human beings are called into the Church precisely in their weakness and sinfulness, so that they may progressively come to the light and reform their lives. This is an ongoing process accomplished with the help of the Holy Spirit and the support of the Church. God is not finished with any of us yet.

It is part of God's wisdom to choose to work through the Church despite the weakness of her individual members. As Paul said in the Second Letter to the Corinthians, "We do not proclaim ourselves; we proclaim Jesus Christ. . . . But we have this treasure in clay jars, so that it may be made clear that this extraordinary power belongs to God and does not come from us" (2 Corinthians 4:5, 7).

God is not indifferent to the human struggle to live as a disciple. God wants to help not only those who already believe, but those who say, like the man whose son was cured of a spirit in the Gospel, "I believe; help my unbelief!" (Mark 9:24). The Holy Spirit is at work to guide all of us as we make our way over, under, through, and around the obstacles to faith. But let us be clear. The faith toward which the Holy Spirit has been guiding people for two millennia is not "religionless Christianity" or a "me and Jesus only" relationship that leaves no room for the Church. These are false conceptions of faith, based on misunderstandings of both religion and the Church.

Religion and Faith

Religion is intended to help people live their faith. The practice of religion is a virtue (see CCC, 1807 and 2095), which means it is a good habit that we can get better at through

human dignity because we are created by God, in the image and likeness of God, each person has a specialness or integrity

religion a set of beliefs and practices followed by those who serve and worship God

MY FAITH

Faith can be our strength.

Faith can be our guide.

Faith can be our light in dark places.

Faith is also often referred to as a journey.

Here are some questions to help you recall and make notes about your own personal journey of faith.

In the beginning . . .

Who or what influenced your faith?

What notions of God were strongest for you?

What worries or concerns did you pray about most?

What religious traditions, rituals, or prayers meant the most to you?

Along the way . . .

What changes did you make in your faith?

What event, conversation, or concept caused you to grow in your awareness and understanding?

Which part(s) of your faith have remained constant?

These days . . .

What word or phrase would you use to describe your faith?

What hope(s) do you have about your faith?

What do you find yourself praying about the most?

How can your faith be sustained?

God willing . . .

How will your faith shape your future?

What kind of adult do you think you will choose to be because of your faith?

Use this space to begin building your own faith portfolio. Make some private notes about your own spiritual growth. Keep track of your faith journey. Mark the spiritual truths, questions, and actions that are important to you. At the end of the course, you will be asked to summarize some of what you have learned or decided about My Faith.

Go to the student site at
hs.osvcurriculum.com

Discipleship . . . within the Body of Christ . . . for the glory of God and the good of the world

practice and God's grace. It is not simply a matter of *going to Mass* or *not going to Mass.* Adoring God, praying to and worshipping him, as well as fulfilling promises to him are all acts that are part of the practice of religion.

God invites a faithful, reverent, worshipful response from us, simply because of who God is. Religion is not the same thing as faith, but it is one of the ways through which faith makes itself known. The practice of religion reinforces our faith. It is also a web of connection among people who believe the same things, and trust in the same God. We are religious beings by nature. We have been made to live in union with God.

Faith, though deeply personal, always takes shape within a community of believers. As

REFLECT

>> Who comprises my community? Who is part of our parish and who preceded us that led to where we are today?

Who are my friends? Do I have friends who share my faith: a lot, a few, or none at all? Am I good friends with someone who belongs to another faith? How does that impact both of us?

In your own words, explain the simile, "faith is like a team sport." Do you agree with the comparison? Why or why not?

the *Catechism* puts it, "The Church's faith precedes, engenders, supports, and nourishes our faith" (CCC, 181). The community of believers—both the contemporary community and the people of the Church through the ages—helps us to keep going in faith. The faith of the Church supports and nourishes our faith, making it possible for us to believe and grow in our relationship with God and others in the Church. The Letter to the Hebrews sums it up: "Since we are surrounded by so great a cloud of witnesses, let us also lay aside every weight and the sin that clings so closely, and let us run with perseverance the race that is set before us, looking to Jesus the pioneer and perfecter of our faith" (Hebrews 12:1-2).

The practice of religion recognizes and emphasizes the communal nature of faith. We are social creatures; faith is something that is meant to be shared with a community of believers. To use an analogy, imagine a basketball athlete who diligently practices shooting hoops. While that individualized practice is important, basketball is really a team sport. Practicing *with* the team is a crucial part of being a good basketball player. The same holds true for a musician or vocalist who is part of a band, ensemble, or orchestra.

Define What is human dignity?

Explain How is the practice of religion a virtue?

SECTION 4 REVIEW

QUICK REVIEW

1a. **Analyze** Why is it easier sometimes to *not* believe than it is to believe?

b. **Evaluate** How do others influence our willingness to act as disciples of Christ?

c. **Interpret** What does the expression "to lose your faith" mean?

2a. **Recall** What allows us to choose between having faith and not having it?

b. **Analyze** How does belonging to the Church change sinners?

c. **Speculate** What would the Church lose if only sinless people belonged to it?

3a. **Interpret** How is Jesus a "treasure in clay jars"?

b. **Connect** How does the Church support individual faith?

c. **Recall** In which country was Father Walter Ciszek imprisoned?

ACT

Jesuit Father Walter Ciszek was imprisoned for his faith for more than twenty years. His story is recounted at the end of the chapter.

○ Write a list of feelings that Ciszek most likely experienced in prison.

○ Pool your list with those of other classmates. Use the lists to write a monologue for Ciszek. Show his inner conflicts over being in prison for his faith's sake.

SELF-ASSESS

Which statement best reflects where you are now?

☐ I'm confident enough about the material in this section to be able to explain it to someone else.

☐ I have a good grasp of the material in this section, but I could use more review.

☐ I'm lost. I need help catching up before moving on.

PRAYER

Prayer for the Virtue of Faith

Jesus, your faith was in God our Father.

Your steadfastness is our living model!

Kindly grant us the richness of such faith

to embrace our Father as our true provider.

Help us to maintain a staunch belief in God's eminent powers.

Help us to remain loyal to the God until our last days.

When our faith shifts, rush to our rescue without any hesitation.

May your presence always be enjoyed, enabling each of us

to shine as a flame of faith.

May our faith reach out to you!

Amen.

Prayer to Be Faithful in Serving God

Father in Heaven,

ever-living source of all that is good,

keep me faithful in serving you.

Help me to drink of Christ's truth.

Send your Spirit to fill my heart with his love

so that I may serve you in faith

and love and reach eternal life.

In the Sacrament of the Eucharist

you give me the joy of sharing your life.

Keep me in your presence.

Let me never be separated from you

and help me to do your will.

Amen.

TERMS

Write a paragraph that incorporates these terms. Your paragraph should show that you know what each term means.

faith

mediator

disciple

Constitution on the Sacred Liturgy

Christian disciples

human dignity

religion

PEOPLE

Identify who best fits each description.

1. Works within us to increase our faith.

2. The person who fulfills God's promise.

3. Touched Jesus' robe so that she could be healed.

4. A blind man who sat in the road and called out to Jesus to be healed.

5. Was healed by Jesus because of his father's faith.

6. Said "I believe; help my unbelief."

7. Called Jesus a "treasure" and his followers "clay jars."

UNDERSTANDING

Answer each question and complete each exercise.

SECTION 1

1. **Analyze** How do you demonstrate faith in your everyday actions?

2. **Synthesize** Why is faith in anything but God futile?

3. **Synthesize** How does faith change during a person's life?

SECTION 2

4. **Analyze** What do the three Scripture stories in this section have in common?

5. **Examine** How does Jesus react to those who demonstrate faith in him?

6. **Explain** What did the man in the Scripture story mean when he said, "I believe; help my unbelief"?

SECTION 3

7. **Describe** How does the Church help us know Jesus?

8. **Interpret** What does the quotation "Christ is still proclaiming his Gospel" mean?

9. **Relate** How do disciples have a role in Jesus' mission?

10. **Analyze** Why is the metaphor of a journey an appropriate description of life with Christ?

SECTION 4

11. **Analyze** What is the relationship between peer pressure and faith?

12. **Connect** How does having freedom affect a person's faith?

13. **Connect** How is justice related to faith?

14. **Analyze** Why do we need a faith community?

CONNECTING

Visual This illustration depicts the author John Bunyan dreaming about characters in his story, *The Pilgrim's Progress*. *The Pilgrim's Progress* is a very famous allegory, or extended metaphor, that tells about travels to the Celestial City.

How does the illustration reinforce the idea of a spiritual journey? What image would you use to describe your own spiritual journey?

Challenge There is a sign at the entrance to your school that reads: "Christ is at the center of everything we do."

You walk into religion class and your teacher has an opening assignment written on the board: "Explain what the sign at the entrance of our school means. How does it require faith? Use at least 75 words to answer."

○ What would you write?

Question After working through this chapter, what advice would you give someone who wants to increase his or her faith?

Imagine You are a reporter and have spoken with witnesses who saw Jesus heal the woman with a hemorrhage, the blind Bartimaeus, and the boy with a spirit. Now you have an appointment to talk with Jesus about the healings.

○ Make a list of questions you would want to ask about the incidents.

○ Consult the original stories in the Bible and see if your questions are answered.

○ Share the unanswered questions with a classmate; try to use what you learned in the chapter to answer them.

SELF-ASSESS

On Your Own Make a list of the most important things you learned from this chapter. Select three things that represent your growth in understanding as you worked through this chapter. Write a paragraph explaining your choices.

With a Partner List what you found most helpful or interesting in this chapter, as well as any other questions that have surfaced.

What might the people in this photo think about the salvation of the world? What do you think they're doing?

CHAPTER **2**

God Comes to Save His People

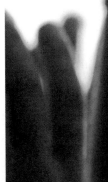

Go to the student site at
hs.osvcurriculum.com

DO

○ View the "big picture" of God's plan for the salvation of the world.

○ Explore examples of God's faithfulness and mercy.

○ Make distinctions between the Persons of the Trinity.

○ Stretch your imagination concerning the Second Person of the Trinity.

○ Describe how the Holy Spirit builds up the Church and makes her holy.

○ Experience contemplative prayer.

○ Explain the Incarnation.

○ Name ways that Jesus teaches us how to live.

DEFINE

logos	Christ
Son of God	Emmanuel
original justice	Trinity
salvation history	communion
messiah	Incarnation
convocation	solidarity
Son of Man	Triune God

Catholic high school students were recently asked this question. Their answers follow:

Which of the three Persons of the Trinity do you find yourself talking to the most: Father, Son, or Holy Spirit?

From a freshman: I find myself talking to the Holy Spirit. Because when I talk to the Holy Spirit, it makes me feel like he's actually with me right now. Sometimes I feel like the Spirit is in my body. When I pray about the sick, he helps them. When I talk to the Holy Spirit, he makes me feel better about myself and also helps me with my problems.

From a senior: I usually find myself talking to the Father. For a while, I was struggling with my Catholicism and simply believed in "some sort of deity." It was easiest to just address whomever I was talking to as "God." Eventually, my faith strengthened, but I still talk predominantly to the Father. Most of the time I pray for comfort, acceptance, and guidance, so it just seems to make more sense to talk to a father figure.

WHAT ABOUT YOU?

Where Are You?				
Choose the response that best reflects where you are right now.				
I know why God sent his Son.	☐ Quite a bit	☐ Somewhat	☐ A little	☐ Not at all
I understand what *salvation history* is.	☐ Quite a bit	☐ Somewhat	☐ A little	☐ Not at all
I understand our belief in the Trinity.	☐ Quite a bit	☐ Somewhat	☐ A little	☐ Not at all
How much does religion shape your decisions?	☐ Quite a bit	☐ Somewhat	☐ A little	☐ Not at all
When I pray, I relate to God the Father.	☐ Quite a bit	☐ Somewhat	☐ A little	☐ Not at all
When I pray, I relate to God the Son.	☐ Quite a bit	☐ Somewhat	☐ A little	☐ Not at all
When I pray, I relate to God the Holy Spirit.	☐ Quite a bit	☐ Somewhat	☐ A little	☐ Not at all

The Turning Point

How is Jesus different from the holy people of other religions?

How can we understand God, who by definition is beyond our comprehension?

What does the Incarnation mean for us?

What does Revelation in Jesus teach us about who God is?

How does the truth about Jesus actually change things here on Earth?

Lyrics from an African-American spiritual contain the words: "You may have all this world, give me Jesus." Many religions have great teachers, prophets, and holy people. We know that Jesus is the most important among these for Christians, but how does our faith explain the difference?

The Church has always had a story to tell—a true story. It was witnessed firsthand, written in Scripture, and passed on by Tradition. It has been told in many different ways, sometimes very simply and sometimes with great elaboration and detail. Sacred art conveys it. Music, song, theater, and dance have been used through the centuries to give it expression. The story of Jesus has been told and retold by people around the globe, in every walk of life. We often call it "The Story." And we describe it as good news.

The story of Jesus doesn't begin with his birth or even his conception. No, the story begins with the eternal God, before creation. In the words of the prologue of the Gospel according to John:

"In the beginning was the Word, and the Word was with God, and the Word was God. He was in the beginning with God. All things came into being through him, and without him not one thing came into being" (John 1:1-3a).

Storytelling

Think of one of your favorite fictional characters from a popular television program, movie, or series of novels and tell that character's story to a partner in exactly one minute.

○ Where did that character's story begin? Where did it end?

○ What did you discover by summarizing the story?

That Word of God—in Greek, *logos*—became incarnate (became flesh) and was born through the Virgin Mary. Jesus, the only **Son of God**, is the Word made flesh. He is God himself, but the title Son of God shows his unique relationship with God the Father.

This chapter focuses on why the Son of God became man. We will also introduce the mystery of the Trinity. The next chapter will discuss our specific understanding of each divine Person of the Trinity—the Father, the Son, and the Holy Spirit—and the Trinity's response to action in the world.

logos a Greek term meaning "word"; in Christian theology, it refers to the Second Person of the Blessed Trinity

Son of God in the Gospel, the term signifies the unique relationship of Jesus to the Father

original justice the harmony inside the human person, between a man and woman and between the first humans and all creation

salvation history the scriptural account of how God over many centuries prepared to heal the separation between God and his People

messiah a Hebrew word meaning "anointed"

In the beginning of the Bible, the Book of Genesis tells how God created the whole world, in all its goodness, beauty, and order. God created our first parents in a state of **original justice** and original holiness. Original justice is described as the harmony that existed inside each human, among each other, and between our first parents and the rest of the world (see *Catechism of the Catholic Church*, 379). Their friendship with God came from the goodness of paradise.

In the Genesis accounts, when the first humans, Adam and Eve, sinned by disobeying God's commands, they separated themselves from God. In doing so, they lost the harmony that existed through original justice and holiness. That loss is known as Original Sin. Sin—"a deliberate thought, word, deed, or omission contrary to the eternal Law of God" (CCC, Glossary)—entered the world, and with sin, death. This transition of the first couple and their descendants from a state of friendship with God to a fallen state is called "the Fall."

Sin is an offense against God. It is disobedience against God that goes against Jesus' own obedience. Because of sin, the world needed a divine intervention to restore humanity to friendship with God. **Salvation history** is the scriptural account of how God, over many centuries, prepared to heal the separation between himself and his People. He entered into separate covenants with Noah and Abraham, and revealed to Moses how to live in the covenant relationship. God reached out to the world again and again. God was actively involved with the Chosen People, through charismatic leaders and kings and the preaching of the prophets. God revealed himself to be faithful and merciful. Through the prophets, he also promised to send the **Messiah**, the Anointed One, who would bring about God's reign. We will fully cover the richness of salvation history later, from Original Sin through the covenants, and the coming of the Messiah.

Eventually God fulfilled this promise by sending his Son to save humans from their sins. Salvation history begins with creation, is clarified in the Old Testament, reaches its fulfillment in Jesus, and continues in and through the Church.

Salvation History Up to the Coming of Christ

Using the timeline of salvation history below, choose one episode and find out more about it from a biblical reference book, such as a dictionary of the Bible or an encyclopedia.

○ What does this episode show us about God?

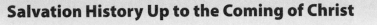

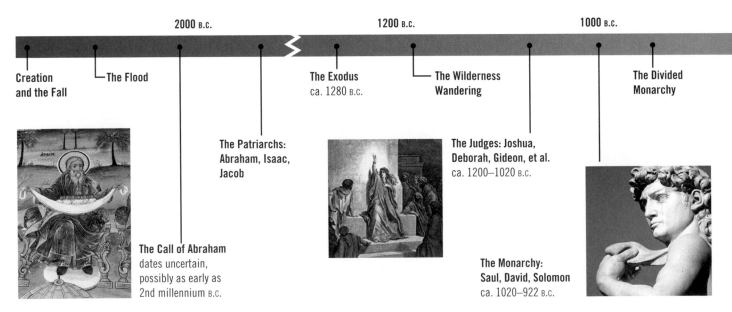

2000 B.C. 1200 B.C. 1000 B.C.

Creation and the Fall

The Flood

The Exodus ca. 1280 B.C.

The Wilderness Wandering

The Divided Monarchy

The Patriarchs: Abraham, Isaac, Jacob

The Judges: Joshua, Deborah, Gideon, et al. ca. 1200–1020 B.C.

The Call of Abraham dates uncertain, possibly as early as 2nd millennium B.C.

The Monarchy: Saul, David, Solomon ca. 1020–922 B.C.

God did all this to prepare the way for the assembly, or **convocation**, of all people in Christ, and through the Church, continues gathering people every day. The word "church" itself means convocation. Today, Jesus is present in our Eucharist, the teachings of the Church, and the way we, as members of the Church, try to serve the world.

Identify When does the story of Jesus begin according to the Gospel according to John?

Explain What is salvation history?

Something More

All the episodes of salvation history prepared the way for the coming of the **Son of Man**, Jesus **Christ**. The term Son of Man is used in visions of the prophet Daniel, where it refers to a mysterious person who will appear at the end of time, coming in the clouds with great glory (Daniel 7:13-14). The community of disciples who followed Jesus gradually came to understand that although he taught and preached and led, he could never be reduced to just one of these roles—or even all of them. He was something far more.

The Gospel according to Matthew shows how Jesus fulfills the promises of God and the hopes of his People. You are likely familiar with the very first chapter of that Gospel that tells how an angel visits Joseph, Mary's husband-to-be, in a dream. The angel announces that Mary will bear a Son, to be named Jesus. The Gospel writer goes on to say that "All this took place to fulfill what had been spoken by the Lord through the prophet: 'Look, the virgin shall conceive and bear a son, and they shall name him **Emmanuel**,' which means, 'God is with us'" (Matthew 1:22-23). The name is a pledge of God's help. It reflects that Jesus is the Messiah. The prophet referred to in this Gospel passage is Isaiah (see Isaiah 9:6).

convocation an assembly of people who have been called together from various places

Son of Man a title recorded in Scripture that Jesus uses to describe himself

Christ from the Greek translation of the Hebrew "messiah," which means "the anointed one"; name proper to Jesus, who is priest, prophet, and King

Emmanuel a name given to Jesus which means "God is with us"

GO TO THE SOURCE

The writer of the Gospel according to Matthew and his community knew the Old Testament Scriptures well. When Matthew tells the story of Joseph, the husband of Mary, Jewish readers would have been reminded of *another* Joseph—the son of the patriarch Jacob.

Read Genesis 37.

○ What skill did the Old Testament Joseph have?

○ How did his brothers react? Why?

○ What do you think of the way Joseph's brothers acted?

○ What attitudes toward Jesus might this story foreshadow?

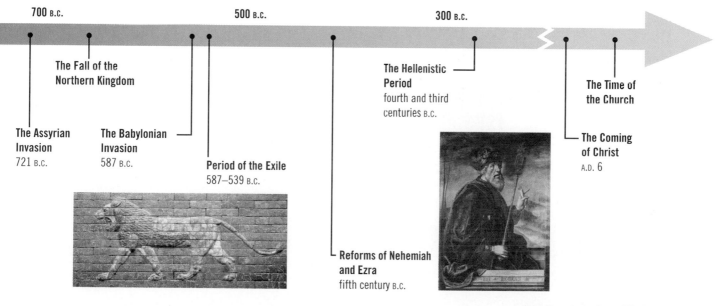

700 B.C.   500 B.C.   300 B.C.

The Fall of the Northern Kingdom

The Hellenistic Period
fourth and third centuries B.C.

The Time of the Church

The Assyrian Invasion
721 B.C.

The Babylonian Invasion
587 B.C.

Period of the Exile
587–539 B.C.

The Coming of Christ
A.D. 6

Reforms of Nehemiah and Ezra
fifth century B.C.

Stained Glass

In the Middle Ages, when most Christians could not read or write and there were few books even available, the Catholic Church used stained glass windows to teach the faith and to help Christians understand Bible stories.

Using colored material as part of window openings can be traced back to 306 B.C. when artisans in the Far East made windows by arranging small gem-like pieces of pot-metal (metal that has a low melting point and can be easily cast) in wooden or stone panels. As early as the twelfth century, the monk Theophilius described the process of making stained glass for decoration.

Subjects for the windows included creation, the Trinity, angels, the Ten Commandments, the Apostles, and the life and death of Jesus (baptism, crucifixion, Resurrection, and Ascension; the Marriage Feast of Cana; the Transfiguration; raising of Lazarus from the dead).

The use of stained glass windows in many Catholic churches continues today. For example, the church of Saint Vincent de Paul Parish in Seward, Nebraska, has eight large windows depicting the Beatitudes. The stained glass windows in the chapel at Saint John's Seminary in Plymouth, Michigan, offer designs depicting duty and inspiration for the young men preparing for the priesthood.

Stained glass windows became very popular during the Renaissance period (A.D. 1400–1600) when Gothic architecture provided churches with large window openings.

A filling strong enough to protect the interior of the church from the weather, yet transparent enough to admit light was needed.

Lead strips held these pieces of glass together.

Artisans either pieced together glass of various sizes and colors or painted the glass pieces.

At that time, glass was only available in small pieces, so artisans created mosaics to fill these openings.

》 What have you learned from stained glass windows you have seen?

If you could build a stained glass window for your school, what would it depict?

The Church continues to affirm that Jesus is God with us. Recall that the word *Christ* is the Greek translation of the Hebrew term *messiah*, which means "anointed." Jesus willingly and faithfully carried out his mission to bring us new life, dying for us on the cross. That mission grew out of the Father's love for us and his willingness to send his Son to make amends for our sins. The heart of Jesus' mission was to bring about salvation for all who believe. He reconciled humankind to God by freely offering himself. The cross is the turning point of the Christian story. It stands at the center of God's plan for the world. It is the symbol of the good news.

The total self-giving of Jesus on the cross proved that God's love for us is without limit. It was truly the Son of God made man who died and was buried. The Resurrection of Jesus shows that God's love has indeed triumphed over evil and is stronger than anything that threatens us.

You know the rest of the story: Jesus ascended to Heaven after his Resurrection. Whenever God sends his Son, he always sends the Holy Spirit, who descended on the disciples at Pentecost. The coming of the Holy Spirit was part of Christ's mission. Our understanding of Jesus would be incomplete without knowing that he sent the Holy Spirit to finish his work on Earth and establish the Church. The Holy Spirit makes a collection of individual disciples into something more: a convocation of people reconciled with God and with one another. In short, he makes us the Church and inspires, builds up, and guides us. The Church then is not an afterthought or an add-on to the plan of salvation. The *Catechism* calls her the Sacrament that unites the Trinity and mankind because God's grace comes to us through the Church. (see CCC, 747). She is the sign of the Holy **Trinity's** continuing **communion** with the human race.

Identify What is the turning point for the Christian story?

Explain Why is the Church a sign of the Trinity's enduring communion with the human race?

Sketch for an Annunciation, Luca Giordano (1634–1705)

Until Christ Comes Again

The Church, through the sending of the Holy Spirit, is assured of God's continual, sustaining presence, until Christ comes again in glory at the end of time. The very last words of the Gospel according to Matthew attest to the presence of God with us in Jesus Christ: "Remember, I am with you always, to the end of the age" (Matthew 28:20).

The Church's mission is the same as the mission of Jesus and the Holy Spirit. The Church draws people into communion with God

Trinity the mystery of one God in three divine Persons: Father, Son, and Holy Spirit; this is the central mystery of the Christian faith and life

communion our calling to share in the life of the Trinity, the inseparable divine Persons who each does what is proper to him (see CCC, 265, 267)

Contemplate

Throughout history, people called mystics have practiced contemplative prayer in order to experience real communion with God. Saint Teresa of Ávila once said, "Contemplative prayer in my opinion is nothing else than a close sharing between friends; it means taking time frequently to be alone with him who we know loves us" (CCC, 2709).

Here's how it works:

○ Begin by putting aside all distractions. Get into a comfortable position. Quiet down. Recall that you are in the presence of God and the Holy Spirit dwells in you. Focus your mind and heart on Christ, the Son of God.

○ Whisper an aspiration such as "Be with Me, Lord" several times, or sing to yourself a familiar verse from your favorite Church hymn.

○ Close your eyes or, if you prefer, focus your gaze on a candle flame or sacred image. Allow five minutes of silence.

○ Afterward, record your insights, emotions, or experience in a journal.

and one another. This is why the period of salvation history in which we now live is called "the time of the Church" (CCC, 732), a time when the Kingdom of God is present but not yet complete. By the Kingdom of God we mean the rule of God, which is present in Jesus and remains among us through the Eucharist. Through the work of the Holy Spirit we build God's Church, which is the beginning of the Kingdom of God on Earth.

To sum it up, Jesus has always existed and will always be with us. He is truly "the Alpha and the Omega" (Revelation 1:8)—the beginning and the end—of the great story of God's love, unfolding through history.

Explain What is the mission of the Church?

Develop Why do we say we are living in "the time of the Church"?

GO TO THE SOURCE

The Bible provides glimpses into the Trinity's eternal presence. Some are found in what is called wisdom literature. For example, Divine Wisdom is personified in several poetic texts of the Old Testament. Wisdom—often used with a feminine pronoun—refers to the third Person of the Trinity: the Holy Spirit.

Read Proverbs 8:22-31.

○ What is Wisdom's role in creation?

○ What is Wisdom's relationship with the human race?

○ How does this passage expand your understanding of the transcendent mystery of the Holy Spirit, who existed from all eternity?

SECTION 1 REVIEW

QUICK REVIEW

1a. Recall When does the story of Jesus begin?

b. Recall What term describes the relationship between God and his People before Original Sin?

c. List Give three examples of titles that refer to Jesus.

2a. Explain Why did the world need divine intervention soon after creation?

b. Demonstrate Give examples of how God reached out to the world.

c. Recall What was the approximate length of the exile after the Babylonian Invasion?

3a. Interpret Why is *Emmanuel* the correct name for Jesus?

b. Recall Which Person of the Holy Trinity completed Jesus' work on Earth and established the Church?

c. Locate Where does the Son of Man, used by Jesus to describe himself, appear in the Old Testament to refer to a person coming in clouds of glory?

Listen and Discuss With a partner, discuss the following.

In this chapter, we said that whenever God sends his Son, he always sends the Holy Spirit.

○ Search through the Gospels to find a passage where all three members of the Trinity are mentioned.

○ Make a list of the role of each member of the Trinity in the event you chose.

○ Why is Jesus the only human who could bring about the Kingdom of God?

Pray Compose a short prayer or write down the lyrics of a song that asks for a closer relationship with Jesus.

SELF-ASSESS

Which statement best reflects where you are now?

☐ I'm confident enough about the material in this section to be able to explain it to someone else.

☐ I have a good grasp of the material in this section, but I could use more review.

☐ I'm lost. I need help catching up before moving on.

Mystery of the Incarnation

When the Church celebrates Christmas, we recall the coming of Christ for the first time as a baby born of the Virgin Mary. This mystery of the union of the divine and human natures is called the **Incarnation.** The accounts of Mary and Joseph and their journey to Bethlehem, the birth of Jesus in a stable, the appearance of shepherds, angels, and Magi— all these narratives are very familiar to us. They are beautiful and comforting. What they are trying to express, however, is a startling fact, when you think about it: God actually became man (see CCC, 479).

The Word made flesh is Son of God and Son of Mary. Salvation is wholly from above, the gift of Heaven, yet it truly springs from our human soil.

—Maria Boulding, spiritual writer

It's not that God became "like" a man or put on a human disguise. In the myths of the ancient Greeks and Romans, for example, gods could appear as any sort of creature, animal or human. Eventually, however, these humans and animals would whip off the disguise and return to their godly status. If Christians had believed something like this, it would not have been remarkable.

Incarnation the fact that the Son of God assumed human nature and became man in order to accomplish our salvation in that same human nature (see CCC, 461)

Scriptures tell us that John the Baptist baptized his cousin Jesus in the Jordan River.

- The Jordan lies at the lowest elevation of any river in the world.
- Christian pilgrims today often visit the traditional site of Jesus' baptism near where the river flows south from the freshwater Sea of Galilee.
- The Jordan River forms the border between Israel and the West Bank.
- The 223-mile river ends at the salty Dead Sea, which is 1,312 feet below sea level.
- The river is a major water source for Israel, Jordan, Syria, and Lebanon, not just for drinking, but also for agriculture.
- At its widest points, the Jordan spans about 60 feet and the deepest parts are only about 17 feet.

Faith & Culture

Go to the student site at **hs.osvcurriculum.com**

What the Gospel tells us about the Incarnation, however, is something very different. God did not take on a costume of human flesh in order to make a theatrical appearance on Earth. God actually became one of us. Another title sometimes used for Jesus is "the Son of Mary," which emphasizes his very real humanity.

Jesus knew what it meant to live a human life, with all its joys and sufferings. He experienced physical hunger, enthusiasm and disappointment, joy and sorrow, energy and fatigue. He had family and friends. He shared in the Jewish religion and followed its observances. He prayed. When Jesus suffered his Passion, the pain and suffering were real. He truly died on the cross.

Jesus took on human nature, but he did so without losing his divine nature (see CCC, 479). Why? If Jesus had only been a man, his life wouldn't have resulted in the Redemption of the world. No human being, no matter how gifted, could save the human race from sin. But because Jesus was also God, he could do what no other human being could do. Christ shared our human nature, so that we could share the divine nature. He made it possible for us to share in God's own life. The *Catechism* states this concisely: "The Word became flesh to make us *'partakers of the divine nature.'*"[2] (CCC, 460).

We know we were created in the image and likeness of God (Genesis 1:26-27), but the Incarnation takes the understanding of human dignity to a whole new level. The Incarnation gives us a sure knowledge of God's **solidarity**, or union, with us, and a new vision of how to be human. And it also helps us understand the value, importance, and potential of the human person in a whole new way: "The Word became flesh *to be our model of holiness*" (CCC, 459). The more we study and meditate on all the events of Christ's life, the more we see reflected in them the good and holy people we ourselves are called to be.

To share in the divine nature of Christ means to imitate Jesus in the way we respond to the challenges we face:

solidarity union of interests, sympathies, and responsibilities

- to forgive when we would rather seek revenge;
- to pray for our enemies when we would rather curse their existence;
- to seek the betterment of those in need as well as our own interests;
- to stop our peers from belittling one another when we would rather join in or ignore it;
- to take a risk for the greater good when we would rather play it safe;
- to apologize for mistakes instead of justifying ourselves;
- to seek purity of mind and heart in an anything goes culture; and
- to gather with the community of disciples in gratitude at Mass when it is easier to think our absence doesn't matter.

Process of Discovery

When we watch any Christmas special on television that depicts the Incarnation, the Holy Family often is pictured with halos, a chorus of angels is singing "Glory to God," and a star shines brightly above the manger, which is all-aglow with God's presence. The magnificence of this scene could prompt a twenty-first century believer to wonder how anyone could doubt that Jesus is the Christ. In reality, this truth—that Jesus is the Messiah—became evident only gradually to those around him.

In Chapter 1, we discussed a threefold understanding of faith: conviction, spiritual trust, and discipleship. Coming to a deep-in-your-heart realization of who Jesus is remains a lifelong passage of discovery for everyone. All along the way, each of us asks questions of Jesus such as, "What do you think is the right thing to do here?" We find out in new ways, for ourselves, who Jesus is by asking ourselves this question.

Recall What is the Incarnation?

Compare How is Jesus different from the classical Greek or Roman gods?

PRIMARY SOURCES

The beginning of article 22 of *Gaudium et Spes* is provided here. The rest of the document is provided at
↗ hs.osvcurriculum.com

The Second Vatican Council issued a statement that addresses the relationship of the Church to the struggles, turmoil, and possibilities of the world around us. It is called "The Pastoral Constitution on the Church in the Modern World." Its title in Latin is *Gaudium et Spes*, which means "Joy and Hope."

↗ Go to the student site at
hs.osvcurriculum.com

22. In reality it is only in the mystery of the Word made flesh that the mystery of humanity truly becomes clear. For Adam, the first man, was a type of him who was to come,(20) Christ the Lord. Christ the new Adam, in the very revelation of the mystery of the Father and of his love, fully reveals humanity to itself and brings to light its very high calling. It is no wonder, then, that all the truths mentioned so far should find in him their source and their most perfect embodiment.

He who is the "image of the invisible God" (Col. 1:15),(21) is himself the perfect man who has restored in the children of Adam that likeness to God which has been disfigured ever since the first sin. Human nature, by the very fact that it was assumed, not absorbed, in him, has been raised in us also to a dignity beyond compare.(22) For, by his incarnation, he, the Son of God, has in a certain way united himself with each individual. He worked with human hands, he thought with a human mind. He acted with a human will, (23) and with a human heart he loved. Born of the Virgin Mary, he has truly been made one of us, like to us in all things except sin.(24)

>> According to the text, what has the Incarnation done?

Is the Incarnation only for believers, or for everyone? Why?

What are we expected to do in response?

How would you summarize the main message?

MY FAITH

When Jesus came into the district of Caesarea Philippi, he asked his disciples, "Who do people say that the Son of Man is?"

And they said, "Some say John The Baptist, but others Elijah, and still others Jeremiah or one of the prophets."

He said to them, "But who do you say that I am?"

Simon Peter answered, "You are the Messiah, the Son of the living God."

And Jesus answered him, "Blessed are you, Simon son of Jonah! For flesh and blood has not revealed this to you, but my Father in heaven."
—Matthew 16:13–17

Take some time answering as honestly as you can. Begin the same way the disciples did by using this outline; only take it a step one step further.

○ Some say you are . . .

○ Others say you are . . .

○ I say you are . . .

○ And so I . . .

This is a good way to sort out some of the different understandings people have while also naming your own. The purpose of the last statement is to help you describe how your belief in Jesus affects you.

Remember that you may choose to share some of this as part of the report you give at the end of this course.

How do you answer Jesus' question: "Who do you say that I am?"

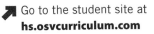

Go to the student site at
hs.osvcurriculum.com

Discipleship . . . within the Body of Christ . . .
for the glory of God and the good of the world

The disciples, one by one, discover who Jesus is by following him. They learn the identity of Jesus gradually, and sometimes amid confusion. Even at the Last Supper, Jesus finds that the disciples still did not completely "get it." Take a look at some of the times when the Apostles were called to follow Jesus and when they didn't quite understand what he was telling them.

Read the following: Matthew 4:18-22; Matthew 16:21-23; Mark 14:66-72; Luke 5:1-11; John 14:8-14.

○ Why did the Apostles accept Jesus' invitation so readily and then later have such a hard time understanding things he said to them?

○ What does it mean to you that the Apostles didn't always understand what Jesus told them?

○ How and when do you have difficulty understanding Christ's calling and his teachings?

SECTION 2 REVIEW

QUICK REVIEW

1a. Contrast How is the story of the Incarnation and Jesus' birth different from ancient myths?

b. Compare What types of experiences does Jesus have in common with us?

c. Interpret What does the *Catechism* mean by the statement, "The Word became flesh to make us 'partakers of the divine nature'"?

2a. Summarize What two things does the Incarnation teach us?

b. Describe How was Jesus' nature revealed to mankind?

c. Synthesize How is our knowledge of Jesus both for everyone and for the individual?

Listen and Discuss With a small group, discuss Jesus' comment to Philip found in John 14:9, "Do you not believe that I am in the Father and the Father is in me?"

○ Why might Philip have had difficulty knowing that the Father was in Jesus?

○ Do we face the same difficulty? Why or why not?

○ What can we do to help ourselves or others understand Jesus' nature?

SELF-ASSESS

Which statement best reflects where you are now?

☐ I'm confident enough about the material in this section to be able to explain it to someone else.

☐ I have a good grasp of the material in this section, but I could use more review.

☐ I'm lost. I need help catching up before moving on.

Jesus Shows Us the Way

All the episodes of Jesus' life are worth meditating on. They contain spiritual wisdom that can help guide us along the path of life.

Consider these two episodes in the life of Jesus from the Gospel according to Matthew.

The Call of Matthew Matthew was a tax collector before he became an Apostle of Jesus. Tax collectors among the Jewish population were responsible for getting the people to pay money to the Roman authorities. They had a reputation for being greedy and corrupt, and were more or less despised by the common people. So when Jesus called Matthew, the other Apostles couldn't make sense out of it. Jesus' explanation reveals something important.

Who Is the Greatest? The disciples came to Jesus with a question: "Who is the greatest in the kingdom of heaven?" (Matthew 18:1). Rank was important to them, as it is in most societies. Again. Jesus' surprising answer reveals something important for the spiritual journey.

Infer Why do you think Jesus called Matthew?

Conclude Why do you think Matthew immediately began to follow Jesus?

GO TO THE SOURCE

Taxes are never popular, but when paying taxes to a foreign power occupying one's country, as the Jews did during the Roman Empire, people felt particularly bitter.

Read Matthew 9:9-13.

○ What do you think Jesus means in verses 12 and 13? What is his mission?

○ What is the spiritual wisdom here and how can that be of help to you?

REFLECT

Think about the episode from the Gospel according to Matthew in which the Apostles wanted to know who was the greatest in God's Kingdom. Remember that Jesus calls us to be childlike, not childish.

>> **What positive qualities of a child would make him or her great in the Kingdom of God?**

What do childlike qualities teach us about humility?

According to Jesus' like-a-child analogy, how is the Kingdom of Heaven different from the "kingdoms" of the world?

Find a song that has this same message, or write a prayer about having the faith of a child.

Identify

○ Name some people you know whose faith in Jesus is obvious.

○ What qualities do they have that show their relationship with Jesus?

○ What actions do they take that let you know they believe in Jesus?

○ When have you noticed one of Jesus' traits in somebody else recently? Was it something that person did or was it something that person said? Explain.

○ Why do you think the disciples wanted to know the answer to this question?

○ What is the spiritual wisdom here and how can that help you?

Go therefore and make disciples of all nations, baptizing them in the name of the Father and of the Son and of the Holy Spirit, and teaching them to obey everything that I have commanded you. And remember, I am with you always, to the end of the age.

—Matthew 28:19-20

Children and the Poor

The Kingdom of God proclaimed by Jesus was not just for the first disciples. In fact, all of us are called to enter the Kingdom. To enter it, one must first accept Jesus' word and believe in him (see CCC, 543). Jesus gave this ongoing challenge to those first disciples, the same people who wondered who was the greatest.

So to whom does the Kingdom belong? God's Kingdom belongs to the poor and most vulnerable among us; those who accept the Kingdom with humble hearts. Jesus shows us the way to the Kingdom because he relates to the poor. During his lifetime, Jesus experienced poverty, homelessness, hunger, and thirst (see CCC, 544).

His mission to bring his message to the poor echoes the words of the Messiah from the Book of Isaiah: "The spirit of the Lord GOD is upon me, because the LORD has anointed me; he has sent me to bring good news to the oppressed, to bind up the brokenhearted, to proclaim liberty to the captives, and release to the prisoners" (Isaiah 61:1). In the Beatitudes of Matthew and Luke, Jesus declares the Kingdom of God is for the lowly and the persecuted. They are blessed (see Matthew 5:3-11; Luke 6:20-23).

GLOBAL PERSPECTIVES

Followers of Jesus wanted to know who ranked highest in Heaven. Jesus answered that the greatest were the least among them. Today, some countries remain among the poorest as they try to pay enormous debts to other nations or global banks. The foreign debt burden on many countries has caused severe problems such as deep cuts in education, more widespread famine, and armed conflicts. The poor often have little or no voice in borrowing the money in the first place. Once a nation's debt is built up, the country has to pay it back. So money that could be used to produce jobs, improve health care, build housing, and purify water resources instead goes out of the country to pay the debt.

Some measures have helped the situation, such as the Heavily Indebted Poor Countries Initiative in the late 1990s, which reduced some debts. Then in 2005, the leaders of the industrialized nations, including the United States and Russia, proposed canceling all the debt owed by qualifying countries.

○ What do you think is the wisest or best way to handle the national debt owed by poor countries?

○ What might be a wrong way to address this issue?

○ Which solution(s) would reflect the values of Christ?

○ How can the poor have a voice among those who decide how much money to borrow?

SOURCE: Catholic Campaign Against Global Poverty

Go to the student site at **hs.osvcurriculum.com**

James McGinnis
(1943–2009)

James McGinnis was a person who took Jesus seriously. In the spring of 1970, he saw the turmoil in the United States and the world and started on the road of peace and justice.

McGinnis was a graduate assistant who taught ethics at St. Louis University. He saw a flyer advertising a talk on peace studies. The discussion sparked a passion for McGinnis. Within eight weeks, he and other professors created an undergraduate curriculum in Peace Studies, with McGinnis as the director of the program.

To complete his doctorate, he and his wife, Kathy, traveled to India to interview many of Mahatma Gandhi's co-workers and delve more deeply into nonviolence as a way of life. McGinnis said the trip had a profound effect on his own call from God to live and teach peace and social justice through nonviolence. He realized that call had been implanted in the late 1960s when he was a member of the Tennessee National Guard in Memphis. In 1968, Dr. Martin Luther King, Jr. was killed. "I sensed that God was calling me to step up to the plate and do what I could to end the war in Vietnam and promote racial and economic justice."

McGinnis and his wife founded the Institute for Peace and Justice in St. Louis in 1975. The Institute promotes peace and justice through education, social action, and prayer. The couple has written books on how to prevent violence and empower people with prayer and peace.

McGinnis didn't live in a bubble of his own lofty theories. He understood that presentations and curriculums needed to evolve when faced with challenges such as the realities of being financially sound, the pervasive power of materialism, and covert and overt racism. These challenges were in addition to fostering a justice and peace movement that continually needs younger voices alongside its aging contingent.

McGinnis found ways to grow and change. He found an outlet in portraying a clown. "I was looking for a way of converting myself, of stretching the limits, of becoming a more compassionate person," McGinnis said in 1988. "I also wanted to become a more courageous person, wanted to become a bolder person in public." The playful side of McGinnis—as an actor, singer and dancer—allowed him to portray peace and justice in another light.

But changes later came in more somber ways. On the night the United States began bombing Iraq in 1991, McGinnis left a gathering of peace activists and walked alone to talk with Jesus. He asked, "What do you want of me in the face of this new violence?" Within in a few moments, McGinnis said he knew the answer: "In the face of escalating violence, escalate love." These words continued to inspire him for the rest of his life. He also carried a "pebble of love," symbolizing tiny acts of kindness and love in everyday life to offset the impact of the "boulders of violence" in the world.

After the terrorist attacks of Sept. 11, 2001, McGinnis said he spent more than a year revising his materials—taking into account the feelings of so many people who no longer felt secure. McGinnis said while there is "no simple answer" to the fear and insecurity people now experience, people can, and should, experience peace in their own daily lives as best they can to make a difference. He applauded students who pray for soldiers and write letters to them, but he also asked educators to encourage students to pray for children involved in conflict regions, suggesting that perhaps they could write letters to legislators that speak about how important it is to work toward peace. McGinnis died in 2009

at the age of 66. Many people who knew him and many he never met left testimonials about how they were inspired by McGinnis' words and actions.

66 Jim's fidelity over his lifetime in being a light, a bridge, a part of a rainbow people has enriched the vision and brightened the flame for many of us. I am counting on his intercession, as he joins the cloud of witnesses, especially when I live through days when my heart is heavy and wants to close up and hide. 99

—Mary Ann Holtz, St. Petersburg, Florida

Think About It In the face of national turmoil, how difficult is it to seek peace and justice? What "pebbles of love" could you do to offset the impact of the "boulders of violence" in your life or the lives of others? What events cause you to turn to Jesus and ask for help, answers, or inspiration?

↗ Go to the student site at **hs.osvcurriculum.com**

The Kingdom also belongs to the children. "At that time Jesus said, ' I thank you, Father, Lord of heaven and earth, because you have hidden these things from the wise and the intelligent and have revealed them to infants; yes, Father, for such was your gracious will'" (Matthew 11:25-26). Anyone who wants to be first in the Kingdom must be last in the world. That person must serve all others.

Children were chosen as examples of the Kingdom of God in much the same way as the poor were blessed in the Beatitudes. Few were more vulnerable and in need of loving care than a child at the time of Jesus.

Historians often note the low status held by children in ancient societies. They were sometimes seen as laborers or property. The fact that the Gospels spoke of including children in the Kingdom of God highlights the message that the Kingdom is open to the everyday people and the least among us.

By using a child and the poor as examples, Jesus indicates that the Kingdom of God belongs to those connected to the most vulnerable. Jesus teaches us to look for him and serve him by seeing and serving those most susceptible to life's hardships. Father Alfred McBride, O. Praem, describes this personal approach. "Personally feeding hungry people, clothing the homeless sitting on the cold pavement, sitting by the side of the sick and comforting them, going to a jail and treating a prisoner as Christ himself, and welcoming strangers into your community are the times you will find Jesus," Father McBride writes.

These are not easy things, and prayer will help give us courage. We cannot separate prayer from acting justly as the prophets and Jesus showed us over and over. Following these teachings of Jesus not only brings a person into new life in the world we live in, but it prepares us for the new life brought about by Christ's Resurrection.

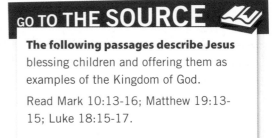

GO TO THE SOURCE

The following passages describe Jesus blessing children and offering them as examples of the Kingdom of God.

Read Mark 10:13-16; Matthew 19:13-15; Luke 18:15-17.

○ What insights do you get from Jesus and children from these accounts about the Kingdom of God?

QUICK REVIEW

1a. Recall Why was the disciple Matthew's occupation significant in the Gospel story?

b. Analyze Tell what Jesus meant when he said, "For I have come to call not the righteous but sinners" (Luke 5:32).

c. Interpret Why was it surprising that Jesus said people would have to become like children to be great in Heaven?

2a. Recall Jim and Kathy McGinnis founded the Institute for Peace and Justice in St. Louis in what year?

b. Summarize What led Jim and Kathy McGinnis to found the Institute for Peace and Justice?

c. Explain What significant revisions did Jim McGinnis make in his materials following September 11, 2001?

ACT

Research on the Internet other programs that serve those who are disadvantaged and neglected.

○ Prepare to give a report on what you find. As part of your report, create a poster or another visual aid that highlights the work of this program and helps others understand its mission.

Pray Write a short prayer about those who are sick and suffering around you, or about your awareness of their suffering.

SELF-ASSESS

Which statement best reflects where you are now?

☐ I'm confident enough about the material in this section to be able to explain it to someone else.

☐ I have a good grasp of the material in this section, but I could use more review.

☐ I'm lost. I need help catching up before moving on.

The Trinity Is Revealed

People have always wanted to know who God is and to be able to put the truth about God into words. But God is beyond definition. God is greater than our human powers of comprehension. Words fall short. Yet there have been many attempts to describe God. It is a natural human desire to want to know who God is, what God is like, and to name the truth about God.

> *You want to know Me? You want to see My face?*
>
> *I do not age with time; I do not fit into a space*
>
> *I transcend the capacity of your eye, so who am I?*
>
> *It is the question of the moment;*
>
> *It is the question for all time.*
>
> —Danielle Rose ("God Is"), youth songwriter

As Catholics, we believe that God has revealed himself. Specifically, God is a Trinity of divine Persons—Father, Son, and Holy Spirit. This is the central mystery of our faith.

As the *Catechism* explains: "The Trinity is a mystery of faith in the strict sense" (CCC, 237), because it is about the inner life of God. We could never have known it unless God revealed it to us. We do not know it by means of our human reason; we could never deduce it from things we observe in nature. And although there are clues to this mystery in the Old Testament, it was not revealed until the coming of Christ.

It is because of what Jesus has shown us, and ultimately the coming of the Holy Spirit at Pentecost, that we come to know God as Trinity. Many passages in the Bible affirm that Jesus is truly God, but different from God the Father.

We also see in the New Testament that the Holy Spirit is promised by Jesus and sent by him. The way in which Jesus speaks shows us that the Holy Spirit is a divine Person distinct from the Father and the Son. Yet all three Persons of the Trinity work together for our salvation. They act as one because they are one God. This is indeed a mystery.

Name What was it that Jesus revealed about the nature of God that we could not have deduced on our own?

Elaborate Why is God impossible to define?

For Our Salvation

An example of the Trinity at work for our salvation can be found in the account of the Annunciation (see Luke 1:26-35). The angel Gabriel appeared to the Virgin Mary and announced that she had found favor with God. He went on to say, "The Holy Spirit will come upon you, and the power of the Most High will overshadow you; therefore the child to be born will be holy; he will be called Son of God" (Luke 1:35). All the Persons of the Trinity are involved, each in a distinct way.

It is clear from Gospel accounts that God alone reveals himself as the Holy Trinity. God the Father comes to us as a voice from Heaven and is described as the Father several times. He is also called the Most High. Jesus is recognized as God's Son. Out of a bright cloud, which is the Holy Spirit, the voice of God says at the Transfiguration:

"This is my Son, my Chosen; listen to him!" (Luke 9:35). Jesus himself talks about the Holy Spirit, who is also described as the Paraclete, meaning Advocate. The Holy Spirit will provide comfort and truth to believers, we are told. Our belief in a Triune God makes us different from many other religions.

Each of the Persons of the Trinity is distinct, but they remain inseparably one God. Many ancient faiths were polytheistic, believing in many gods. The Christian faith is monotheistic. As we affirm in the Creed, "I believe in one God."

The Transfiguration of Our Lord, Russian icon from the Holy Theotokos Dormition Church, Novgorod, Russia

The Attributes of God

The attributes of God are common to each Person of the Trinity, because each Person is fully divine. Saint Thomas Aquinas discussed the following attributes of God in his first volume of *Summa Theologica*.

○ Choose the top two or three attributes of God mentioned in the graphic that best reflect your experience of God.

○ What words would you add?

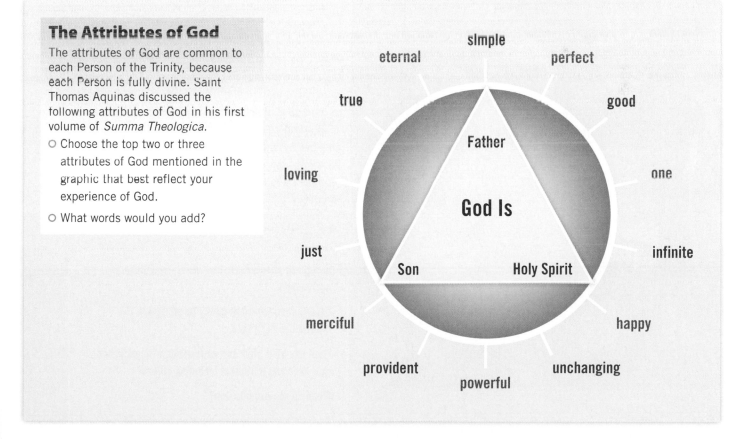

"Do you not know that your body is a temple of the Holy Spirit within you, which you have from God, and that you are not your own? ... Therefore glorify God in your body."

—(1 Corinthians 6:19-20)

Everybody

EVERYBODY DESERVES TO BE included, particularly those in need of physical or mental assistance. This care for others reflects Catholic teaching that every human life deserves respect and protection from the moment of conception. God created us in his image and likeness and loves us with all of our limitations and abilities.

In *Welcome and Justice for Persons with Disabilities,* the U.S. Catholic Bishops explain, "Positive recognition of these differences discourages discrimination and enhances the unity of the Body of Christ".

Some of us—in an honest desire to be polite—try to ignore the differences of people with disabilities. Our hearts may be in the right place, but avoiding these differences doesn't actually work. For one thing, we're lying to ourselves and others when we do this. For another, it's actually *disrespectful* of their dignity. It disrupts the communion of persons created by God for us.

> God saw everything that he had made, and indeed, it was very good.
>
> —Genesis 1:31

Others are awkward and rude. They may even use the words "retarded" or "crippled" in a joking fashion insensitively dismissing both the gifts and struggles of people with disabilities. Worse still is the mocking: when disrespect turns ugly. Verbal abuse can be a step along the path of violence and evil.

A commitment to seeing the image of God in everybody requires us to "acknowledge the dignity and positive contributions of our brothers and sisters with disabilities" (*Welcome and Justice for Persons with Disabilities*). In fact, as a communion of persons, the Christian family must learn to care and take responsibility for those among us who have illnesses or disabilities.

One way to do this is by acting with compassion for all—disability or not. We know how it feels to be excluded. We know how it feels to be judged. Human compassion requires us to be conscious of the situation of others and the desire to alleviate distress.

>> Everybody deserves respect. Everybody deserves compassion.

Comment on your own ability to recognize differences positively.

What has been your own experience with exclusion? How have you worked at including others?

When do you exclude God?

How well do you practice compassion for all?

Our **Triune God** is the origin and goal of all human life. This is part of the story that Christians have to tell. Firsthand witnesses passed it on verbally and then put it in writing. The accounts are passed down to us by the Tradition of the Church. We see it in sacred art and hear it in music. Our senses are filled with the story.

A Fruitful Mystery

The *Catechism* assures us that believing in and loving God wholeheartedly "has enormous consequences for our whole life" (CCC, 222).

- Belief means acknowledging the greatness and majesty of God. This enables us to stand in awe and wonder before God.

- Belief means living in thanksgiving and being grateful for everything God has given us.

- Belief logically leads to affirming the unity and dignity of all people because all are made in God's image and likeness.

- Belief logically leads to trusting God, even when we experience hardship and suffering.

- And, belief means honoring God by making good use of what God has given us: our lives, our bodies, our talents, and our planet.

The Triune God calls all people into communion with himself. In the next chapter we will take a closer look at each of the three Persons of the Trinity as we continue to explore what God has revealed through Jesus Christ.

Identify What is the Annunciation?

Explain How does the Transfiguration show us the Trinity?

Triune God One God in three Persons with God the Father, Jesus the Son, and the Holy Spirit

GO TO THE SOURCE

Two more examples of the Trinity at work in the Bible are the baptism of Jesus and the Transfiguration of Jesus.

Look up the baptism of Jesus in Matthew 3:1-17; Mark 1:1-11; and Luke 3:1-22.

Read about the Transfiguration in Matthew 17:1-13; Mark 9:2-8; and Luke 9:28-36.

○ How is the Trinity identified in each account?

○ What does God say about Jesus in both instances?

QUICK REVIEW

1a. Assess Why is it impossible for humans to describe God?

b. Recall How do we know about the Trinity?

c. Name Whom did Jesus promise to send?

2a. Summarize Retell one of the following stories, showing how it reveals the presence of the Trinity: the Annunciation, the baptism of Jesus, the Transfiguration.

b. Define Select three qualities from the Attributes of God graphic organizer and define them.

c. List What are five consequences of believing in God?

ACT

Think about of the five consequences of believing in God listed in the chapter. Which do you already practice well?

○ Which ones do you want to further develop? Make a few notes and try to specify how and when you can do this.

SELF-ASSESS

Which statement best reflects where you are now?

☐ I'm confident enough about the material in this section to be able to explain it to someone else.

☐ I have a good grasp of the material in this section, but I could use more review.

☐ I'm lost. I need help catching up before moving on.

PRAYER

Gracious God,

I ask you to plant a seed of stillness in my soul.

Everything in my life moves ever more quickly and I am continually expected to fit more things into time that is already brimful with activity. Even when I have moments that require nothing of me, my mind races and I seem unable to locate a switch to turn it off.

Give me, each day, the desire and capacity to breathe in the wonder of air, to envision a still lake on a windless dawn, to drop deep into the well of my own being and find there the peace of your presence.

I ask this in the name of your love.

Amen.

Scripture

Ponder it on your beds, and be silent. (Psalm 4:4)

Now during those days [Jesus] went out to the mountain to pray; and he spent the night in prayer to God. (Luke 6:12)

[Jesus] woke up and rebuked the wind, and said to the sea, "Peace! Be still!" (Mark 4:39)

Be still, and know that I am God! (Psalm 46:10)

I have calmed and quieted my soul, like a weaned child with its mother. (Psalm 131:2)

Then Jesus was led up by the Spirit into the wilderness. (Matthew 4:1)

After he dismissed the crowds, he went up the mountain by himself to pray. (Matthew 14:23)

He withdrew from there in a boat to a deserted place by himself. (Matthew 14:13)

Be silent, all people, before the Lord. (Zechariah 2:13)

The Word of the Lord. Thanks be to God.

Closing Prayer

Let us go in peace to experience the stillness and nurture what needs to come to life. Thanks be to God.

CHAPTER 2 REVIEW

TERMS

Use each of the following terms in a sentence that shows you know what the term means. You may include more than one term in a sentence.

logos	Christ
Son of God	Emmanuel
original justice	Trinity
salvation history	communion
messiah	Incarnation
convocation	solidarity
Son of Man	Triune God

PEOPLE

Identify the person or persons who best fit each description.

1. The couple who brought sin into the world.

2. Patriarchs who had covenants with God.

3. God promised through these teachers that he would send a messiah.

4. The Mother of Jesus.

5. Learned in a dream that Jesus would be born to Mary.

6. Baptized Jesus.

7. A tax collector who followed Jesus.

8. Announced the Incarnation to Mary.

9. Made a list of God's qualities.

10. Witnessed the Transfiguration.

UNDERSTANDING

Answer each question and complete each exercise.

SECTION 1

1. **Recall** Which word was used in the beginning of the Gospel according to John to refer to the Second Person of the Trinity?

2. **Interpret** Why did the prophet Isaiah predict that Jesus' name would be Emmanuel?

3. **Analyze** Why is the cross the turning point of the Christian story?

4. **Interpret** Why is the current period of salvation history called "the time of the Church"?

SECTION 2

5. **Analyze** How do the terms "Son of God" and "Son of Man" reflect Jesus' divine and human natures?

6. **Assess** Why does the Incarnation give us a new vision of humanity?

7. **Interpret** What did Jesus mean when he said, "Do you not believe that I am in the Father and the Father is in me?"

8. **Evaluate** Why would God reveal Jesus slowly to the world?

SECTION 3

9. **Analyze** Why did Jesus eat with sinners?

10. **Summarize** What did Jesus teach about status in Heaven?

SECTION 4

11. **Identify** How do we know about God?

12. **Recall** Who has taught us about the Trinity?

13. **Analyze** If we have a Triune God, why is the Christian faith considered monotheistic?

CONNECTING

Visual This painting, *Batême de Jésus* by James Tisson (1836–1902), depicts the baptism of Jesus. How does this painting interpret this occasion? Point out the major figures and interpret the symbols.

Challenge You are working on questions in this chapter when a friend asks a question:

> **Friend:** Why would Jesus want to live on Earth? Didn't he have it made in Heaven?
>
> **You:** Maybe he wanted to show us something.
>
> **Friend:** Like?

○ What is your next reply?

○ Continue the conversation, including at least two more questions your friend might ask and how you would answer. Use information from the chapter in your answers.

Question After working through this chapter, what advice would you give someone who has trouble understanding how Jesus is true God and true man?

Imagine You are in charge of a movie about Jesus' life. The current scene you are working on depicts the Transfiguration (Mark 9:2-8). As part of your planning process, answer these questions:

○ In what ways could you depict Jesus to show his divinity?

○ How would you position the three disciples to show their reactions to Jesus' transformation?

○ What sort of music would you use to enhance the feelings in the scene?

SELF-ASSESS

On Your Own Make a list of the most important things you learned from this chapter.

Select three things that represent your growth in understanding as you worked through this chapter. Write a paragraph explaining your choices.

With a Partner List what you found most helpful or interesting in this chapter, as well as any other questions that have surfaced.

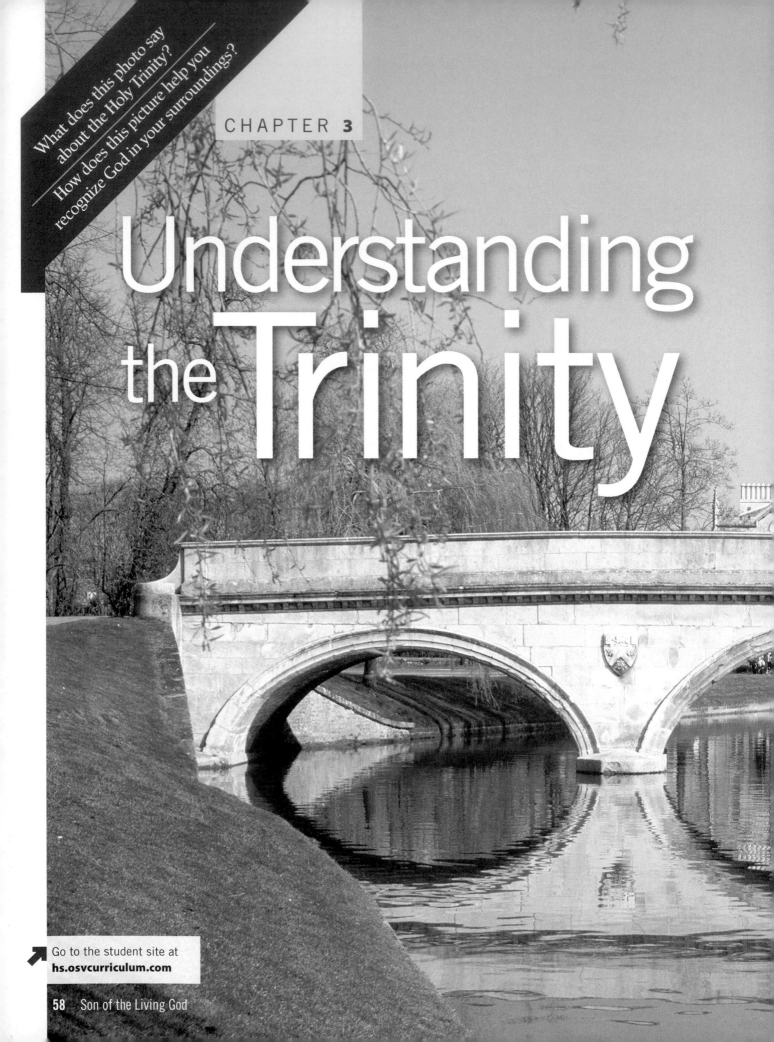

What does this photo say about the Holy Trinity?

How does this picture help you recognize God in your surroundings?

CHAPTER **3**

Understanding the Trinity

Go to the student site at
hs.osvcurriculum.com

- Name the distinguishing characteristics of each Person of the Trinity.

- Connect the early controversies about Christ's nature to today.

- Give reasons why Jesus Christ is the Son of God.

- Explain the challenge associated with the problem of evil.

- Name some causes of evil and see how they are separated from God.

- Describe the Christian perspective on evil.

theology
consubstantial
begotten
the fullness of time
Christology
procession
pneumatology

A priest holds up an egg as he begins his homily. "Can everyone see this?" he asks as he raises the egg up over his head. "I've got one egg here, right? Just one egg, right?" Children nod as teens and adults watch. "How many parts make up my one egg?" After several responses, someone finally calls out the right answer.

"Correct!" he grins. "And today is Trinity Sunday, the first Sunday after Pentecost. I brought this egg to Mass today because it reminds me of the Trinity."

How so?

HOW DO YOU RESPOND?

Where Are You?				
Choose the response that best reflects where you are right now.				
I understand why Jesus has both a divine and a human nature.	☐ Quite a bit	☐ Somewhat	☐ A little	☐ Not at all
I understand how Jesus is the one and only *mediator* between God and humankind.	☐ Quite a bit	☐ Somewhat	☐ A little	☐ Not at all
I've experienced the presence of the Holy Spirit.	☐ Quite a bit	☐ Somewhat	☐ A little	☐ Not at all
I'm okay seeing God as mystery.	☐ Quite a bit	☐ Somewhat	☐ A little	☐ Not at all
I have seen evil at work in the world.	☐ Quite a bit	☐ Somewhat	☐ A little	☐ Not at all

God the Father

What does it mean to call God our Father?

Why have there been theological controversies about the Trinity?

Who is the Holy Spirit?

If God is all-good, why is there evil?

What does it mean to call Jesus the Son of God?

Don't theological definitions take away from the mystery of God?

According to estimates of astronomers today, the universe is about 13.73 billion years old, and is at least 93 billion light years in diameter. Who could create this vast and intricate world? What sort of power would be necessary to set all of this in motion? It is truly beyond human imagining. It requires nothing less than the power of God.

> God made the two great lights—the greater light to rule the day and the lesser light to rule the night—and the stars.
>
> —Genesis 1:16

To better understand the Trinity, we will spend time discussing each of the three Persons—Father, Son, and Holy Spirit. The Father maintains the universe he created through his Word—the Son—and by his "Creator Spirit, the giver of life" (*Catechism of the Catholic Church*, 320). If this is hard to grasp, don't worry. It's a mystery. We can't completely understand it. What we can say is this:

- God alone is the creator of everything that exists.

- God created everything through his Word, Jesus the Son.

- The Old Testament suggests and the New Testament confirms the creative action of the Son and the Holy Spirit. They are inseparable from the Father.

> *Here in this time, here in this place,*
> *here we are standing face to face.*
> *Here in our hearts, here in our lives,*
> *our God is here.*
>
> —Lyrics from "Our God Is Here"
> by Chris Muglia

"'There exists but one God . . . he is the Father, God, the Creator, the author, the giver of order. He made all things *by himself*, that is, by his Word and by his Wisdom, 'by the Son and the Spirit' who, so to speak, are 'his hands.'[3] Creation is the common work of the Holy Trinity" (CCC, 292).

The Triune God is understood as the Creator. God as three divine Persons working together created the universe freely and of God's own divine power. The creation of the world was part of the Triune God's plan of loving goodness. The universe is not the expression of random forces or blind chance.

Think about how many conditions had to be just right for life to exist on Earth. The wonder of the created world gives glory to the Triune God, who formed us all. Our God communicates his glory by creating the world. Through it we share in his truth, goodness, and beauty.

Next, let's look at this quotation from the Book of Job.

> *But ask the animals, and they will teach you; the birds of the air, and they will tell you; ask the plants of the earth, and they will teach you; and the fish of the sea will declare to you. Who among all these does not know that the hand of the Lord has done this? In his hand is the life of every living thing and the breath of every human being.*
>
> —Job 12:7-10

Nothing would exist without the Triune God. We therefore call God "the creator of Heaven and Earth." But the Triune God did not create the universe and then step out of the picture. God the Father keeps the world in existence through his Word, the Son, and through the Holy Spirit, the giver of life. Creation is attributed to God, but all three divine Persons of the Trinity "are the one, indivisible principle of creation" (CCC, 316).

List

An unknown number of conditions had to be just right for Earth to support life—the distance from the sun for example.

- Make a list of at least five things that had to be just right for life to exist on our planet.
- What does this say about the Earth's place in the universe?
- What does this say about the Glory of God?

When we try to comprehend the magnitude of God, our lives may seem like a single drop of water in the ocean. Like the psalmist, we may wonder: "What are human beings that you are mindful of them, mortals that you care for them?" (Psalm 8:4).

We usually think that the Old Testament teaches us about God the Father's power, strength, and glory. We find many terms used to describe God along those lines, such as "Lord," "Almighty," "Holy One," "Rock," "Stronghold," and "Savior."

But the Old Testament Scriptures also express God's guidance, protection, and interest in us. God is called "Father of orphans and protector of widows" (Psalm 68:5). "God gives the desolate a home to live in; he leads out the prisoners to prosperity" (Psalm 68:6). Often we describe our relationship with God in personal ways that tell how he cares for us. We are not insignificant to God.

In the Book of Exodus (4:22), God shows he is like a parent by calling the people of Israel his "firstborn." Occasionally, in the writings of the Old Testament prophets, God is called "Father" to the people (see Isaiah 63:16, 64:8, and Jeremiah 31:9). God is portrayed as "Father" to the king of Israel, too (see 2 Samuel 7:14 and Psalm 2:7, 89:26).

Compare and Contrast

- List at least five titles, names, or images used to describe God the Father.
- Next to each, write down what that word says about God the Father. Compare and contrast each of them. Do they each say something different or do they all say the same thing?
- What are the strengths of each different way of thinking about God the Father?
- How do you think of God the Father most of the time?
- What images or metaphors do you find helpful?

PRIMARY SOURCES

View the image of Rublev's icon first, and then read Father Nouwen's meditation from "The Icon of the Holy Trinity: Living in the House of Love."

A famous artistic work depicting the Trinity is an icon painted by the Russian artist, Andrei Rublev, in 1425. Father Henri Nouwen (1932–1996), a Dutch Catholic spiritual writer who lived many years in the United States and Canada, wrote a meditation about this icon. He described how the icon could lead us to prayer and peace.

↗ Go to the student site at
hs.osvcurriculum.com

Andrei Rublev painted this icon not only to share the fruits of his own meditation on the mystery of the Holy Trinity but also to offer his fellow monks a way to keep their hearts centered in God while living in the midst of political unrest. The more we look at this holy image with the eyes of faith, the more we come to realize that it is painted not as a lovely decoration for a convent church, nor as a helpful explanation of a difficult doctrine, but as a holy place to enter and stay within. As we place ourselves in front of the icon in prayer, we come to experience a gentle invitation to participate in the intimate conversation that is taking place among the three divine angels and to join them around the table. The movement from the Father toward the Son and the movement of both Son and Spirit toward the Father become a movement in which the one who prays is lifted up and held secure . . .

Through the contemplation of this icon we come to see with our inner eyes that all engagements in this world can bear fruit only when they take place within this divine circle. The words of the psalm, "The sparrow has found its home at last. . . . Happy are those who live in your house" (Ps 84: 3, 4) are given new depth and new breadth; they become words revealing the possibility of being in the world without being of it. We can be involved in struggles for justice and in actions for peace. We can be part of the ambiguities of family and community life. We can study, teach, write, and hold a regular job. We can do all of this without ever having to leave the house of love. . . . Rublev's icon gives us a glimpse of the house of perfect love (Nouwen 20-22).

» **Return to the image.**

What do you see in the picture that you did not see before?

What do you think it means to "move from the house of fear into the house of love"?

Share your insights in small groups.

GO TO THE SOURCE

The Bible also uses feminine images to reveal God. In these three passages, we read about some of God's qualities and characteristics through feminine analogies.

Read Isaiah 49:14-15, Isaiah 46:3-4, and Luke 15:8-10.

○ Explain how God is depicted in each account.

○ What do these passages say about our relationship with God?

○ How do they impact your image of God?

Fatherhood, as a natural metaphor, suggests some specific features of God's relationship with us. Just as the bond between the ideal father and children is strong, so is the bond that exists between God and us. Thinking of God as Father can also remind us that we are made in God's image and likeness. Everyone resembles his or her parents in some way. People resemble God, too. The Church reminds us that we all come into the world with the natural ability to sense God's presence.

Recall How old do astronomers estimate the universe to be?

Connect How does God stay "in the picture" with the universe that he created?

The Father in Theology

We use the title "Father" as the divinely revealed name for the first Person of the Trinity. **Theology**, the study of God, has a specialized vocabulary, like any other discipline. Therefore, it is important to learn how words are used in precise ways to express truths about God.

In the New Testament, Jesus frequently refers to God as his Father. When Jesus taught his disciples to pray, he told them to

theology the study of God, based on divine Revelation

GO TO THE SOURCE

In the Sermon on the Mount, Jesus gives everyone some insights about the characteristics of God the Father.

Read Matthew 6:5-14, 25-34, and 7:7-11.

○ Make a list of three things that these passages tell us about God the Father.

address God as "Abba." One translation for Abba is "Our Father." Abba was a very familiar way of addressing God and less formal than the title of "Father." It is more like "dad," a more intimate way to speak to God. These simple facts place the term "Father" above other metaphors and images. Because Jesus called God his Father, Christians have treasured this expression.

Sometimes we simply refer to the first Person of the Trinity as "God," especially in some of the prayers used in the Mass and other Sacraments. However, this does not mean that the Son and the Holy Spirit aren't God, too.

Every time we pray the Lord's Prayer, we affirm that God is *our* Father as well as the Father of Jesus Christ. As the New Testament tells us, there is "one Lord, one faith, one baptism, one God and Father of all" (Ephesians 4:5). This describes God the Father's unique property, meaning that the Church teaches one God and Father from whom everything exists (see CCC, 258).

In previous chapters, we studied how Jesus is the one and only mediator between God and humankind. Those who are not baptized can also experience God's mercy and love. "This is right and is acceptable in the sight of God our Savior, who desires everyone to be saved and to come to the knowledge of the truth" (1 Timothy 2:3-4). God invites all humans, through Jesus and the Holy Spirit, to share their lives with him. This is the heart of the Church's missionary role, and Jesus saw how this could be accomplished: "Let your light shine before others, so that they may see your good works and give glory to your Father in heaven" (Matthew 5:16).

National Migration Week

God is just and we have studied our relationship with God the Father as a parent. The Church also works for justice and cares for people as a parent might. Advocating for justice has been a primary expression of faith throughout modern Catholicism. In recent years, we have expressed our faith by standing up for nuclear disarmament, welfare for the poor, the right to life, medical ethics, the end of genocide, and other matters of justice.

In 1980, the U.S. Catholic Bishops set aside the first week of January as National Migration Week (NMW), a time of reflection and prayer about the causes of migration and the plight of migrants, refugees, and other displaced persons in the United States and around the world.

People migrate because they are often desperate and unable to find a safe and secure life in their own land. They endure many hardships and dangers in their search for a safe home. NMW activities urge Catholics to provide a welcoming community for migrants and a reminder that we are all united in one family of God.

Originally NMW was celebrated on the parish level. However, today it is marked in Catholic elementary and secondary schools, colleges and universities, and religious education classes. Educational booklets and posters provide statistics on migrants and refugees, discussion questions, and activities. Some parishes offer multicultural liturgies and ethnic food festivals.

Grants are awarded every year to Catholic groups who educate others about the problems migrants and refugees face around the world. For example, in Memphis, Tennessee, the diocese sponsored "Building Bridges of Welcome," a program that highlighted the music and art of other cultures, a multicultural dinner, a panel discussion, and training sessions to help build mentoring skills.

Pope Benedict XVI said, ". . . those who have to leave everything, sometimes even their family, to escape from grave problems and dangers . . . [should find] the Church as a homeland where no one is a stranger." (*Angelus*, 2005)

>> When it comes to immigration, what do you need to do in order to properly express your faith?

Does it require increasing your knowledge, adjusting your attitude, or changing a behavior? Elaborate.

↗ Go to the student site at
hs.osvcurriculum.com

> *Can a woman forget her nursing child, or show no compassion for the child of her womb? Even these may forget, yet I will not forget you.*
>
> —Isaiah 49:15

To call God our Father is not to confuse God with an earthly father. Even though we always refer to God as "He," God trancends human categories and is neither male nor female. Human parents have their faults, as we all do. But their shortcomings must never cast a shadow on our understanding of the fatherhood of God. God's paternal tenderness is sometimes compared to that of a mother, but his divinely revealed name is Father.

Recall What title for God have Christians always treasured?

Elaborate Why can those who are not baptized experience God's mercy and love?

SECTION 1 REVIEW

QUICK REVIEW

1a. **Infer** What do the things that God created tell us about him?

b. **Analyze** What does it mean to say that God "maintains" the world that he has made?

2a. **List** Make a list of qualities that humans have that reflect God's nature.

b. **Define** What is theology?

3a. **Recall** What is significant about the word Abba, which Jesus uses to refer to God the Father?

b. **Analyze** How is God different from human parents?

ACT

Ask one of your parents:

○ How has being a parent changed your view of God?

○ What image of God did you have as a child and what image of God do you have now?

Pray Compose a short prayer that honors God the Father.

SELF-ASSESS

Which statement best reflects where you are now?

☐ I'm confident enough about the material in this section to be able to explain it to someone else.

☐ I have a good grasp of the material in this section, but I could use more review.

☐ I'm lost. I need help catching up before moving on.

God the Son

All of us can appropriately consider ourselves sons and daughters of God because of our Baptism. The theological expression "Son of God" (with a capital "S") applies to Jesus alone, whose relationship to the Father is eternal, without beginning or end. The Son is one in being with the Father.

At the fourth-century ecumenical councils (gatherings of worldwide bishops, under the approval of the Pope, to discuss issues of belief and practice) in Nicea and Constantinople, the Church stated that the Son is **consubstantial**. This means the Son is one in being with and of the same essence as the Father. With the Father, the Son is one and the same God. This dogma, or principle of the Church, is expressed in the Nicene Creed, and we continue to affirm it today. The Nicene Creed states that Jesus Christ is "the Only Begotten Son of God, born of the Father before all ages. God from God, Light from Light, true God from true God, begotten not made, consubstantial with the Father" (CCC, 242). It is also true that Jesus is consubstantial with us in his humanity. He is like us in all things but sin.

What is the relationship between the Father and Son like? As we look into this, remember that we can't begin to really understand the inner workings of the Trinity, but God has revealed some things about the mystery. The Church, in trying to tell people about the Trinity, had to come up with its own vocabulary.

Take the word *consubstantial*. Con means "with." The root word "substantial" comes from the Latin meaning "that which stands under." The *Catechism* refers to the "consubstantial Trinity," meaning one God in three Persons (CCC, 253). It also explains the Trinity like this: that the Father is "wholly" or entirely in the Son and the Holy Spirit; the Son is wholly in the Father and the Holy Spirit; and the Holy Spirit is wholly in the Father and the Son. Each divine Person is love (see CCC, 255).

The *Catechism* points out that our human words never adequately describe God. "Since our knowledge of God is limited, our language about him is equally so" (CCC, 40). Sometimes an analogy can help us understand God. One that describes the relationship of the Persons in the Trinity uses a painter as God the Father; his talent as God the Son; and his imagination as God the Holy Spirit. The analogy is not perfect because talents and imagination are usually things a person might possess. The Father, Son, and Holy Spirit are living, divine Persons, but talent and imagination are not living beings. The analogy, however, offers some understanding of the relationship among the Persons of the Trinity.

First there is an artist (God the Father). That artist sculpts human figures. They are very lifelike, but they are not made of the same substance as the artist himself. The figures, however, *are* made in the image and likeness of the artist.

consubstantial with the Father, the Son is one and the same God

This oil on paperboard painting is titled, "Mount Calvary"

JUSTICE AND DISCIPLESHIP

Jesus tells us that discipleship involves praying to the Father, studying his teachings and following his example, participating in the Eucharist, and living the virtues. He also calls us to act for justice.

HAVE YOU EVER BEEN THE VICTIM OF RACISM? Do you make assumptions about a person because of his or her race or ethnic origin? What about when someone tells a racist joke? Do you laugh or not? Is racism a sin?

Racism excludes people. It is a pervasive way that groups or individuals deny that someone else is a son or daughter of God.

Racism is the belief that another person is inferior (or less than human) because of skin color or ethnic origin. Differences in physical characteristics (skin color, hair texture, eye shape) are used to support a system of inequities. Throughout history to today, we sometimes ignore the fact that God created all of us, and Jesus is the mediator for every human. Racism has influenced slavery, unjust legal codes, wars, violence, and genocide. In addition to bullying in schools and violence in communities, racism has led to discrimination—favoring the few self-proclaimed *superiors* and excluding the rest. Although racial discrimination may now be illegal, victims of racism continue to feel its effects. In the United States, decades of job discrimination have affected generations of Americans. The cycle of exclusion can have long-term effects.

The United States Conference of Catholic Bishops addressed the evil of racism in its letter, *Brothers and Sisters to Us.*

As a matter of justice, you have the choice to act.

Educate Learn about backgrounds different than your own. Become knowledgeable; provide as much accurate information as possible to reject harmful myths and stereotypes.

Awareness Check yourself from time to time. What are you thinking as you pass someone of a different race or hear people of a different race give their opinion?

Advocate Speak out against jokes and slurs that target people or groups. Silence sends a message that you are in agreement. It implies tacit approval on your part. It is not enough to refuse to laugh.

Go to the student site at **hs.osvcurriculum.com**

Racism is a sin: a sin that divides the human family, blots out the image of God among specific members of that family, and violates the fundamental human dignity of those called to be children of the same Father . . . It mocks the words of Jesus: "Treat others the way you would have them treat you" (Matthew 7:12). Indeed, racism is more than a disregard for the words of Jesus; it is a denial of the truth of the dignity of each human being revealed by the mystery of the Incarnation.

Hatred between ethnic groups in the Balkans led to conflicts in the 1990s that killed more than 100,000 people.

You can be for justice without being a disciple, but you cannot be a disciple without being for justice.

Using this analogy, the human race is indeed a masterpiece. God the Son, however, is uncreated. He and the Father have the same substance. As we mentioned, the Nicene Creed says that the Son was "begotten, not made." The Son is not God's created handiwork, as humans and the rest of creation are. Jesus the Son is **begotten** from all eternity. We can say that an artist produces works of art with talent. Just as the artist has talent, God the Father has God the Son. Works of art can be taken away from the artist, but talent can never be apart from the artist.

Now we have said that the artist, God the Father, is of the same substance as the talent, God the Son. Now suppose that the artist's talent *becomes* a piece of art, so that all the pieces of art in the world (all of us) may know their purpose. The talent comes from the artist and the talent knows the artist. The talent was always there from the beginning of the creation of the artist's work. In fact, the artist creates through his talent.

One day, the piece of art that is the talent is destroyed, but the artist makes it new again.

A little later, the talent leaves this world to be with the artist, but in the talent's place he sends the imagination of the artist (the Holy Spirit) so that all the pieces of art in the world (us) can share in the artist's glory.

Here are two essential things to remember about the Son of God. As we've said, he was begotten ("from the beginning") and then manifested in the Incarnation. The Incarnation describes what happened when the Son of God became flesh in the womb of the Virgin Mary to begin his human life. Without losing his divine nature, the Son assumed a human nature. The Incarnation brings about important consequences.

begotten the eternal relationship between Jesus and God the Father, meaning Jesus is the only Son of God and he is God himself. The Father generates, the Son is begotten, and the Holy Spirit proceeds (see CCC, 254).

Research

Using historical maps, pinpoint the location of the cities in the Near East where the councils of Nicea, Antioch, Ephesus, and Chalcedon took place in the third, fourth, and fifth centuries.

○ What do all these cities have in common geographically?

○ Why would this have been important?

Christological Controversies

In the early centuries of the Church's life, many controversies arose about what precisely we should believe concerning Jesus and the Trinity. By working out the answers to some difficult questions, theologians and bishops carved out a pathway of understanding. The resolutions of the early controversies do not offer answers for every question, but they keep us on track. This chart shows the heresies of four different groups and when and how various Church councils met and responded.

The Group	What They Said	The Council that Decided	The Orthodox Response
Arians	The Son is not of the same substance as the Father and is not true God.	Nicea (A.D. 325)	The Son is divine. The Father and the Son are one.
Gnostics	Jesus was not a true man. In him, it was as if a spark of divinity assumed a human costume.	Antioch (A.D. 264)	Jesus is God's Son by nature and truly assumed a human nature.
Nestorians	Jesus was a human person joined to the divine Person of God's Son.	Ephesus (A.D. 431)	He is one divine Person with two natures (human and divine).
Monophysites	God's divine nature overwhelmed Jesus' human nature so that only the divine nature remained.	Chalcedon (A.D. 451)	Jesus Christ is one divine Person with two natures (human and divine).

the fullness of time a time fixed by God in which divine prophecies about the Messiah's coming on Earth are fulfilled

Christology the branch of theology devoted to the study of Christ

One consequence is that because Jesus has in his divine Person both a human and a divine nature, he is the one and only mediator, or intermediary, between God and humanity. Jesus is the one who "stands between" and becomes a bridge. Through Jesus our sins can be forgiven and we can have eternal life. "He has rescued us from the power of darkness and transferred us into the kingdom of his beloved Son, in whom we have redemption, the forgiveness of sins" (Colossians 1:13-14).

The *Catechism* uses the word *mystery* one hundred eighty-six times. There are many mysteries, but the central one in Christian life is the Trinity. Only God can tell us about the Trinity as the Father, Son, and Holy Spirit. It is one of those mysteries hidden in God. We know something about the Trinity from creation and from the Revelation that we have been given, but God's inner self remains unknown to us (see CCC, 237).

Jesus Christ, the Son of God, also became the Son of Mary at a particular moment in history. There is a biblical and theological name for this moment. It is called **the fullness of time**. It's not like chronological time, which can be divided into minutes, hours, days, and years. God had prepared for the coming of Christ through many generations.

Jesus' humanity is very important to our understanding of who he is. Not only is he the mediator between God and people, he is also the example of how to live as a human.

The branch of theology devoted to studying Jesus Christ is called **Christology**. Like theology, Christology has a specialized vocabulary and uses some specific categories to discuss who Jesus is, and what he means for us. Studying Christ is important for having a living relationship with Jesus.

Describe How is Jesus' humanity important to our understanding of him?

Conclude Why was Christ's birth a crucial moment for the world?

SECTION 2 REVIEW

QUICK REVIEW

1a. Recall What does begotten mean?

b. Contrast How is the idea of Jesus being begotten different from the idea of his Incarnation?

c. Explain How is Jesus a mediator?

2a. Contrast How is chronological time different from God's time?

b. Recall What is the name of the branch of theology that studies Jesus?

c. Analyze How have councils helped us know Jesus better?

3a. Infer Why have there been so many controversies over Jesus' nature?

b. Infer How have the controversies over Jesus' nature helped the Church's teachings?

c. Analyze Why were the Monophysites incorrect?

Listen and Discuss In a small group, read the Lord's Prayer aloud, then discuss the following questions:

○ What does the prayer tell us about God?

○ What does the prayer tell us about Jesus' view of God?

Pray Compose your own short prayer along the lines of the Lord's Prayer by beginning with the words "Our Father."

SELF-ASSESS

Which statement best reflects where you are now?

☐ I'm confident enough about the material in this section to be able to explain it to someone else.

☐ I have a good grasp of the material in this section, but I could use more review.

☐ I'm lost. I need help catching up before moving on.

God the Holy Spirit

The third Person of the Blessed Trinity is God the Holy Spirit, who is consubstantial to the Father and the Son. Signs of the existence of the Holy Spirit are present throughout the Old Testament. In the story of creation, for example, the biblical author of Genesis says, "a wind from God swept over the face of the waters" (Genesis 1:2). Wind or breath is a common noun in Hebrew, *rūah*, which is also translated "spirit." So the very way in which the story is told affirms that the Spirit of God was present and active in creation. Breath and wind are natural symbols of God's presence and action in the world. Wind is mysterious and powerful, but it can also be gentle. Breathing is necessary for life, yet pure air is invisible, just as the Spirit of God is invisible.

In the Old Testament, references to the "Spirit of God" exist side by side with metaphors for God's action such as the "hand of God" and the "finger of God." The Scriptures reveal

GO TO THE SOURCE

The Holy Spirit is revealed in the New Testament through symbols and actions. Read Matthew 3:13-17, Mark 9:2-8, John 20:19-23, and Acts 2:1-11.

○ What symbol represents the Holy Spirit in each of these four passages?

○ What is the Holy Spirit's action in each of these passages?

○ What role does each member of the Trinity play in each passage?

○ How would you describe the Holy Spirit?

○ What images or words would you use based on your own experience?

○ How are these images different from how you would have described the Holy Spirit when you were very young?

Faith & Culture

Wind has always been a symbol of the Holy Spirit. Recently, a national effort has begun to develop the potential use of turbines to harness the wind as a new form of "green" energy. Proponents of these turbines point out the power and free natural energy found in the wind.

In a speech at the Los Angeles Religious Education Congress in 2007, noted Catholic theologian and storyteller John Shea said the experience of the Holy Spirit can be recognized in three dynamics:

"The Spirit illuminates your mind: you understand something better or differently than before. The Spirit gladdens your heart: you experience joy over it. The Spirit activates your will: you are motivated to act upon it. These three things are the signs of being 'inspired' or 'in-Spirited.' And all three of these dynamics are needed." What Shea describes is the grace of the Holy Spirit, which helps prepare us to exercise our spiritual freedom. This gift of grace makes us free collaborators in the Holy Spirit's work in the Church and the world.

○ What kind of power and energy does the Holy Spirit bring?

○ How would you describe the way the Holy Spirit helps people?

↗ Go to the student site at **hs.osvcurriculum.com**

that God's Holy Spirit could transform a human person, and make that individual capable of great things, as he did with Israel's judges and kings. And in the Book of Isaiah, the world was told that the promised Messiah would receive the Holy Spirit in an especially intense way. The Spirit of God would not only descend on him, it would remain with him (see Isaiah 11:2). The passages that speak of God's Spirit prepared the way for our Christian understanding of the Holy Spirit.

procession a theological term for how the Spirit proceeds from the Father and the Son as from a single principle

The Holy Spirit in Theology

Christians believe that the Holy Spirit always existed and was revealed as a divine Person in the Trinity through events in Jesus' life. This Revelation of the Holy Spirit came about fully when Jesus was glorified, after his death and Resurrection. As the time drew near for his glorification, Jesus promised that he would send the Holy Spirit from his place with the Father. He also promised to remain with us forever.

The Holy Spirit *proceeds* from the Father and the Son eternally. The Nicene Creed includes the statement: "I believe in the Holy Spirit, the Lord, the giver of life, who proceeds from the Father and the Son." The theological term used to describe the relationship of the Holy Spirit to the Father and the Son is **procession**.

The *Catechism* explains that the Holy Spirit and the Son share a joint mission. The Holy Spirit carries on the mission of the Son with the Son because when God sends the Son, he also sends the Spirit:

> *The Son and the Holy Spirit are distinct but inseparable. To be sure, it is Christ who is seen, the visible image of the invisible God, but it is the Spirit who reveals him.*
> —CCC, 689

God the Father and God the Holy Spirit were at work throughout the life and ministry of Jesus Christ.

GO TO THE SOURCE

Read about Jesus' promise of the Holy Spirit in these passages from the Gospel according to John: 14:16-17, 26; 15:26; 16:7-15; 17:26.

○ What are the words Jesus uses to describe the Spirit?

○ What does he say the Spirit will do for the followers of Jesus?

Read about the Holy Spirit descending on Jesus' disciples in John 20:21-22 and Acts 1:8.

○ Why do you think this happened?

○ How does the Holy Spirit help you to be a witness for Christ?

According to Saint Paul, the Holy Spirit helps us to pray. The reality of the Trinity is not far away, but very near.

Read Romans 8:26-27.

○ Who is praying?

○ Who is listening to the prayer?

○ When have you ever wanted to pray, but could not find the words?

○ What emotion do you feel when you read this passage?

Using the metaphor from Section 2, we can see the talent of the artist at work. His imagination, however, we cannot see. Jesus gave us the Holy Spirit so his mission may continue in all of us. The Church continues the work of Jesus by the power of the Holy Spirit. The community of believers gathers for the Sacraments and serves in their homes, in their workplaces, in their communities, in their nation, and in their world. The Holy Spirit makes present the redemptive power of Jesus so that we may all work together to bring the world back to the original justice and holiness that is the Kingdom of God.

The Holy Spirit continues to unite God the Father's People with Christ the Son. It is the Holy Spirit who makes us sharers in God's own life. We become open to the gift of faith and united to Christ through the Sacraments, where we meet Jesus and experience God's grace through the work of the Spirit. Because the Greek word for spirit is *pneuma*, the branch of theology devoted to the study of the Holy Spirit is called **pneumatology**.

pneumatology the branch of theology devoted to the study of the Holy Spirit

THINKING THEOLOGICALLY

Truths About Faith

In a crowded underground Boston subway stop called South Station, thousands of people wait to catch trains to work and back. This handwritten poster was taped to the wall across the tracks where people waiting for trains would see it. Whoever wrote it had to jump down into the pit, cross the tracks, attach this sign to the wall, run back across the tracks, and climb back up out of the pit before another train came.

I believe in Christianity as I believe the sun has risen:
not only because I see it,
but because by it I see everything else.

—C.S. Lewis

>> What are two truths about faith found in this quote?

When have you ever experienced God in an out-of-the-way place, like a subway?

MY FAITH

The wind blows where it chooses, and you hear the sound of it, but you do not know where it comes from or where it goes. So it is with everyone who is born of the Spirit.

—John 3:8

Take time to try and describe the presence of the Holy Spirit in your life. What experiences of the Holy Spirit have you had?

○ When have you felt the Holy Spirit's presence?

○ How could you tell? Was it a strong presence or a gentle one?

○ What effect did the Holy Spirit have in that situation?

○ In whom do you see or feel the Holy Spirit's presence?

○ Based on your experience, what words would you use to describe the Holy Spirit?

Use the questions to help you write a few paragraphs (or pages) about the Spirit in My Life.
Remember that you may choose to include this as part of the report you give at the end of this course.

Go to the student site at
hs.osvcurriculum.com

Discipleship . . . within the Body of Christ . . . for the glory of God and the good of the world

The Trinity Teaches Us

The Persons of the Trinity are inseparable in who they are and in what they do. Everything accomplished by them in the world is the work of one God. God is a community of three Persons; their life together is a perfect expression of love. Community is basic to the nature of God and originates with the Trinity. Because of this, the Christian faith is not primarily individualistic, but is based on and oriented toward being together with others in a community.

Our God remains a mystery despite all that we know about the Trinity and all that has been revealed through Jesus. Theological definitions can keep us from being misled by mistaken ideas about God, but they do not take away his mystery. Nor do they take away the fact that our God is personal. He wants to be with us. Humility is always essential in the way we speak about and relate to God. The mystery of the Trinity is inaccessible to the human mind. It is part of our faith only because Jesus Christ revealed it, as the divine Son of the eternal Father.

Define What is the meaning of the Hebrew word *rūah*?

Develop How was the Holy Spirit's role in salvation revealed by Jesus?

Discover

The Trinity and the fact that God allows evil to exist are two mysteries of God.

○ In small groups or pairs, find two or three other examples that point out how God is a mystery.

SECTION 3 REVIEW

QUICK REVIEW

1a. Explain Why is wind an appropriate metaphor for the Holy Spirit?

b. Compare How did awareness of the Holy Spirit increase between Old Testament times and New Testament times?

c. Summarize In the New Testament, how was the Holy Spirit revealed?

2a. Define What is the meaning of "procession" as it relates to the Holy Spirit?

b. Recall What is pneumatology?

c. Explain How is the Holy Spirit at the heart of the life of the Church?

3a. Analyze Where does the concept of community originate?

b. Assess Even though we study the Trinity, why will it always remain a mystery?

Listen and Discuss Talk with other students about church buildings that have inspired you.

○ Describe how their architectural materials and style symbolize the Trinity.

○ Share your thoughts about why these buildings helped you relate to the Triune God.

○ If possible, find an image of the Trinity on the Internet to share with the class.

SELF-ASSESS

Which statement best reflects where you are now?

☐ I'm confident enough about the material in this section to be able to explain it to someone else.

☐ I have a good grasp of the material in this section, but I could use more review.

☐ I'm lost. I need help catching up before moving on.

The Trinity's Response to Evil

How can it be that God is good, yet the world he created and sustains is scarred by so much hurt, loss, and violence, not to mention sickness and death?

> God whispers to us in our pleasures, speaks to us in our conscience, but shouts to us in our pains: It is his megaphone to rouse a deaf world.
>
> —C.S. Lewis, *The Problem of Pain*

At the beginning of this chapter, we reflected on how God created the world in goodness and wisdom, and described God's continuing role in "holding the world in being." Yet when we look around us, often enough, we do not just see goodness or wholeness.

This is the problem of evil. We believe in a God who is all-powerful and perfectly good, yet our lives and our world are imperfect. People are too often afflicted by suffering and evil. The fact that God allows evil is a mystery, but one that God sheds light on through his Son, Jesus Christ, who died on a cross and rose from the dead to defeat evil. Every generation of believers has confronted evil and wrestled with it. Our faith tells us, however, that God would not allow any evil if he did not also allow good to come from it. We will not fully understand this until we reach eternal life.

> Angels and men, as intelligent and free creatures, have to journey toward their ultimate destinies by their free choice and preferential love.
>
> —CCC, 311

God allows evil because he respects the freedom of those he has created. Somehow—we don't know how—God can extract good from the evil people often choose.

We are certain that God is not the source of evil. He does not bring about evil, or send evil into the world—not even to teach us a lesson. God abhors wickedness. But Scriptures tell us that God himself has at times become so disgusted by evil that he wanted to sweep it away and start the world all over again. Recall the story of Noah and the great flood and the account of Sodom and Gomorrah.

God promised Noah that he would never again destroy the Earth or its inhabitants with water. This was a renewal of God's blessing all living things, which had already taken place at the dawn of creation. Then with Abraham, this divine blessing became part of human history and redirected people toward God and the start of salvation history (see CCC, 1080).

So, from where does evil come? In reflecting on this situation, Christians have identified at

GO TO THE SOURCE

Read the beginning of the story of Noah and the Ark found in Genesis 6:9-22 and the beginning of the story of Sodom and Gomorrah found in Genesis 18:20–19:5.

○ What do these passages tell you about God's view of evil?

○ Why do you think evil exists? Where does it come from?

Suffering in the world often results from human actions or inaction. We misuse our free will or don't exercise it enough. Arguably the most heinous misuse is genocide, or the killing of a large group of people because of their race or nationality. This is not really a new concept. The Romans, for instance, tried to exterminate Christians from their empire in the early days of the Church. We know about the Holocaust when six million Jewish people and others died under the Nazis during World War II. The killing has continued in recent decades. Millions have been murdered in places such as Cambodia, Bosnia, Iraq, Rwanda, and Sudan.

○ Research a case of genocide and list the causes that led to it.
○ What response does our faith call us to in regard to genocide? Be specific.
○ Outline three actions you are willing to support in order to stop or prevent genocide.

⬈ Go to the student site at **hs.osvcurriculum.com**

---

least two basic facts. Evil is sometimes the result of sin. It comes from human deeds that misuse the gift of free will. Some evil and suffering is the work of Satan and fallen angels who, though in no way equal to God, try to thwart the plan of God and distort human life with lies. We renounce Satan at Baptism, and must always resist him.

Some suffering comes from the Original Sin of our first parents. Through their sin, death entered the world. Original Sin destroyed the condition of original justice and original holiness, which we discussed in Chapter 2. Sometimes natural disasters are made worse by human failure to respect and care for the environment, or the failure to care for one another in a time of need. Evil can be complex and have many sources, but none of these sources is God.

Some evils in nature are simply due to the fact that the world is incomplete. The world is "in a state of journeying" toward its final goal (CCC, 310), and suffering is part of that process. Evil that results from this condition is not sent from God as a punishment or an expression of divine displeasure. Because both nature and humanity are imperfect, the innocent suffer, along with the guilty.

Tell What does God promise at the end of the story of Noah?

Explain How has Jesus changed our relationship with God?

Discuss
○ Give an example of what you see as an evil act, person, group, or attitude.
○ Can you think of any instances in history when good was brought out of evil?

The Story of Job

The Book of Job in the Old Testament is part of the wisdom literature of the Bible. It is not a historical book, but rather a story written to lead us into deeper understanding of life and faith. It deals with the problem of evil and innocent suffering.

The main character in the story is Job. He is a good man, a true servant of God, and innocent of any wrongdoing. But he suffers terrible losses. Job's children die, his wealth disappears, and he experiences illness so severe that he hates his life. Everyone rejects him, even his family. He wishes he had never been born.

Job's friends reason that he must have done something wrong to deserve his suffering. They argue with him and try to convince him of their reasoning. Job knows he is innocent, but does not know why his suffering came

Explain
You will be assigned one of the following statements to explain. Prepare to make a case for that perspective even if you don't agree with it.
○ The presence of evil raises questions about the existence of God.
○ Evil comes from human imperfection and our free will.

Trinity Monastery,
FUJIMI, JAPAN

Catholics are a tiny minority in Japan, where most people are Shinto or Buddhist. Japanese Catholics make up about one-half of one percent of the total population. In 2005, for the first time, the Catholic population reached one million. Half of those were from outside the country.

Is Catholicism therefore just a "foreign import" religion? The Catholics of Japan say no. Though small in number, Japanese Catholics have a long history, including saints and valiant martyrs. Today, Japanese culture and Catholic

faith have new opportunities to enrich one another. Here is one example.

When a community of Benedictine monks, from Germany and the United States, living in the city of Tokyo wanted to build a monastery, they took very seriously the task of designing something that would be authentically Japanese. They could have copied American or European buildings. Instead, they created a plan in the style of the architecture of Japan. They chose a beautiful site on a mountain in Fujimi, in the center of

Honshu, the largest and most central island of Japan. All the materials and design elements were selected with care. The result, Trinity Benedictine Monastery, was so impressive that the architect, Tenjiro Takagaki, won a grand prize for architecture in 2002 from the Tokyo Architects Association.

The decision to name the monastery after the Trinity was also an intentional bridge to the wider community. The monks' English-language website describes it this way:

> We have named our monastery the Sanmi Ittai Benedikuto Shuudooin (Trinity Benedictine Monastery). The human penchant for organizing reality into sets of three is probably a universal phenomenon. Among the Japanese people, however, there seems to be a special attraction to triads. At the very heart of Japanese culture are the 'Three Jingi,' that is, the Three Sacred Treasures—a mirror, a sword, and a crescent-shaped jewel—that have been in the possession of the Imperial Household since mythological times.

Because of the Japanese people's special predilection for threes, the doctrine of the Trinity resonates well with the culture. Furthermore, the Christian portrayal of God as a mystery of three distinct Persons relating to one another in perfect and creative unity offers monks a model and goal for their community life.

Think About It Why is it important that the Catholic faith is perceived to be not only European or American, but belonging to everyone?

Why is the role of architecture so important to the Trinity Benedictine Monastery?

If you came upon a beautiful building in a scenic mountain vista, would you want to look inside and meet the people who live there? Why or why not?

What in your own church building reminds you of the Trinity?

➤ Go to the student site at
hs.osvcurriculum.com

In one of the most dramatic passages in the Bible, God speaks to Job from out of the whirlwind. Later, Job answers God with humility and satisfaction as he realizes we can't always understand the ways of God.

- Read Job, Chapter 38. What is God trying to say to Job?
- Then read Chapter 42:1-9. What is Job's response? Why will God hear Job's prayer, but not the prayer of his friends?

upon him. In his struggle, Job longs for death to end his suffering, but in the end he falls silent—not in defeat, but in recognition of God's greatness and unknowable ways. Job is vindicated when God hears Job's prayer and restores his fortunes beyond what he lost.

God permits evil to exist for reasons that are mysterious to us and that can only be shown by his Son Jesus Christ, who died and rose to vanquish evil. As C.S. Lewis is quoted at the start of this section, God shouts at us in our pain. But evil will never triumph over goodness. In the next chapter, we will see the reasons behind that conclusion. It started with the Resurrection of Jesus that ultimately assures us of victory over evil, sin, and death. As Saint Paul said in his Letter to the Romans: "Who will separate us from the love of Christ? Will hardship, or distress, or persecution, or famine, or nakedness, or peril, or sword? No, in all these things we are more than conquerors through him who loved us" (Romans 8:35, 37).

Identify What type of literature is the Book of Job?

Infer What does Job's silence mean?

REFLECT

Name someone you know who has been troubled by suffering, tragedy, or illness for most of his or her life.

>> **What effect has the suffering had on that person?**

What spiritual questions or truths do you see in this situation?

SECTION 4 REVIEW

QUICK REVIEW

1a. Analyze How can we reconcile the goodness of God's creations with the presence of evil in the world?

b. Recall How does God feel about wickedness?

c. Recall What did God promise after the flood?

2a. Analyze Where does evil come from?

b. Define What is "original justice" and "original holiness"?

c. Explain How is the world in a "state of journeying"?

3. Summarize How do you explain the mystery of evil? How should we approach it and handle it? What seem to be the unanswered questions about it? And what hope do we have?

Listen and Discuss With a partner, discuss what you wrote in the Section 4 Quick Review about the mystery of evil and listen to your partner's perspectives.

- What did your partner say that enhances your understanding of evil?
- What would you like to think about or discuss further with the rest of the class?

Pray Compose a short prayer regarding evil in the world.

SELF-ASSESS

Which statement best reflects where you are now?

☐ I'm confident enough about the material in this section to be able to explain it to someone else.

☐ I have a good grasp of the material in this section, but I could use more review.

☐ I'm lost. I need help catching up before moving on.

Consecration to the Trinity

O everlasting and Triune God,
I consecrate myself wholly to you today.
Let all my days offer you ceaseless praise,
My hands move to the rhythm of your impulses,
My feet be swift in your service,
My voice sing constantly of you,
My lips proclaim your message,
My eyes perceive you everywhere,
And my ears be attuned to your inspirations.
May my intellect be filled with your wisdom,
My will be moved by your beauty,
My heart be enraptured with your love,
And my soul be flooded with your grace.
Grant that every action of mine be done
For your greater glory
And the advancement of my salvation.
Amen.

CHAPTER 3 REVIEW

TERMS

Use each of the following terms in a sentence that shows you know what the term means. You may include more than one term in a sentence.

theology

consubstantial

begotten

the fullness of time

Christology

procession

pneumatology

PEOPLE

Identify the person who best fits each description.

1. The members of the Trinity.

2. Russian artist who painted a famous icon of the Trinity.

3. Jesus serves as this between God and humanity.

4. Believed that Jesus was not of the same substance as God the Father.

5. Believed Jesus was not a true man.

6. Believed Jesus was a man with two natures, human and divine.

7. Believed God's divine nature overwhelmed Jesus' human nature.

8. Japanese architect who designed the Trinity Benedictine Monastery.

9. Biblical man who suffers greatly, but is vindicated by God.

UNDERSTANDING

Answer each question and complete each exercise.

SECTION 1

1. **Recall** How is God's current relationship with creation described?

2. **Explain** How is the parent/child metaphor a good description of God's relationship with humans?

3. **Recall** Why are God the Father, the Son, and the Holy Spirit of the same substance?

4. **Assess** What does creation tell us about God?

SECTION 2

5. **Interpret** Why does the Nicene Creed say that Jesus was "begotten, not made"?

6. **Interpret** What does "the fullness of time" refer to?

7. **Explain** What does begotten mean? How does that describe Jesus as part of the Trinity?

8. **Summarize** Give information about one controversy about Jesus and tell how and when it was resolved.

SECTION 3

9. **Synthesize** How has knowledge of the Holy Spirit changed through the ages?

10. **Analyze** Why is the term "community" used to express the relationship between members of the Trinity?

11. **Explain** How is the action of the Trinity a divine unity?

12. **Apply** Why isn't the Christian faith individualistic?

SECTION 4

13. **Explain** Why did original justice end?

14. **Assess** What are the sources of evil?

15. **Analyze** What assurance does the story of Job promise God's servants?

16. **Recall** What does Jesus' death and Resurrection teach us about evil?

CONNECTING

Visual The tapestry shown below is from an altarpiece showing the Trinity with Saint Sebald and the Archangel Michael.

How do the figures and their placement show the importance of the Trinity?

Challenge You are online with two friends talking about a tragedy that happened to someone at school.

> **Friend A:** When something so sad like that happens, I wonder whether God is paying attention.

> **Friend B:** I hear you. Look at wars and starvation. Is God taking care of the world or not?

○ Based on the discussions in this chapter, how do you answer your friends?

Question After working through this chapter, how would you explain the three Persons of the Trinity to someone who is not a Catholic?

Imagine You have been commissioned as an artist to design a building or altarpiece that honors the Trinity.

○ What images or ideas will you base your design on?

○ How important will the opinions of people who see your design each day be to you?

○ Make a sketch of your design.

SELF-ASSESS

On Your Own Make a list of the most important things you learned from this chapter.

Select three things that represent your growth in understanding as you worked through this chapter. Write a paragraph explaining your choices.

With a Partner List what you found most helpful or interesting in this chapter as well as any other questions that have surfaced.

CHAPTER 4

Describe the hands you see in this photo. What reflection of God can you see in this picture?

Knowing
Jesus

Go to the student site at
hs.osvcurriculum.com

DO

○ Reflect on the face of Jesus you see in others.

○ Research the House of Saint Joseph and the Sanctuary of the Annunciation.

○ Explain the various aspects of Jesus' humanity.

○ Identify how the Gospels show that Jesus' life was a Revelation.

○ Relate a time when you were faced with significant consequences for doing what was right.

○ Consider what changes discipleship requires of you.

DEFINE

public ministry

parables

obedience

actualization

signs

hypostatic union

Gentiles

Recently, Catholic high school students were asked: **"If you could ask Jesus one question, what would it be?"** Here are a few of their responses:

"I would ask Jesus how he stayed strong through it all. The whole time he was being disliked by the community and while being put to death, he never faltered once, which I'm amazed by. I believe that if I could be strong, just like Jesus, that maybe I could make a real difference in this world."

"I would ask Jesus why he loves us so much. I'd like to know how, even when we sin so constantly, he can still love us unconditionally. It is hard for me to understand by myself, so I would ask him why."

"If I could, I would ask, 'God, can you help those people who are poor? Today, many families don't have anything to eat and don't have a place to live. If God can, can you help us get past this moment?'"

"If I could ask Jesus one question, I would ask, 'If you say you love us all, why are there people dying because of no food, no water, and no shelter?'"

"I would ask Jesus what he thinks about there being so many different churches with different beliefs based around him."

"I would ask Jesus how my grandfather is doing. He died six years ago. I would want to know if he went to Heaven or is in the process of going. We miss him very much."

WHAT WOULD YOU ASK?

Where Are You?				
Choose the response that best reflects where you are right now.				
I know a lot about Jesus.	☐ Quite a bit	☐ Somewhat	☐ A little	☐ Not at all
I can list his personality traits.	☐ Quite a bit	☐ Somewhat	☐ A little	☐ Not at all
I understand his parables.	☐ Quite a bit	☐ Somewhat	☐ A little	☐ Not at all
I know what he *reveals*.	☐ Quite a bit	☐ Somewhat	☐ A little	☐ Not at all
I have witnessed or know of miracles.	☐ Quite a bit	☐ Somewhat	☐ A little	☐ Not at all
I'm interested in discipleship.	☐ Quite a bit	☐ Somewhat	☐ A little	☐ Not at all

Jesus of Nazareth

What do we really know about Jesus of Nazareth?
What kind of a person was he?

What is he asking of us?
How does knowing him make a difference?
How is it that the life of Jesus is relevant to people today so many years after his time on Earth?

By today's standards of biographies and background checks, we really know very little about Jesus of Nazareth. Most of the information we do have focuses on a mere three years of his life.

It is significant that historians of Jesus' time confirm some events found in the New Testament Gospels. Though we cannot get many specifics on his life, cultural studies of the times in which Jesus lived do give us valuable background information.

Cultural understanding helps paint a picture of a real time, a real place, and a real human being who called his parents Mommy and Daddy when he was very young, played with his cousins in the village, and was consoled by his mom when he scraped his knee. When he grew older, he went to work with his earthly father to learn the carpentry trade.

Growing up in the village of Nazareth would have involved working on a farm among an extended family of aunts, uncles, and cousins. Nazareth was a cross between a village and a family farm. Excavations have found three watchtowers set up to help protect the harvest. It would be a good guess that Jesus spent many nights looking at the stars as he watched over the village's crops. Just four miles away set high on a hill was the city of Sepphoris, one of the capital cities for the ruler Herod Antipas. Sepphoris could be

Modern-day Nazareth

seen from Nazareth. It was here that Joseph and Jesus would go to ply their carpentry skills as Herod built his city.

Just as we have been influenced by some degree by historical events such as terrorist attacks, economic recessions, or natural disasters, so too Jesus was likely influenced by the events of his time. Jesus grew up

Whoever finds Jesus finds a rich treasure, and a good above every good.

—Father Thomas à Kempis,
The Imitation of Christ

Interview
Imagine you are the host of a popular talk show and your next guest is Jesus.

○ What questions would you ask?

○ What kind of answers would Jesus offer?

○ Would he be serious or funny?

○ Write out the interview dialogue between Jesus and you.

during the occupation of oppressive Roman rule. He witnessed the crucifixions of many of his countrymen, including those who resisted the Roman Empire. He saw and experienced the oppression of the working class of society to which he belonged. It was out of the reality of Jesus' real time and real place that his message took shape and grew.

Reflecting on the historical time and place helps make Jesus more real to us. It can also make us wonder why God would send his Son to live the hardships of the day. The Kingdom of God was not going to come about according to the rules of worldly power, but according to the power that is not of this world and through those who are not addicted to the power of this world. Jesus changed the game.

The Gospels do not provide a biography of Jesus in the modern sense. They talk about his birth, but give almost no information about his childhood and upbringing. We find nothing about what sort of a teenager Jesus was. Only one story from his youth appears in the whole New Testament (see Luke 2:41-52). Many of the questions we

GO TO THE SOURCE

The Gospel according to Matthew jumps from Jesus as a baby to his baptism by John the Baptist. The Gospel according to Luke also includes an Infancy Narrative, and is the only one to include a passage about Jesus' life as an early adolescent. Except for that one account in Luke, the Evangelists skip almost thirty years of Jesus' life.

Read Luke 2:41-52.

○ Why do you think the Evangelists included only this account of Jesus as a young person?

○ Identify something you can take from the passage in Luke to apply to your own life.

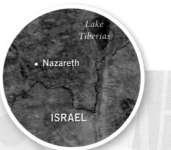

Faith & Culture

Scripture tells us that Jesus grew up in Nazareth. The Annunciation took place there when the angel Gabriel told Mary that she would give birth to a son. Today, Nazareth serves as a trade center and a pilgrimage site. Two important shrines there are the House of Saint Joseph and the Sanctuary of the Annunciation. Franciscans built a church in 1730 over the spot where the Annunciation is thought to have taken place. Researchers found a church built by the Crusaders during excavations for a new basilica on the same spot. There was also a fifth-century church unearthed and a Christian structure from about A.D. 200. Graffiti found on the early Christian structure included the words "Hail Mary." While Jesus lived there most of his life, the Gospels point out that he was not well received in Nazareth: "And he did not do many deeds of power there, because of their unbelief" (Matthew 13:58).

○ Research the House of Saint Joseph and the Sanctuary of the Annunciation.

○ What do these help us to see?

➚ Go to the student site at **hs.osvcurriculum.com**

might ask about his personality, daily life, habits, and tastes were never recorded. The Gospel writers were not interested in such details, but they were passionately interested in who Jesus is for all of us—the Christ.

The Evangelists who wrote the Gospels did, however, record important historical facts about Jesus. It was a rock-solid understanding for them that he was a historical human being. King David was his ancestor. Mary was his Mother, and Joseph his adoptive father. He was born in Bethlehem, and grew up in Nazareth, a town in Galilee, which is in the northern part of Israel.

We know that Jesus began his **public ministry** at about the age of thirty. He preached the Good News, healed the sick, and cast out demons. He called disciples to follow him, shared his life and message with them, and worked miracles. They traveled with him as he went from place to place on his mission.

We also know the content of his preaching: Jesus announced the Good News of God's Kingdom. He invited people into relationship with God and one another. He called people to conversion, to return to his Father. He forgave sins, as only God can do. He called them to account for their failures to love God and neighbor. At times we have a record of what Jesus said during his ministry on Earth. His followers remembered many of his sayings and handed them down to others.

Jesus was a compelling storyteller. In fact, Christ's whole life was a constant teaching. For example, he spoke in **parables** to explain the Kingdom of God. These short, memor-

able stories or comparisons used elements of everyday life to provide insights into God's Kingdom. Parables are short, allegorical stories that convey a hidden truth or meaning. They often question commonly held perspectives. They also made Jesus' listeners see how their assumptions and actions might need to change in order to welcome the Kingdom of God.

The Gospels include a lot about Jesus' humanity. He showed concern for the people he encountered. He experienced a full range of human emotions. Episodes in the Scriptures show that Jesus got angry, felt sorrow and compassion, and expressed joy. Jesus was like us in all things but sin (see *Catechism of the Catholic Church*, 470).

The Apostles were so familiar with Jesus' humanity that when Peter, James, and John saw Jesus transfigured on the mountaintop, they were amazed at this glimpse of his divinity. Most of the time, Jesus appeared to

REFLECT

Through the centuries, people have created countless images of Jesus. You might hear someone say that others reveal Christ to us because we see Christ in the way they act toward us. "By this everyone will know that you are my disciples, if you have love for one another" (John 13:35).

We often say that we see Christ in the innocent, in those treated unjustly, or in those needing help. Jesus reminds us: "When you did this for the least of my people, you did it for me" (see Matthew 25:45).

>> **Where do you see Christ: in others who have helped you, in the poor, the lonely, or elsewhere?**

Write about a time when you might have been "Christ" to someone else.

public ministry the approximately three years following his baptism in which Jesus publicly preached the Good News of salvation

parables allegorical stories with hidden truths or meanings that question commonly held perspectives and were used by Jesus to provide insights into the Kingdom of God

GO TO THE SOURCE

The parable of the Good Samaritan is one of Jesus' best-known parables. But are we sure we know *everything* the parable is saying? Read Luke 10:25-37 and pay special attention to the introduction (verse 29) and the conclusion (verse 36).

○ How does Jesus reframe the lawyer's question?

○ Why is it necessary to reframe the question?

○ What is Jesus telling us here?

be very much like all people are. He was one of us, with personal friends such as Mary, Martha, and Lazarus.

Recall What was the content of Jesus' teaching?

Infer Why did the Gospel writers not include many details about Jesus' daily routines and opinions?

Human Qualities of Jesus

Jesus remained truly God when he became man. The Gospels give us a picture of his human nature. One of his most obvious traits was **obedience** to God the Father. He experienced agony when he was about to suffer his Passion and death, but he remained obedient—even when he felt abandoned by his Father on the cross. Capuchin Father Raniero Cantalamessa, preacher to the Pope, says that obedience is the key part that explains the suffering of Christ. The Letter to the Hebrews says Jesus learned obedience through suffering, Father Cantalamessa pointed out. "The Passion was the proof and measure of his obedience."

> *And being found in human form, he humbled himself and became obedient to the point of death—even death on a cross.*
>
> —Philippians 2:7-8

The Gospels give us a picture of some of his other human qualities, too. Jesus was generous and loving. He welcomed everybody, including outcasts and sinners. For example, Luke 15:1-10 talks about tax collectors and sinners gathering to listen to Jesus. This upset the Pharisees and scribes, so he told them the parables of the lost sheep and the lost coin.

obedience Jesus' compliance with God the Father's plan for salvation

GO TO THE SOURCE

Sinners came to hear Jesus talk and the local leadership didn't think he should welcome these people, let alone eat with them.

Read Luke 15:1-10.

○ What do these two parables say about Jesus' attitude toward sinners?

○ Why is there more joy for the one sinner who repents than for the ninety-nine righteous people?

Christ: Aspects of Human Nature

○ Read the Scripture passages listed on the graphic organizer.

○ Analyze and list all the ways that each passage illustrates either the love, work, thoughts, or will of Jesus.

○ Identify something you would like to know more about concerning this aspect of Jesus' humanity.

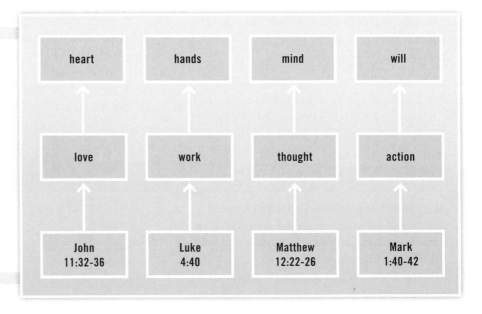

heart	hands	mind	will
↑	↑	↑	↑
love	work	thought	action
↑	↑	↑	↑
John 11:32-36	Luke 4:40	Matthew 12:22-26	Mark 1:40-42

But Jesus also was no stranger to conflict or division. He had enemies, such as those same local leaders who had problems understanding Jesus' actions. He was uncompromising in confronting evil and hypocrisy, but gentle and kind with those who were meek. He welcomed the poor and children, greeting and blessing them even after his disciples tried to turn them away (Mark 10:13-15). Jesus did not "lord it over" others despite his greatness. He was their servant. He cooked for them and even washed their feet. He said to his disciples: "The Son of Man came not to be served but to serve, and to give his life a ransom for many" (Matthew 20:28). He came to bring about our salvation (see CCC, 461).

Imagine

Saint Francis of Assisi loved to imitate Christ, especially in his poverty, which he saw as a positive trait. It was Saint Francis who invented the Christmas crèche, so that people could imagine the birth of Jesus.

For centuries, it has been a folk custom for people in Italy to include small figures representing their own everyday lives as part of the Christmas crèche. A worker might place a replica of his tools. A cook might place a small model of her kitchen table. The town square with a fountain where people visit their neighbors might be represented, and so on. Think about your own everyday life, into which Christ "is born" by faith, and share your answers to these two questions:

○ What sort of figures would you place around the crèche?

○ When you visualize this, what does it make you think about Christmas?

GLOBAL PERSPECTIVES

Jesus came to save the whole world, whether or not everyone on Earth accepts him as his or her Savior. There are more than six billion people living on planet Earth. Of those, just more than two billion are Christians. According to research nearly 1.2 billion people are Muslims; 811 million people are Hindu; 385 million are Chinese folk-religionists; and 360 million are Buddhists. Other major religion populations include twenty-three million Sikhs, fourteen million Jews, twelve million Spiritists, and six million Confucionists. The same research lists more than 900 million nonreligious and atheists.

○ How do you feel about statistics that show Christians make up about a third of the world's population? Then turn that around: How do you feel about the fact that two-thirds of the global population do not follow Jesus?

○ Make a prediction: How do you see these statistics shaping up ten years from now? And why?

↗ Go to the student site at **hs.osvcurriculum.com**

The Face of Jesus

Many people have found their own hopes, struggles, and dreams reflected in the face of Jesus. Think of someone who believes in God's reign or longs for a better world. Witness people who treat others with love and concern. See others who confront evil and suffer unjustly. All of these will find in Jesus a person who knows their struggles. People whose faith brings them joy and laughter will see the smiling face of God in Jesus.

So it's not surprising that those who put themselves first and only look out for their own comfort in this life will find that Jesus stands in opposition to their lifestyle and choices. Like the prophets of the Old Testament, Jesus is an uncomfortable reminder to people about what *truly* matters and what does not matter. We are confronted

Compare and Contrast

There are many different depictions of the face of Jesus in art, icons, and popular images. Find four images of Jesus and compare them.

○ What aspects of Jesus' identity does each image emphasize?

○ What reaction do you have as you look at each image?

○ What do you think each artist wanted to convey about Jesus, and how does each contrast with the other depictions you found?

GO TO THE SOURCE

One person who went away feeling uncomfortable and sad was the rich young ruler who asked Jesus: "Good Teacher, what must I do to inherit eternal life?" (Luke 18:18).

Read Luke 18:18-30.

○ Why did the rich young ruler end up feeling the way he did?

○ What does this story say about what really matters?

○ Put yourself in the rich young ruler's shoes right now. What are you valuing more than what *really* matters?

○ When opportunities and situations come your way, how do you decide between those that will build up the Kingdom of God and those that are contrary to Jesus' message?

with important decisions in life. Jesus was clear that those who choose *not* to love God and neighbor are not living as God intended.

During Jesus' time, most people were reluctant to resist authority figures. The strong political and military powers of Jesus' day discouraged any open resistance. Some, however, such as the Zealots, resisted militantly and fought back from time to time. Others who made up the service class sometimes tried to change peoples' hearts and minds. Jesus belonged to the service class as did John the Baptist. It was out of this grassroots movement that God chose to give birth to the salvation of the world. The Gospel message through Jesus was born. Instead of privilege, the concept of service was promoted and became the model for the Kingdom of God.

Describe What did the Son of Man come to do?

Summarize What kind of man was Jesus?

QUICK REVIEW

1a. Recall What is the best source of information about Jesus' life?

b. Analyze What did the Gospel writers focus on with regard to Jesus?

c. List Tell some of the things that Jesus did as he preached.

2a. Tell Describe what Jesus was like as a person.

b. Evaluate Why would Jesus have enemies?

3a. Infer What does Jesus' humanity reveal about God?

b. Analyze Why would Jesus make people uncomfortable?

Listen and Discuss With a partner, talk about these questions:

○ If Jesus lived during our time, how do you think people would react to him?

○ Would you be comfortable in Jesus' presence? Explain your answer.

Pray Write a short prayer—no more than three lines—that asks Jesus to help you be more like him. See if you can pray it once a day at the same time every day—maybe when you get up, on the way to school, when you open your locker, in home room, or before you go to bed at night. You decide.

SELF-ASSESS

Which statement best reflects where you are now?

☐ I'm confident enough about the material in this section to be able to explain it to someone else.

☐ I have a good grasp of the material in this section, but I could use more review.

☐ I'm lost. I need help catching up before moving on.

A Lifetime of Revelation

Throughout our lives we continue to develop our personal relationship with this interesting, deep, loving, and real Person; Jesus of Nazareth. As we do, we find that every aspect of Jesus' life can teach us something essential about God and about ourselves. The *Catechism* affirms this.

actualization taking something that was once potential and putting it into action or making it actually happen

The whole of Christ's life was a continual teaching: his silences, his miracles, his gestures, his prayer, his love for people, his special affection for the little and the poor, his acceptance of the total sacrifice on the Cross for the redemption of the world, and his Resurrection are the **actualization** *of his word and the fulfillment of Revelation.*

—Pope John Paul II, in the CCC, 561

Silences, Miracles, and Gestures of Jesus

1 *Silences* Sometimes Jesus is silent when asked to defend himself.

Read Matthew 26:59-63 and 27:11-14. These are perhaps Jesus' strongest moments of silence. Here we can find ourselves wanting to urge him to "Speak up!" "Tell him the truth!" "Save yourself!" But Jesus' silence is a refusal to participate in an unjust trial and an indictment against those who accuse him. And deeper still, it also indicates who Jesus is. We can go back to the Old Testament to understand these silences.

Read Isaiah 53. Isaiah is prophesizing about Jesus. In the Acts of the Apostles, Philip explains to the Ethiopian court official that this passage from Isaiah is about Jesus (Acts 8:26-40). Jesus fulfilled the word of the prophet, Isaiah. He is the Suffering Servant, who saves the people from their sins.

signs in a broad sense, actions or events that convey meaning by pointing to something other than themselves

2 *Miracles* In the Gospel according to John, the miracles of Jesus are called **signs**. In a broad sense, signs reveal who Jesus is.

Read John 2:1-11 to see the first of these signs.

○ How is "the good wine served last" a fitting symbol of God's gift of Jesus to the world?

○ What is the outcome of the story for the disciples?

○ Do you think "saving the best for last" applies to other aspects of real life? Explain your opinion.

3 *Gestures* Some of Jesus' gestures are very elemental and even shocking to modern sensibilities. Yet they show that he came to save us just as we are. Some of these happen to bring about miracles.

Read Mark 7:31-36 about Jesus healing a deaf and mute man.

○ What do you think his gestures symbolize?

The spiritual power of Jesus was not disembodied, but came down to Earth.

Other gestures didn't involve miracles.

Read John 8:1-11 about Jesus put to a test.

○ What might be the significance of his gesture here?

PRIMARY SOURCES

Here are the opening paragraphs from Chapter 1 and Chapter 8. Read the full excerpts for each at hs.osvcurriculum.com.

Father Thomas à Kempis (1380–1471), an Augustinian monk who lived in the Netherlands, wrote a collection of meditations called *The Imitation of Christ*. This work has been a very influential book in Christian history, a spiritual classic. Not only did it influence a number of great saints, such as Saint Thomas More and Saint Ignatius Loyola, it also speaks to ordinary believers. It is arranged in four "books" each with a number of chapters.

⬈ Go to the student site at
hs.osvcurriculum.com

Book 1, Chapter 1

Imitating Christ and Despising All Vanities on Earth

"He who follows Me, walks not in darkness," says the Lord. By these words of Christ we are advised to imitate His life and habits, if we wish to be truly enlightened and free from all blindness of heart. Let our chief effort, therefore, be to study the life of Jesus Christ.

The teaching of Christ is more excellent than all the advice of the saints, and he who has His spirit will find in it a hidden manna. Now, there are many who hear the Gospel often but care little for it because they have not the spirit of Christ. Yet whoever wishes to understand fully the words of Christ must try to pattern his whole life on that of Christ.

Book 2, Chapter 8

The Intimate Friendship of Jesus

When Jesus is near, all is well and nothing seems difficult. When He is absent, all is hard. When Jesus does not speak within, all other comfort is empty, but if He says only a word, it brings great consolation.

Did not Mary Magdalen rise at once from her weeping when Martha said to her: "The Master is come, and calleth for thee"? Happy is the hour when Jesus calls one from tears to joy of spirit.

>> According to the first chapter, what does following Christ enable us to do?

Why is knowledge useless without virtue?

According to Chapter 8, what sort of attitude must we have in order for Jesus to come to us and remain with us?

What benefits does friendship with Jesus bring to us?

Dr. Martin Luther King, Jr., once said, "Occasionally in life there are those moments of unutterable fulfillment which cannot be completely explained by those symbols called words. Their meaning can only be articulated by the inaudible language of the heart."

>> Recall a time when something left you "speechless." Was it due to awe, wonder, joy, or surprise? Explain.

What did this experience of silence tell you?

As the Word made flesh, Jesus communicates not only through spoken words but also through actions.

What about other aspects of Jesus' life? If Jesus' life most fully reveals the Father, then every episode can tell us something about God. Sometimes this Revelation is "spoken" nonverbally, that is, without words. Let's look at some examples of the first three elements of Jesus' life listed in the *Catechism* text quoted on page 94. They are: "his silences, his miracles, his gestures."

Understanding the Mystery

We may have heard these Gospel stories often enough that we haven't bothered to stop and think about the details. Can you imagine spitting and touching someone's tongue, for example? Jesus even cooked for his disciples on another occasion in John 21:1-14. He was on the beach one day after his Resurrection. He had a fire going and asked some of the disciples to bring the fish they had caught.

Miracles were a significant part of Jesus' ministry on Earth and miracles are an important part of our faith today.

These questions can help you describe the role miracles play in your spiritual life.

Take your time and remember that you may choose to share some of this as part of the report you make at the end of this course.

1. Where are you when it comes to miracles? What has been your experience? When have you sensed a **small** miracle had taken place in your life? Was it for you or for someone else? Which area of your life did it affect: relationships, tasks, health, or emotions?

2. How about a **big** miracle?

3. When have you really prayed for a miracle, only to get a response from God you didn't expect? How did you handle it?

4. When you look back at your experience, what insight has come to you about miracles?

Miracles and Me: Notes to self.

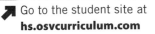
Go to the student site at
hs.osvcurriculum.com

Discipleship . . . within the Body of Christ . . . for the glory of God and the good of the world

SOLIDARITY

> For I was hungry and you gave me food, I was thirsty and you gave me something to drink, I was a stranger and you welcomed me, I was naked and you gave me clothing, I was sick and you took care of me, I was in prison and you visited me.
>
> —Matthew 25:35-36

The spiritual practice of solidarity means "standing with" and supporting those in need or those trying to do the right thing. We are all brothers and sisters, and we have a responsibility to one another, no matter how similar or different. When we stand in solidarity with the poor and vulnerable, we stand in solidarity with Jesus. It is more than compassion, pity, or empathy. Solidarity is a Christian virtue that may include those things. It shares spiritual as well as material goods. It involves building awareness and examines how to alleviate problems or oppression on behalf of people who are hurting. It leads to caring for the needs of others.

But solidarity can be hard to do. We may want to offer solidarity but don't know how—or we can't find something specific to do.

If you want to develop the practice of offering solidarity, you "must have":

- *Eyes to see*, which means *looking around and noticing* what other people are going through.

- *Ears to hear*, which means *taking the time to listen* to those who need help or fair treatment.

- *Hands to help*, which means actually *doing something* to support someone.

- *Hearts to hold*, which means *praying or sacrificing* for that person.

Try it:

Eyes to see: Write down the name of a person or group that you notice is in need—or is in the process of trying to do something good.

_____

Ears to hear: Whose story do you need to listen to, or what issue do you need to get more informed about?

_____

Hands to help: What can you do to offer solidarity to either of the two situations above?

_____

Have a heart: In what manner will you pray for either of the two situations above?

_____

>> **What have you noticed about your response to someone in need of help or support?**

Circle the one(s) true about you:

I try to understand	I listen	I offer encouragement
I change the subject	I ask what's wrong	I become uncomfortable
I am sympathetic	I ask what I can do	I try not to get involved

How would you describe your approach to offering Solidarity?

There are many more examples in the Scriptures of how the whole life of Jesus most fully reveals the Father. The meaning of the sign that Jesus performed at Cana, for example, goes far beyond rescuing a newlywed couple from a shortage of refreshments at their party. An abundance of wine is a sign of the new and joyful times that the coming of the Messiah would bring. Examples like these help us understand the mystery of the Incarnation. They show us the ways of God.

Name Give three aspects of Jesus' life that show his life on Earth was continual teaching.

Apply How are Jesus' non-verbal actions examples for your life?

Discuss

Studies have shown that babies need to be touched and held in order to thrive. When people become elderly, fewer people touch them—especially if they do not have close family or live in a nursing home—and the loss of human touch can have a negative effect.

○ Why is touch so important?

○ What does this say about human nature?

○ How does Jesus touch people today?

SECTION 2 REVIEW

QUICK REVIEW

1a. Explain How was "the whole of Christ's life . . . a continual teaching"?

b. Infer Why would Jesus remain silent at times?

2a. Recall Who was the Suffering Servant?

b. Interpret How did Jesus resemble the Suffering Servant?

c. Connect What do Jesus' signs (or miracles) show in the Gospel according to John?

3a. Infer Why would Jesus perform miracles?

b. Analyze Why did Jesus use gestures to cure?

c. List Describe some gestures Jesus used and tell how people might feel about them.

ACT

Recall some of Jesus' miracles and make a list of them.

○ Identify the miracle you think teaches the most about Jesus.

○ Find images that depict this miracle.

○ Make an electronic presentation about the miracle, using the images you found and your thoughts about it.

SELF-ASSESS

Which statement best reflects where you are now?

☐ I'm confident enough about the material in this section to be able to explain it to someone else.

☐ I have a good grasp of the material in this section, but I could use more review.

☐ I'm lost. I need help catching up before moving on.

True God and True Man

We've been talking about all the ways Jesus modeled what it means to be truly human. In his daily life, we see aspects of Jesus' very real and true human nature. It really helps to remember that Jesus understands our human experiences—our joys, challenges, temptations, frustrations, and excitement. But what makes this so powerful for us is that Jesus was more than human. Jesus was divine, too. This union of divine nature and human nature is key to our understanding of Jesus and what it means to profess faith in him. The Son of God had to be both in order to redeem us.

So, the Second Person of the Trinity assumed human nature without losing his divine nature, without ceasing to be God. He did not suspend his divinity in order to embrace humanity. He is true God and true man. Yet, he cannot be subdivided into parts. It would be incorrect to say, "the divine Jesus did this" and "the human Jesus did that," as though there were two separate beings at work.

"The union of the divine and human natures in the one divine person (Greek: hypostasis) of the Son of God, Jesus Christ" (CCC, Glossary) is described in Christian theology by a technical Christological term: the **hypostatic union**. The word *hypostasis* in Greek originally meant reality or actuality. As Christian theology developed, it used the term *hypostatic union* to describe the union of the divine and human natures of Christ in the one divine person of the Son of God.

Our understanding of the two natures of Jesus helps us better understand what it means to be human—and what it means for God to be God. Because the hypostatic union is a mystery, we might unintentionally downplay Jesus' human nature and focus only on the divine. For instance, when studying the agony in the garden (Luke 22, Matthew 26, Mark 14), we often make the assumption that Jesus knew of his impending death because he was divine. In reality, however, Jesus was practicing the very human skill of being aware of the consequences of his actions. He knew that anyone who continually challenged the reigning authority of his day with strong words and impassioned followers would surely get himself killed.

The fact that God could and did become man also tells us something about God. Jesus' humanity was not shed by him at his death, nor at his Ascension into Heaven. Instead, the Ascension is the entry of Jesus' humanity into divine glory. Jesus has forever bridged the divide between God and humanity.

Like Us in All Things but Sin

We are familiar with the statement that Jesus was human like us in all things but sin. He acted as a human in every part of his human life. Because Jesus became a man to do what his Father wanted, even the smallest thing he did brought God's love to us (see CCC, 516).

Jesus experienced joy and happiness with his family and friends. Among other things, Jesus experienced extreme hunger and thirst, the heavy grief of losing a friend, and mental anguish before facing suffering. He showed us the capacity of human virtues by facing all of it willingly and without hesitation. He demonstrated love for us.

hypostatic union in Christology, the union of the divine and human natures in the one divine person of the Son of God, Jesus Christ

The Lives of Saints

Artists through the centuries have painted portraits of saints. A recent project by modern day, Los Angeles-based artist and author J. Michael Walker followed the lives of ordinary people whose actions and resolve Walker describes as "saintly."

Born and raised in Arkansas, Walker first traveled to Mexico before settling in Los Angeles. He said the city's history and inhabitants intrigued him.

In 2008, Walker completed the book, *All the Saints of the City of the Angels: Seeking the Soul of L.A. on Its Streets*. After eight years of research and exploring the history and lives of Los Angelans, Walker said the journey was "a great gift." He describes his exploration of Los Angeles as an open-ended road trip.

"I gave myself the simplest of mandates," Walker wrote. "To research the history of the streets named for saints, research the stories of those saints, then visit the streets and see how the two histories converge, in whatever ways they might meet—in essence, to try to find the spirit of the saint on her or his namesake street."

The process was profoundly spiritual, Walker said, as he followed wherever the Spirit led him. He connected the stories of people whose lives resonated with the saints' lives. One such story occurred with the mothers of imprisoned youths. Walker connected their suffering with the loving Santa Monica, mother of Saint Augustine. The hard-working gardeners and day laborers along San Ysidro Drive in Bel Air, reflected the spirit, beauty, and sun-hardened face of Saint Isidore, their patron saint.

"By the time I was completing the manuscript for my *All the Saints* book, it became next to impossible not to see in the thousand daily trials and tribulations of the everyday people surrounding me a spiritual profundity that evoked the lives of the saints," Walker said. "For some people, I came to understand, just making it through the day is miracle enough."

J. Michael Walker

Walker creates "narrative, or iconic, representational art." He said he has long thought of each piece he draws or paints as "a quiet space for reflection and contemplation." His work is very meditative and he spends as much time looking at the unfinished work as he does when he brings the work to completion. He contemplates each step before taking it.

"When I am drawing or painting a face, I feel as though I am in conversation with that person," he wrote. "I fall in love with them. I read emotions and stories in their eyes, in their faces."

While his art is a reflection of himself, Walker said he continually works with the help of the Holy Spirit. The Los Angeles father and husband said he values the spirituality in his art. He sees himself as a vessel of the gift he possesses.

"I often feel like the work is creating itself and I am simply the channel for that to occur," he said. "When you're in the proper attitude it is as if you disappear, only to reappear at the end to observe, and wonder in, what was created."

Think About It Tell about a time when you felt the Holy Spirit was working through you. When have you seen someone perform an act you considered saintly? What kind of act was it? Was it something you would have done yourself? Which of the saints do you connect with and why?

Go to the student site at hs.osvcurriculum.com

The agony in the garden is a very familiar passage to many of us. Jesus asked the Father three times to "let this cup pass from me," but each time added that he wanted to do the Father's will. In his prayer in Gethsemane, Jesus expressed the horror that suffering and death signified for him and for us as well. Other accounts depict Jesus' compassion, sorrow, and happiness. In short, it is the Son of God who actually became man. He assumed our human nature so we could become sharers in his divinity.

> *O marvelous exchange! Man's Creator has become man, born of the Virgin. We have been made sharers in the divinity of Christ who humbled himself to share our humanity.*[8]
>
> —Liturgy of the Hours, Antiphon I of Evening Prayer for January 1

Explain Why is it incorrect to say "the divine Jesus did this" and "the human Jesus did that"?

Elaborate What does the fact that God became man say about God?

Relate

Recall a time when you, like Jesus, were fully aware of the consequences of doing the right thing.

○ Describe the situation.

○ At what point did you realize what was going to happen to you?

○ Did being "aware of the consequences" cause you to hesitate or reconsider what you were doing (or what you were about to do)? Why or why not? Jesus was facing crucifixion for doing the right thing. What consequences were you facing?

○ How do we use the words "crucified" or "crucifixion" today? What's the significance, and do you think we use it too lightly?

GO TO THE SOURCE

Everyone has been hungry or thirsty at one time or another, but few of us have experienced the extreme conditions that Jesus did in the desert. Read Matthew 4:1-11.	○ Why would Jesus go into the desert in the first place? ○ How much more difficult would it be to resist the temptations that Jesus faced in the desert after fasting for forty days?
Re-read each of the temptations: Matthew 4:3, 4:6, and 4:9.	○ With what exactly did Satan tempt Jesus?
Anyone who has lost a family member or friend knows the empty pain that seems like it will never end. Jesus experienced such pain. Read John 11:1-44.	○ Why did Jesus not go immediately to Bethany when he heard Lazarus was sick? ○ What does Jesus say to God the Father just before raising Lazarus from the dead? ○ How does Jesus react when they show him Lazarus' tomb? Explain what this says about Jesus' human nature.
Jesus also felt the very human agony in the Garden of Gethsemane just thinking about what was about to happen to him. Read Matthew 26:36-46.	○ How do you think praying similar prayers three times helped Jesus? ○ Share with the class, or a partner, a time when you prayed that something wouldn't happen to you.

QUICK REVIEW

1a. Analyze Why was Jesus sent to a world that did not always accept him?

b. Recall What is the hypostatic union?

2a. Interpret What is the result of Jesus keeping his humanity even after the Ascension?

b. Recall What did Jesus ask of the Father three times during his agony in the garden and what did he really want?

c. Infer What happened as a result of Jesus assuming our human nature?

Listen and Discuss Think about how you would film Jesus' life.

○ With a partner, discuss which scenes would be important to have.

○ Talk about who should play the key roles; these could be famous people or people you know.

○ Discuss where you would film the movie.

SELF-ASSESS

Which statement best reflects where you are now?

☐ I'm confident enough about the material in this section to be able to explain it to someone else.

☐ I have a good grasp of the material in this section, but I could use more review.

☐ I'm lost. I need help catching up before moving on.

Called to Follow

We can know things *about* Jesus from the Gospels and other people, but discipleship requires an additional step. In a very real way, this additional step is God's grace. Discipleship is a response to something about Jesus himself that awakens our spirit, calls to our soul's deepest longing, and makes us want to know him better. The additional step of discipleship is a "Yes" to his call. As we mentioned in Chapter 1, a disciple is someone who studies the teachings of the One and tries to live by those teachings.

Usually, following the call of Jesus means making changes in one's life or it involves sacrifice: giving up things we are used to doing. The first disciples of Jesus made a break with the past when they answered the call to follow him. They were called away from their homes and occupations. They had to leave behind what they knew in order

REFLECT

>> What does discipleship mean to you and what does it require?

What challenges are there to being a disciple today?

How much does answering the call of discipleship change a person's lifestyle, attitudes, or priorities?

How much would it change your lifestyle, attitudes, or priorities?

to follow Jesus. The fishermen, Peter, James, and John, had to leave their nets and their jobs. Matthew was a tax collector. He had to leave a good-paying job and endure the suspicion people had about tax collectors.

Not everyone was called to leave home or change jobs, but they all made important changes in their lives. Though he stopped persecuting Christians, the Apostle Paul kept working as a tentmaker. You might recall that we use the title "apostle" with Paul even though he wasn't one of the twelve. We honor him with the title, however, because of his importance in spreading the Gospel in the early Church. Because of his preaching efforts, he is sometimes called the Apostle to the **Gentiles**.

Gentiles members of "the nations," that is, anyone not belonging to the Jewish community

Catholic Charities

The *Catechism* describes holiness as the perfection of charity. It also calls charity the pathway for love of God and neighbor. It is charity that makes us capable of practicing justice (see CCC, 1889).

The help offered by Catholic Charities includes food services, such as food banks and pantries, soup kitchens and other dining services, as well as home-delivered meals. Helping to feed the hungry in the United States is the largest portion of the organization's work, but they also help millions of people with other needs.

Catholic Charities builds strong local communities. These services include social support, education, socialization and neighborhood services, and help for at-risk people. The agencies also provide some health-related services.

Family services are also a big part of the Catholic Charities mission. The agencies provide help with counseling and mental health, immigration and refugees, addiction, pregnancy, and adoptions.

Housing is another area where Catholic Charities provides services. The organization provides counseling and assistance, temporary shelter, supervised living, permanent housing, and transitional housing.

> One way the Church in the United States practices justice is by helping people in need through the more than 170 Catholic Charities agencies.

> These agencies include more than 1,600 branches and affiliates.

> In 2007 the agencies provided aid for 7.7 million people.

> Some of the people needed help more than once, so that number stands at nearly 14 million times Catholic Charities provided services that year.

>> What types of these services are needed in your community?

What do you think happens with the demand for these services when the economy experiences a downturn with higher unemployment and/or a recession?

What does an organization like this say about Catholics and the Catholic Church?

Research where the Catholic Charities office is located in your diocese and what types of services it provides to your community.

Everyday life challenges you to think about right and wrong, to sort out the good from the bad, and to inform and form your conscience. Here's an example . . .

A high school sophomore walks three blocks from the bus stop to the school and passes homeless people every day. The student decides to start dropping some change for the homeless every day. One day, the student gets a ride with an older brother, but asks to stop the car in front of the homeless in order to quickly drop some change again. The brother asks what's up. The student says quietly: "My own little way of helping out." The brother replies: **"Maybe you're only helping the homeless stay homeless."**

The brother's right.

Good intention.
Bad result.

Homeless people would work if they could.

Charity is a good thing!

The student is making a selfish decision just to feel good.

If it helps the homeless get through the day, it can't be wrong.

How do you respond?

Going Moral

Paul continued his trade in order to support himself on his preaching mission and so he would not be a burden to the communities he visited. One of the first Gentile converts to Christianity, Lydia, was a dealer in purple goods. She was the head of a household. She answered the call to follow Jesus not by leaving her home, but by welcoming people into it. She opened her home to Paul, Silas, and Timothy. Another convert was the Ethiopian court official who met the Apostle Philip while he was traveling. He too decided to follow Jesus and was baptized. After his baptism, Scripture says he "went on his way, rejoicing" (Acts 8:39). There is more than one way to travel the path of discipleship.

Though everyone is not called to change in the same way, once someone decides to be a disciple of Jesus, some kind of important change will be made, even if it is an important change in beliefs or attitudes. There is an old saying based on what we read in the Gospels, and it extends forward into the present: "No one ever met Jesus and stayed the same."

Sometimes we focus on the call of Jesus best when we make a break from the ordinary. We go on a retreat or a mission trip. We experience a lock-in, a concert, or an overnight with the parish youth group. We might even travel abroad to take part in a World Youth Day. We might have an intense experience of service with the disadvantaged, helping to build a house in a deprived neighborhood, or digging a well in a developing country. Experiences such as these can give us "new eyes," and we bring home a new sense of purpose and energy.

We all have heard the Gospel message Jesus gave to humanity: "I stand at the door and

Share

Take a poll. What events or experiences have shaped the spirituality of the different members of your class? Answer these questions:

○ What was the event or experience?

○ What was the most important or memorable part of the experience?

○ What was the difference in the way you felt before and after the event?

○ What truth did the event help you to see?

knock." Believers let Christ into their hearts, and discipleship is about the next step. After we open the door and let Christ into our heart, he points outside and invites us to go live like him in the world.

When Paul preached in Athens, he taught that from the beginning, God made all nations from one ancestor. God put into all humankind the need to search for God and to find him. Paul reminded the first disciples about something that applies to all of us, but which is easy to forget: "indeed he [God] is not far from each one of us. For 'In him we live and move and have our being;' as even some of your own poets have said" (Acts 17:27-28).

It is comforting to know that in the Holy Spirit we "have our being." The task is to learn how to open ourselves to the Holy Spirit's voice, hear it from within and from others, and let it direct us.

List What does it take to hear the voice of the Holy Spirit and what increases the ability to hear the Spirit?

Select Name someone you know who seems to be in touch with the Holy Spirit in his or her life. Explain why you say this about this person.

GO TO THE SOURCE

We do not rely on our own efforts to respond to the call of Jesus. Jesus made us a promise.

Read John 14:15-17 and 25-27 and John 16:7-15.

○ What does Jesus promise?

○ What does Jesus' use of the term "Advocate" tell you about the Holy Spirit?

○ What effect does this have on how you relate to the Holy Spirit?

QUICK REVIEW

1a. Recall How did some of Jesus' disciples change their lives to follow him?

b. Infer What does a list of Jesus' disciples' occupations tell about them?

2a. Explain How does getting out of everyday routines help us follow Jesus?

b. Analyze How do good everyday actions increase our faith?

c. Analyze What might Saint Paul have meant by his comment that God "is not far from us"?

Listen and Discuss Write down one of your favorite stories or quotes from Jesus and explain why it stands out for you.

Pray Compose a short prayer about discipleship.

SELF-ASSESS

Which statement best reflects where you are now?

☐ I'm confident enough about the material in this section to be able to explain it to someone else.

☐ I have a good grasp of the material in this section, but I could use more review.

☐ I'm lost. I need help catching up before moving on.

PRAYER

God of my heart, my whole desire is in loving you.

I give myself to you without reserve.

I give you my heart.

Receive it as an offering of love and unite it to your heart. I desire to
dwell with you all my days.

I give to you my will.

May it be joined to yours in all things.

May my deepest desire be to do what is pleasing to you.

May your Spirit guide me in the way of obedience and may selfish
desires not find a home in me.

I give to you my understanding.

May I see with your eyes and choose what is life-giving.

May I forego all that is false and passing that I may embrace what is true
and enduring.

Let me desire the good and all that brings the good to birth.

May your grace bring my desire to realization.

I give to you my memory.

Let me always remember your goodness and beauty.

I shall take delight in remembering your favors—the love and mercy you
have shown to me.

May my heart be forever grateful.

I give to you my body. Make me a worthy dwelling for your Spirit, Jesus.

I give you all that I am and I accept whatever limitations, sickness,
sorrows, and death will be mine.

Let me desire what you desire.

No matter how painful the cross that is mine to carry, I receive it with
confidence in your strength and grace.

May I accept it with lively gratitude and carry it with joy and constancy.

Do with me what you will. I give to you all that I can—joys, sorrows, life
and death—to offer you my love and to witness to others the joy of
loving you.

May I serve you with devotion, relying on the help of your grace.

May I be yours without reserve until the last moment of my life.

Amen.

TERMS

Use each of the following terms in a sentence that shows you know what the term means. You may include more than one term in a sentence.

public ministry

parables

obedience

actualization

signs

hypostatic union

Gentiles

PEOPLE

Use information from the chapter to tell why each person or place is significant.

1. King David

2. Saint Francis of Assisi

3. Isaiah

4. J. Michael Walker

5. Lydia

6. Philip

7. Paul

UNDERSTANDING

Answer each question and complete each exercise.

SECTION 1

1. **Analyze** What sort of information does New Testament Scripture contain about Jesus?

2. **Describe** What actions did Jesus perform during his public ministry?

3. **Summarize** What were some important messages that Jesus shared as he preached?

4. **Evaluate** What effect did Jesus have on the people he met?

SECTION 2

5. **Infer** What did Jesus' silence before his accusers demonstrate?

6. **Recall** How did Jesus' silence connect him with Old Testament teachings?

7. **Analyze** How did miracles further Jesus' teachings?

8. **Infer** Why were gestures important when Jesus cured people?

SECTION 3

9. **Interpret** Why might God the Father have sent Jesus to a world that didn't always want him?

10. **Recall** How long did Jesus keep his human nature?

11. **Recall** Which term describes the union of the human and divine natures in the one divine Person of the Son of God?

12. Infer Why was it important for Gentiles to convert to Christianity?

13. Analyze What are some benefits that come from trying to break out of our routines and find God?

14. Evaluate What is the difference between a believer and a disciple?

15. Explain Interpret the statement from Saint Paul that in God we "live and move and have our being."

CONNECTING

Visual This image is a modern painting of Jesus.

Explain why you like or dislike this image.

How would you describe Jesus' expression? Why do you think the artist chose to use so many colors?

Challenge You have a conversation with a good friend of yours who goes to the local public school.

Friend: What do you talk about in religion class?

You: We're talking about Jesus right now.

Friend: What about Jesus?

You: You know, the miracles, like healing people.

Friend: How much of that stuff is made up? Or are they saying it's all true?

○ What do you say next?

○ Construct the conversation with at least two more comments from your friend and your responses. Take the conversation a little deeper and reflect information from the chapter.

Question After working through this chapter, what advice would you give someone who is curious about Jesus?

Imagine You are designing the homepage of a website on the Gospels. Think about how you would present the contents of the Gospels with the elements available for a website.

○ What sort of images would you include on the homepage?

○ Which font would you choose? What qualities of the Gospels would you want the font to convey?

○ Try to find an illustration and typeface that represent your ideas, and make a sketch or drawing of your homepage.

SELF-ASSESS

On Your Own Describe how your understanding increased in two of the following topics covered in this chapter:

○ Jesus' human and divine nature

○ Jesus' parables

○ His personality

○ His miracles

○ The call to discipleship

○ The presence of the Holy Spirit

With a Partner List what you found most helpful or interesting in this chapter as well as any other questions that have surfaced.

What are the people in this photo committed to?

What effort is involved in this commitment?

CHAPTER **5**

Understanding Ourselves

Go to the student site at
hs.osvcurriculum.com

DO

- Identify truths regarding the human condition.
- Discuss the Christian understanding of creation and the Fall.
- Explore the reality of the soul and identify ways to nurture it.
- Learn the concepts of salvation, justification, sanctification, and Redemption.
- Identify Christ's presence in different aspects of Catholic Tradition.
- Decide how to add spiritual discipline into relationships.
- Begin to unpack the concept of the Paschal Mystery.

DEFINE

creation	conversion
Redemption	holiness
disordered affections	Christian anthropology
grace	steward
salvation	soul
justification	particular judgment
sanctification	Paschal Mystery
almsgiving	

Your good friend never keeps his/her word. This friend promises to meet you at a certain time but is always a half-hour late. This same friend makes weekend plans with you during the week but bails out when the weekend comes. Your friend doesn't help with the class project you're supposed to be doing together, which means you have to do it yourself in order to earn a decent grade. When you finally call your friend on it, the response you get is: "Give me some credit. God didn't make any of us perfect! Right?!"

When an eleventh-grade religion class is asked "What's your favorite Catholic season or symbol?" a student answers: "The Easter candle. It reminds me that Christ is always with us." Another says, "The Alpha and Omega. Christ was there when we began this life and will be there in the next." A third junior responds: "Crucifix. When I look at it, it reminds me of what Christ did for us, and it reminds me to do the same."

A panel of three guest speakers comes to school to talk about conserving the Earth's resources, practical ways to save energy, and the importance of protecting the environment. The panel closes its presentation by saying, "We want to leave you with this: Choosing to ignore the needs facing our planet and choosing not to do your part in protecting the environment is a sin."

HOW DO YOU RESPOND?

Where Are You?			
Choose the response that best reflects where you are right now.			
I understand the human condition.	☐ Quite a bit	☐ Somewhat	☐ A little	☐ Not at all
I can explain the Fall.	☐ Quite a bit	☐ Somewhat	☐ A little	☐ Not at all
I know what is meant by Original Sin.	☐ Quite a bit	☐ Somewhat	☐ A little	☐ Not at all
I have experienced spiritual growth during Lent.	☐ Quite a bit	☐ Somewhat	☐ A little	☐ Not at all
I believe we are responsible for each other.	☐ Quite a bit	☐ Somewhat	☐ A little	☐ Not at all
I'm committed to taking care of the Earth.	☐ Quite a bit	☐ Somewhat	☐ A little	☐ Not at all

Created in God's Image

Spiritually speaking, what is the meaning and purpose of life?

Speaking of Jesus, what does "he redeemed us" mean?

Where is my life taking me?

Does following Jesus Christ really help me understand myself and my life?

Why do we need redemption?

"The glory of God is man fully alive," wrote Saint Irenaeus of Lyon in *Against Heresies*. We can go through life passively, or we can search for answers along the way. And the most important answers are the ones that explain who we are, why we are here, and how we are to live. The wisdom offered by Catholic Tradition does not resolve all of life's difficulties, or make it particularly easy to find our path. But Catholic Tradition does offer us some answers and direction.

Catholicism provides a vision of life that makes sense of both the ordinary and the holy. Each person is unique. But all people have certain things in common, such as intelligence, free will to decide their own behavior, and the ability to love one another. We also have a common calling to do what is right and just, and to live in peace with one another. The *Catechism of the Catholic Church* affirms that we are all called to the same end—God (see CCC, 1878).

The story of the human person begins at **creation**, when God alone created every thing that exists outside of himself. The biblical accounts of creation in the Book of Genesis tell us that everything God created was good. Human beings, we are told, were in fact created in the divine image. We are meant to know and love God, and to live in friendship with him. But in the end, it is Jesus who best helps us understand what it means to be human.

The Old Testament, especially the Book of Genesis, describes how the first humans and their descendants chose to live contrary to the way God intended. They broke their relationship with God through sin. Prophets tried to help people see the right way to live throughout the B.C. period of history, but it is Jesus who taught the human race how to live the way God intended. Then he restored our relationship with God through his death and Resurrection. That is what we mean when we say "he redeemed us."

creation the act by which God alone, from nothing, brought into being all that exists outside of himself freely, directly, and without any help

The ancient Greek city of Corinth served as a major trade center from the eighth century B.C. until the Romans sacked the city in 146 B.C.

○ The Romans rebuilt the city in 44 B.C., and Corinth had a community of early Christians in the first century A.D.

○ The Book of Acts records two visits of Paul to Corinth. Today the ruins of the ancient city are a short drive from modern Corinth.

○ Among the ruins is the Temple of Apollo, built in the sixth century B.C. The temple was still in use during the time of Paul's visits, but only thirty-eight of its columns still stand because of earthquakes.

Faith & Culture

Corinth is located on the strip of land that connects the Peloponnese, or southern Greece, with northern Greece.

↗ Go to the student site at **hs.osvcurriculum.com**

It is possible for us to live in a relationship of friendship and intimacy with God because of Jesus. We also believe that Jesus provides all of us with a new creation that begins when we are baptized and remains available throughout our lives. As Paul wrote to the Christian community at the Greek city of Corinth:

If anyone is in Christ, there is a new creation: everything old has passed away; see, everything has become new! All this is from God, who reconciled us to himself through Christ, and has given us the ministry of reconciliation.

—2 Corinthians 5:17-18

GO TO **THE SOURCE**

Two letters of Saint Paul to the Church in Corinth are included in the New Testament.

○ Read the first two chapters of Paul's First Letter to the Corinthians (1 Corinthians 1-2).

○ Explain how these chapters shed light on some of life's most important questions.

Connect
Write a paragraph that describes the connection Jesus has to:

○ the purpose of life

○ Redemption

○ ongoing spiritual renewal

But there is more. Our Catholic Tradition teaches us that Jesus will lead the human race into a new creation at the end of time. The author of the Book of Revelation describes his vision of the new creation in glowing terms:

Then I saw a new heaven and a new earth; for the first heaven and the first earth had passed away, and the sea was no more. And I saw the holy city, the new Jerusalem, coming down out of heaven from God, prepared as a bride adorned for her husband . . . And the one who was seated on the throne said, "See, I am making all things new."

—Revelation 21:1-2, 5

Everyday life challenges you to think about right and wrong, to sort out the good from the bad, and to inform and form your conscience. Here's an example . . .

}

A nine-year-old pitches so fast that nobody in the youth league can hit the ball. Opposing parents protest. League officials ask the young player to "play up" in the older league. The kid's parents say no. League officials then ask that the pitcher play another position. But the kid's parents cry foul. The League disbands the pitcher's undefeated team and makes the second-place team the champs.

The League remains firm, but lawsuits are threatened.

The kid should have gone with one of the suggestions.

Tell me this really didn't happen.

The other kids in the league should have protested *for* the kid.

The kid's parents were selfish.

The opposing parents were wrong.

How do you respond?

Going Moral

Jesus' life and teaching assures us that the origins and destiny of the world, and of each human being, are in God's care. In between the first creation and the new Heaven and Earth, the whole drama of sin and the **Redemption** is played out. We become a new creation at Baptism. Yet, we still experience sin and struggle in our own lives. This is the result of Original Sin, which we discussed earlier in this course. We have times of darkness and confusion, but we have the means for forgiveness. And we know that something good awaits us, if we trust in God.

Redemption Christ's work in freeing us from the domination of evil and sin

Name What does the *Catechism* say is the end to which all people are called?

Explain How has our relationship with God been renewed because of Jesus?

Compare and Contrast

Popular songs often are written from the experience of love gone wrong.

○ Find an example of a song about someone who failed to love as he or she should have, or a song in which someone loved or desired something he or she should not have.

○ What insights or solutions do the songwriters offer for these human dilemmas?

○ How would you respond with a Catholic perspective?

Help Is in Order

Another of the consequences of Original Sin is that human affections are disordered. **Disordered affections** are emotions and passions directed toward what they should not be. Two examples of ideas that can become disordered are the desire to be liked or wanting to succeed.

The human desire to be liked is perfectly natural and "in order." But if you let your desire to be liked cause you to do something you know is wrong, then that desire becomes out of order, or disordered. The same can happen with wanting to succeed, which is also natural and "in order," until we let this desire cause us to cheat or hurt someone. Then wanting to succeed becomes out of order, or disordered. Some disordered affections are extremely destructive, such as addictions, while others are more like distracting obsessions, such as a fixation we might have toward a person, an activity, a technological gadget, or a collection of items.

disordered affections the emotions and passions of the heart which are not directed toward their proper objects

grace our participation in the life of God and his free help that allows us to respond to his call to become his children

We are created with natural goodness, and we have to work at using these good tendencies properly. Faith in God means we always rely on him alone because there is no substitute. This is a balancing act, and the tension that comes with it is part of what we call the human condition.

Our help comes from God through Jesus and the Holy Spirit. We call this help **grace**, which allows us to respond to God's call to become his children. Grace introduces us into the life and love of the Trinity as we respond to God's call. And because of Jesus, we can be forgiven for the times when we let our natural emotions and interests get out of order. The Holy Spirit is with us, as Jesus promised. We are not alone. This is our faith.

Discuss

How does your image of God impact what you think about yourself and others?

What does the last line from the first quotation say about human beings?

Which disordered affections do you see creating the most pain or problems today?

The Church points out two truths about the human condition:

"Our holy mother, the Church, holds and teaches that God, the first principle and last end of all things, can be known with certainty from the created world by the natural light of human reason." . . . Man has this capacity because he is created "in the image of God."

—CCC, 36

The human mind, in turn, is hampered in the attaining of such truths, not only by the impact of the senses and the imagination, but also by disordered appetites which are the consequences of original sin.

—CCC, 37

Saint Augustine, in his autobiography *The Confessions*, told a story from his own life that illustrates disordered affections. When he was sixteen, he and some friends decided to steal pears from one of his neighbors' trees. In those days, stealing fruit was a much more serious crime than it is today. They didn't really want the pears. They had plenty of pears at home. They just wanted the thrill of stealing. So they went at night after playing in the streets and pulled all the pears off the tree. They carted them away and threw them to the pigs.

Thomas Merton, in his autobiography *The Seven Storey Mountain*, also told a story from his childhood. He had a brother, five years younger than himself, and regarded him as a baby. He didn't want him around when he was playing with his friends. One day he even threw rocks at his younger brother, and he and his friends shouted at him to go away. Yet the younger boy stood there. "And there he stands, not sobbing, not crying, but angry and unhappy and offended and tremendously sad . . . [H]is tremendous desire to be with us and do what we are doing will not permit him to go away. The law written in his nature says he must be with his elder brother and do what he is doing; and he cannot understand why this law of love is being so wildly and unjustly violated in his case. Many times it was like that. And in a sense, this terrible situation is the pattern and prototype of all sin. . . ."

As Catholics, we understand ourselves as being born with the goodness of God within, and also being in need of help. We humans are flawed.

Discuss

○ Why do these two stories from Saint Augustine and Thomas Merton tell us about disordered affections?

○ Why did Thomas Merton call his actions unjust?

○ Can you relate to Saint Augustine's desire to do something just because you know it's wrong? Or can you relate to Thomas Merton's story of excluding someone? Were you the one doing the wrong or were you being wronged? Explain your answer.

○ Have you made an effort at reconciliation with the people involved? How hard or how easy was it? Explain.

We are all born into an imperfect world. Jesus, however, has shown us the way to live as God intended. Through his life, Passion, death, Resurrection, and glorious Ascension, he has restored our relationship with God. Through him we have an opportunity for new life. This is the Good News of our **salvation**. We are saved from sin and its consequences by the cross and Resurrection of Jesus.

Identify What became part of life after sin entered the world?

Analyze What word or phrase would you use to describe the human condition?

salvation God's gift of forgiveness of sins and the restoration of friendship with God

GO TO THE SOURCE

The Book of Genesis gives us a way to help us overcome sin and the impact of disordered affections.

Read Genesis 1:26-27.

○ Describe how the fact that we were created in God's image and likeness might help in facing temptation and disordered affections.

○ In what way does this affect the way you view others in the world?

○ How does Jesus' life answer these questions?

○ What impact do you think this had on Saint Augustine and Thomas Merton in their observations described on this page?

SECOND *Chances*

A spiritual practice for the life of discipleship

God gives us second chances when the world distracts us. That's one of the messages revealed throughout the Scriptures, and it's a big part of the Good News. And it is something we experience when we receive the Sacrament of Penance and Reconciliation.

God expects us to give each other second chances as well.

People are happy to give a child a "do-over" because children are innocent and inexperienced. As we get older, however, people are less willing to give us another chance. And we begin to stop asking for one.

The spiritual practice of second chances helps us return to that childlike sincerity to courageously ask for an important second chance. Asking for a second chance improves your spiritual life because it requires honestly admitting that you messed up, demonstrating your willingness to make things right, and trusting in the other person or group's kindness.

That's just half of it. The practice of second chances also includes being willing to grant someone else a do-over. This is hard to practice when you are still hurt or angry. But giving a second chance improves your spiritual life because it requires that you show mercy, let go of past hurts, and put someone else's wishes ahead of your own.

So the practice of asking for, or giving, second chances requires righteous decisions. That's why it's a good exercise for your spiritual growth. It's also a way to model that God is with us and God wants us to be with each other.

>> On a scale of one to five, where five equals very good, rate the following:

How good are you at asking for second chances? _____

How good are you at granting second chances? _____

From whom do you need to ask for a second chance, and about what?

Who wants you to grant him or her a second chance?

QUICK REVIEW

1a. Recall What did God intend for creation, and what made his plans change?

b. Interpret When does the new creation begin for each person?

2. Analyze How do Jesus' teachings help us expand our ideas about the significance of our lives?

3a. Define What are *disordered affections*?

b. Assess Can humans break the cycle of sin and evil? Explain your answer.

Listen and Discuss With a small group, discuss the following:

○ Share a time in your life when you felt the meaning of this quotation from Saint Irenaeus of Lyon: "The glory of God is man fully alive." In other words, when have you felt most "alive"?

Pray Write a prayer of praise in thanksgiving for the ways you experience the different aspects of being human.

SELF-ASSESS

Which statement best reflects where you are now?

☐ I'm confident enough about the material in this section to be able to explain it to someone else.

☐ I have a good grasp of the material in this section, but I could use more review.

☐ I'm lost. I need help catching up before moving on.

Redeemed in Christ

Ash Wednesday begins the season of spiritual renewal leading to Easter. Ashes that we receive on our foreheads at the beginning of Lent remind us that we come from God, will return to God, and are to live our lives in harmony with God. Lent itself reminds us of our need for God, our need for Redemption, and the importance of penance, sacrifice, and eternal life.

What does it mean to be redeemed? To *redeem* literally means "to buy back." When we redeem a gift card, essentially we are taking back what was promised to us. A broader meaning of the word *redeem* involves becoming free. Free from what? Free from all that holds you back, particularly freedom from something harmful or hurtful. Redemption is about overcoming something that is detrimental to our well-being.

Sin is harmful, hurtful, and damaging to oneself, to one's relationship with others, and to God. When we sin, we cause damage that is beyond our comprehension. Think of a time when someone betrayed your trust and his or her sin damaged your relationship. Even with a sincere apology, it's often hard for someone to understand the depth of hurt. Broaden that dynamic of hurt and damage to all human beings throughout all of history, and you may get a glimpse of what is meant by the effects of Original Sin.

justification God's gracious action that "[cleanses] us from our sins" and communicates "to us the righteousness of God through faith in Jesus Christ" (Romans 3:22) (CCC, 1987)

sanctification the work of the Holy Spirit to make human individuals holy with our cooperation

GO TO **THE SOURCE**

Saint Paul explains the Redemption by comparing two people.

Read Romans 5:12-19, then discuss:

○ What is the comparison, exactly?

○ What gets overturned?

○ Who benefits?

How can we possibly break free of the consequences of sin? The idea of breaking free from the consequences of our own sin is overwhelming enough, let alone all of Original Sin. However, that is exactly what Jesus did.

In Catholic Tradition, Redemption is the word that describes our being set free from the bonds of sin. By his death on the cross, Jesus Christ took on himself the punishment that should have belonged to us sinners, and in turn set us free and achieved our Redemption. Jesus did this once for all. This is the reason for our joy. Redemption is what we celebrate together at Mass.

We participate in that Redemption by living with gratitude for the graces gained by Jesus, acknowledging our faults and sins, and asking for forgiveness.

With Redemption comes justification and sanctification. The term **justification** refers to be like God's gracious action that "[cleanses] us from our sins" and communicates "to us 'the righteousness of God through faith in Jesus Christ'" (Romans 3:22) (CCC, 1987). Granted to us through Baptism and won for us by Christ's Passion, justification means not only having our sins forgiven, but also growing in holiness by learning how to receive God's grace. It is the most excellent form of God's mercy, meant to glorify God and grant us eternal life (see CCC, 2020).

Sanctification is the action through which we are made holy and renewed through faith in Jesus Christ by the power of the Holy Spirit. Sanctification is an ongoing process of growth in holiness, aided by the Sacraments. The Holy Spirit, who guides our inner life, does the work of sanctification to make us holy. But it is up to us to engage in the ongoing and lifelong process of sanctification.

Imagine

Catholic Tradition has long meditated through art, music, and prayer on the redemptive suffering of Jesus. It has also reflected on the sufferings of Mary, the Mother of Jesus, as she watched her Son suffer and die.

○ Look at the images of Jesus as the *Man of Sorrows* and Mary as the *Mater Dolorosa* or Sorrowful Mother and choose one that appeals to you.

○ Quietly reflect on the image. After several minutes of quiet prayer, write down your thoughts in a journal.

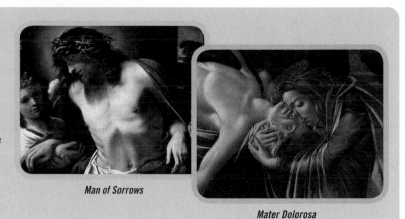

Man of Sorrows

Mater Dolorosa

Justification was done for us, through Christ, once and for all. Sanctification, which happens through the help of the Holy Spirit, requires our efforts to nurture our souls, examine our lives, and seek God's grace.

Springtime for the Church

The word *Lent* means "spring." The season of Lent is when catechumens—adults and children of catechetical age who have decided to become Catholic—begin final preparation for Baptism. Lent is also when we prepare to renew our baptismal promises at Easter. During Lent, prayer, fasting, and works of charity purify our hearts and lead us to **conversion**, the lifelong process guided by the Holy Spirit of turning away from sin and realigning ourselves with God. We ask forgiveness for our sins in the Sacrament of Penance. We practice self-denial by fasting. We are aware of our own disordered affections, and we ask God in prayer to purify our hearts and help us to love, as God wants us to love.

We also practice being more aware of the needs of others. The Lenten tradition of almsgiving is more than simply making donations. It means helping the poor with their material needs and working for justice, motivated by love. True **almsgiving** includes respecting the dignity of the poor as human people called to eternal life and happiness with God, just as we all are.

The concepts covered so far—Redemption, conversion, sanctification, and Justification —all lead to holiness. When our actions follow the example of Christ, we act properly and do good. Because God created us with free will, we are free to act as we want. The grace of God prepares and calls for our response to seek and love him. We have God's help to decide on our actions, but we remain free, and responsible, to choose. Grace perfects that freedom (see CCC, 2022). We mature in the grace of God to the point where we are holy and our initial reaction to any event is wise and loving.

almsgiving money or goods given to the poor out of love

conversion the lifelong process guided by the Holy Spirit involving a fundamental reorientation of life toward God and away from sin

Lenten Disciplines		
Practices	Why do we do that?	Examples
prayer		
fasting		
almsgiving		

Fill in the blank boxes with your understanding of these Lenten disciplines, and some concrete examples of each. In groups, share your responses and add to your chart any insights or examples that enrich your own understanding.

PRIMARY SOURCES

Catholicism is a multidimensional experience of faith. Part of what makes Catholicism different from other faiths is that it intentionally celebrates redemption, conversion, sanctification, justification, holiness, and God's grace with many different symbols, rituals, Sacraments, and seasons.

↗ Go to the student site at
hs.osvcurriculum.com

Some fundamental guidelines concerning the liturgical year are contained in a Vatican document called *General Norms for the Liturgical Year and the Calendar* (1969). They apply to the whole Church, everywhere in the world. Each liturgical year celebrates the history of salvation. We mark the passing of time in relation to Jesus. The Church year begins on the first Sunday of Advent, followed by the Christmas season. Lent arrives, soon followed by Easter, which is not just one feast among others, but the greatest and oldest Christian feast. The *Catechism* calls it the feast of feasts. Easter can be as early as March 22 and as late as April 25. There are two phases of ordinary time between the other seasons.

Look up the sections in the General Norms concerning Lent and Easter (Articles 18 to 31) on the student site at ↗**hs.osvcurriculum.com**. Here is an excerpt from Article 18.

18. Christ redeemed us all and gave perfect glory to God principally through his paschal mystery: dying he destroyed our death and rising he restored our life. Therefore the Easter Triduum of the Passion and resurrection of Christ is the culmination of the entire liturgical year. [7] Thus the solemnity of Easter has the same kind of preeminence in the liturgical year that Sunday has in the week. [8]

>> What is the Easter Triduum?

Why do you think the Easter Triduum is celebrated in this way?

What does it mean to say that the Sundays of Easter are "one 'great Sunday'"?

Go to the ↗student site and review Article 27, which describes the purpose of Lent. What is supposed to happen to the catechumens and to the faithful during this season?

What is your favorite liturgical season and why?

Holiness, then, is the perfection of charity (CCC, 1709). That means we are compassionate, concerned, and kind in all that we do. As disciples of Jesus Christ, we are called to travel the path of life that is grounded in love. The more we love and serve, in imitation of Christ, the more we share in the glory of his Passion and Resurrection.

Describe How is Lent an intense season spiritually?

Infer Give an example of how Sacraments aid in the process of growing in holiness.

holiness the perfection of charity

SECTION 2 REVIEW

QUICK REVIEW

1a. Recall What do ashes symbolize?

b. List How do we participate in our Redemption?

2a. Recall What is *justification*?

b. Compare How does sanctification relate to justification?

3a. Analyze Why is it appropriate for Lent to be in spring?

b. Describe Tell how Lent helps in our conversion.

c. Recall What is *holiness*?

ACT

Begin outlining your spiritual growth plan for the next Lent. Determine how much of it should focus on prayer, fasting, sacrifice, or service.

SELF-ASSESS

Which statement best reflects where you are now?

☐ I'm confident enough about the material in this section to be able to explain it to someone else.

☐ I have a good grasp of the material in this section, but I could use more review.

☐ I'm lost. I need help catching up before moving on.

Visions of the Human Person

> *In spite of everything, I still believe that people are really good at heart.*
>
> —Anne Frank, *The Diary of a Young Girl*, July 15, 1944

Who are we? Why are we here? What is the meaning of life? Have you ever pondered these great mysteries? Philosophers and theologians have been questioning the meaning and significance of humanity for millennia.

As Christians, we have a set of beliefs about what it means to be human, why we are here, and the meaning of life. The technical, theological term for this is **Christian anthropology**. It refers to understanding what it means to be human in relationship to God. The term is something that Pope John Paul II often discussed during his pontificate. "One cannot think adequately about man without reference . . . to God," he wrote in his book *Crossing the Threshold of Hope.* He echoed the Vatican II document *Gaudium et Spes*, "Pastoral Constitution on the Church in the Modern World." Jesus elevates our dignity beyond compare in the world. "For, by his incarnation, he, the Son of God, has in a certain way united himself with each man."

Christian anthropology the study and understanding of what it means to be human in relationship to God

We see the human as a child of God made up of mind, body, and soul. Humans are creatures of God, with mental, physical, and spiritual sensitivities. The human being is destined to have a relationship with God while on Earth and into eternity. And through Christ we can achieve true happiness and the deepest fulfillment of our nature.

> *Any man's death diminishes me, because I am involved in mankind. And therefore never send to know for whom the bell tolls. It tolls for thee.*
>
> —John Donne, *Devotions Upon Emergent Occasions, XVII*, 1624

The Catholic view of the human person sees us related to each other. From the moment of conception until death, we are sacred because God created each and every one of us in his own image and likeness. Male and female, we are equal while there is a complimentarity between us intended and created by God. We shape our own individual lives and pursue our own goals, but we are not meant to be free from caring for each other. We rediscover our right relationship to our brothers and sisters when our relationship with God is restored in Christ. Through Jesus, we see that human solidarity and caring for one another is essential in life. Likewise, we deepen our relationship with Christ when we love one another as Christ loved us (John 13:34).

GLOBAL PERSPECTIVES

There are more Catholics in the United States and the world than there were forty years ago. In 1965, there were more than 46.6 million U.S. Catholics. That number grew to 52.3 million by 1985, then to 62.4 million by the turn of the millennium. Statistics show that number rose in 2008 to 67.1 million, which represents twenty-two percent of the U.S. population. The worldwide Catholic population has grown from 653.6 million in 1965 to more than 1.045 billion by the year 2000, or about seventeen percent of the number of people living on Earth.

○ Why do you think the Catholic population in the United States and around the world has risen? What does that say about the Catholic religion?

○ What does it mean to you to be part of such a large community?

↗ Go to the student site at **hs.osvcurriculum.com**

JUSTICE AND DISCIPLESHIP

Jesus tells us that discipleship involves praying to the Father, studying his teachings and following his example, participating in the Eucharist, and living the virtues. He also calls us to act for justice.

SOME SHRUG THEIR SHOULDERS at environmental issues such as climate change because they feel there's nothing they can do. Some don't believe it's happening, while others adopt "green" or eco-friendly lifestyles. Natural factors can cause climate change, but arguments erupt when questions arise about the human factor and what to do about it.

On the national level, the U.S. Conference of Catholic Bishops does not dispute that climate change exists. Instead the bishops deal with how actions will impact the most vulnerable among us. Why? A vital connection exists between nature and people. Respect for both of these elements of God's creation can generate peace.

> Action to mitigate global climate change must be built upon a foundation of social and economic justice that does not put the poor at greater risk or place disproportionate and unfair burdens on developing nations.
>
> —*Global Climate Change: A Plea for Dialogue, Prudence, and the Common Good,* U.S. Conference of Catholic Bishops, June 15, 2001

God appointed all of us to govern the Earth.

> God blessed them, saying: "Be fertile and multiply; fill the earth and subdue it. Have dominion over the fish of the sea, the birds of the air, and all the living things that move on the earth."
>
> —Genesis 1:28

In essence, the children of God have always been called to be "green," to be stewards of the Earth. How will we use that God-given authority?

> Experience shows that disregard for the environment always harms human coexistence, and vice versa. It becomes more and more evident that there is an inseparable link between peace with creation and peace among men.
>
> —*World Day of Peace,* Pope Benedict XVI, para. 8. January 1, 2007

As a matter of justice, you have the choice to act

Educate yourself and others: read the U.S. Bishops' letter, *Global Climate Change.*

Participate in caring for the environment: volunteer for highway cleanup, broaden recycling efforts, or plant trees. Cut back on Styrofoam, conserve water, conserve energy, etc.

Advocate for public policies that protect the environment: contact your elected officials and ask what they are doing to care for creation.

Give thanks for the Earth's many gifts: make it part of your daily prayer.

Create a prayer service to celebrate Earth Day: use Scripture readings and Catholic symbols that demonstrate solidarity with and gratitude for the Earth.

↗ Go to the student site at
hs.osvcurriculum.com

You can be for justice without being a disciple, but you cannot be a disciple without being for justice.

Discuss

○ What do movies and music most often tell us about caring for creation?

○ What does the link between humans and nature reveal about how God created the world?

○ If your group were in charge of the planet, what would you do about caring for it? Make a list and then ask yourselves what consequences each decision would have.

people. As God's first Revelation, the story of the Earth is the story of the People of God (see CCC, 288).

Rapid communications through the Internet, faster travel around the world, and increased trade with global agreements has had an impact on our role as stewards. Pope John Paul II explained the situation this way:

> *In a world that is increasingly interdependent, peace, justice, and the safeguarding of creation must be the fruit of the common effort of all in pursuing together the common good.*
>
> —Pope John Paul II, Angelus, August 25, 2002

We are destined to be with God, who gave us a soul, intellect, and free will. Basic to our understanding of human dignity is the belief that each and every human person has been given a spiritual soul, and created to be in relation to God:

> *Endowed with "a spiritual and immortal" soul,[5] the human person is "the only creature on earth that God has willed for its own sake." From his conception, he is destined for eternal beatitude.*
>
> —CCC, 1703

We are called to walk with God and to walk with each other. We are called to discipleship that is best lived out within a community of disciples. And we are called to serve the world. The chance to answer this call never happens all at once or once and for all. Spiritually speaking, we have to keep paying attention to this call and keep checking in on how well we are responding to it.

Tell Why is human solidarity and care for one another essential?

Imagine What would life be like if Jesus hadn't taken on human form and died for our sins?

Human Dignity

"Let us make humankind in our image, according to our likeness," says God in the first creation story of the Book of Genesis (1:26). God gives people "dominion" over the animals of the Earth. What does that mean? Pope John Paul II said we are appointed as **stewards** of the Earth in order to cultivate and protect the planet. "From this fact there comes what we might call their 'ecological vocation,' which in our time has become more urgent than ever," the late Pope said in August 2002. Our creation by God and our role as stewards of the Earth and of each other gives us our human dignity.

We are called to affirm the goodness of the created world, and we are responsible to care for the Earth where God has placed us. The Earth and the Heavens belong to God, but God has made us stewards of creation. The seventh Commandment not to steal teaches us that justice and love for God, each other, and future generations ought to direct use of the world's riches and the production of

This **soul** is created directly by God, and is spiritual, individual, and immortal. Soul and body make up the human person. At death, the soul does not die, but returns to God. It will be reunited with the body at the final judgment, when each person will be called to account for his or her deeds. This should not be confused with particular judgment, which we will discuss more in Chapter 8. **Particular judgment** takes place at the moment of death when Jesus determines whether a person's soul will go to Heaven, Purgatory, or Hell.

steward someone who takes on the responsibility God gave humans to take care of the Earth and everything in it

soul the spiritual principle of a human person; each human soul is individual and immortal, and created by God immediately

particular judgment the judgment of each individual at the moment of death by Christ that determines the immediate entrance of the soul into Heaven, Purgatory, or Hell

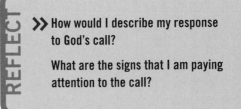

REFLECT

>> How would I describe my response to God's call?

What are the signs that I am paying attention to the call?

People around the world believe in Jesus, study his teachings, and follow his ways because he speaks to their souls. But the world is also full of distractions that make it easy to neglect the spiritual longings of the soul. However, God's grace and the gift of Holy Spirit are here for us. We just have to open ourselves up and seek it.

Define What does it mean to be a steward of creation?

Summarize How does God's first Revelation give us our human dignity?

REFLECT

>> What "noise" in your life makes it hard to hear the Holy Spirit's voice, the will of God, or the soul's longing?

MY FAITH

In this chapter we discussed Lent and took note of the spiritual discipline that comes with our various Lenten practices.

Spiritual discipline can nurture the soul, just as physical discipline can nurture the body.

Remember you may choose to share some of this as part of the report you give at the end of the course.

The Care and Feeding of a Strong Soul

The supreme achievement of reason is to realize that there is a limit to reason. Reason's last step is the recognition that there are an infinite number of things which are beyond it. It is merely feeble if it does not go as far as to realize that.

Blaise Pascal,
Pensées

Given the busy pace of your life, it is hard to deliberately take time to stop and think about how to care for and feed your soul. So here's an opportunity to give serious thought to one or two ways you can intentionally nurture your soul. Just remember that whatever you decide to do, you will have to do it for a while in order for it to help you. It requires spiritual discipline.

You get the idea. Think about it awhile before you decide. See if you can hear the whisper of what the Holy Spirit might suggest.

- Conduct my own private Bible study once a week for _____ minutes.
- Fast every Friday by giving up _____
_____
- Establish the practice of saying prayers before letting my feet touch the floor every morning.
- Add faith-based music to my playlist and listen to it at least once a week to or from school.
- Maintain a list of moments when I noticed or felt God's love.
- Collect quotes that speak to the soul.
- Donate _____ to
_____ once every
_____
- Visit the school chapel or another sacred space the same day every week before homeroom.
- Give up _____
_____
- Reach out to _____ at least once
_____.

_____
_____
_____
_____
_____
_____
_____
_____
_____

Go to the student site at
hs.osvcurriculum.com

*Discipleship . . . within the Body of Christ . . .
for the glory of God and the good of the world*

Getting at the Painful

Flannery O'Connor (1925–1964) has been called one of America's greatest fiction writers. She was born and raised in Georgia and lived for most of her life in the South. She was a keen observer, and she had an ear for southern dialect as well as a good sense of irony and humor. A chronic illness called lupus struck her at a young age, and she died at just 39 years old. She was by no means an invalid, however. One of her more remarkable interests was peacocks. She kept more than forty peacocks on her Georgia farm, along with other birds. Visitors came from miles around to see her fantastic birds.

O'Connor took her Catholic faith very seriously. Her stories and novels depicted the reality of sin and grace in the quirky and even horrible circumstances of her characters' lives. Her writing has sometimes been classified as "grotesque." As one commentator pointed out, "O'Connor made frequent use of violence and shock tactics." She argued that she wrote for an audience who, for all their Sunday piety, did not share her belief in the Fall of humanity or its need for Redemption. In her short story "Revelation," for example, a horribly self-centered and racist woman is called to self-awareness by a complete stranger who throws a book at her and tells her "Go back to hell where you came from, you old wart hog."

Being a Catholic novelist did not mean writing uplifting stories about the Church for O'Connor. It meant getting at the truth, however painful, to be found in the world as we know it. "We Catholics are very much given to the Instant Answer," she wrote. "Fiction doesn't have any. It leaves us, like Job, with a renewed sense of mystery."

All my stories are about the **action of grace** on a character who is not very willing to support it, but most people think of these stories as hard, hopeless and brutal.

—Flannery O'Connor

Truth

"The poet is traditionally a blind man," O'Connor observed, "but the Christian poet, and storyteller as well, is like the blind man whom Christ touched, who looked then and saw men as if they were trees—but walking. Christ touched him again, and he saw clearly. We will not see clearly until Christ touches us in death, but this first touch is the beginning of vision, and it is an invitation to deeper and stranger visions that we shall have to learn to accept if we want to realize a Catholic literature."

Think About It Why was it significant that Flannery O'Connor chose not to write stories about the sunny side of life?
When you observe the facts of the world around you, what signs do you see of sin? Of grace?
Have you ever read a story or novel that changed your outlook in some way? What was it? How did it affect you?

Go to the student site at
hs.osvcurriculum.com

QUICK REVIEW

1a. **Analyze** Why are there so many ideas about what the human person is?

b. **Explain** Why is an understanding of human nature that ignores God incomplete?

2a. **Connect** Why is human solidarity based on God?

b. **Analyze** Why is our response to God's call to us a life-long process?

3a. **Analyze** How does having a good relationship with God affect our view of creation?

b. **Recall** Which principle in every human is immortal?

c. **Recall** How does Jesus help us make good choices?

ACT

Create a slogan or saying that describes (pick one):

○ what it takes to nurture a soul

○ being a steward of the Earth

○ our responsibility to each other

SELF-ASSESS

Which statement best reflects where you are now?

☐ I'm confident enough about the material in this section to be able to explain it to someone else.

☐ I have a good grasp of the material in this section, but I could use more review.

☐ I'm lost. I need help catching up before moving on.

The New Life of Baptism

Baptism is the original Sacrament of forgiveness of sins and the gateway to all the other Sacraments. It is considered one of the Sacraments of Initiation because through Baptism a person becomes a child of God who is welcomed into the Church community. We take on a new life in Christ, which he told us is necessary for salvation. Every Baptism in the Catholic Church is celebrated in the name of the Trinity because through Baptism we are united to the Triune God.

The signs and symbols of the baptismal liturgy remind us of creation, when the Holy Spirit moved over the waters and when God created light and life. Immersion in water or pouring of water is a symbol of cleansing and rebirth as we are baptized in the name of the Father, the Son, and the Holy Spirit. Light and water are repeatedly used as symbols in Scripture. The light and dark, for example, have their places in creation. Water and land are separated at the dawn of creation. Other examples include the flood that cleanses the sin-filled Earth; the column of fire that helps the Israelites flee the Egyptians; the Red Sea, which parts to allow the Israelites to pass through; and the water that springs forth when Moses strikes a rock.

The giving of a lighted candle and a new garment underscores the dignity of the newly baptized, and symbolizes the life of faith that Baptism engenders and supports. These signs also direct our thoughts to the end of time, when Christ will come again in glory. The newly baptized are given a lighted candle and told, "When the Lord comes, may you go out to meet him with all the saints in the heavenly kingdom" (RCIA, 230). The candle is lit from the large Easter Paschal Candle, which signifies the light of Christ, who illuminates our hearts and minds. The white garment worn by the newly baptized is a symbol of putting on the life of Christ.

The symbols used at Baptism are a good example of the multidimensional nature of Catholicism mentioned earlier. We express our belief with deep and thoughtful religious imagination.

Each year, we renew our baptismal promises at Easter, which is the most fitting time of year to celebrate and renew Baptism because the **Paschal Mystery** of Jesus brought us salvation. The Paschal Mystery refers to the way in which our Redemption was accomplished through Christ's Passion and death on the cross, his Resurrection, and Ascension. Through our Baptism, we share in his passage from death to new life. Easter

Paschal Mystery Christ's work of Redemption accomplished through his Passion, death, Resurrection, and Ascension

Exodus, 1999 (oil on canvas), by Richard McBee

Paschal Mystery

At the very center of Christian theology is the dying and rising of Jesus Christ. A closer look at Jesus' words during the paschal journey from the cross to Resurrection reveals much about the nature of God. Below are four of the seven things Jesus said while on the cross. What do they reveal about Jesus?

"My God, my God, why have you forsaken me?" (Matthew 27:46)

"Father, forgive them; for they do not know what they are doing" (Luke 23:34).

"Truly I tell you, today you will be with me in Paradise" (Luke 23:43).

"Father, into your hands I commend my spirit" (Luke 23:46).

The Resurrection accounts in the four Gospels include the statements:

"Do not be afraid"
—Matthew 28:10

"Peace be with you"
—Luke 24:36 and John 20:19

>> **What can we learn about Jesus and the nature of God from these words?**

Go to the student site at
hs.osvcurriculum.com

is marked with joy as we celebrate the Resurrection and remember Christ's victory over death.

The prayers of the Church at Easter often speak about the glory of the Resurrection. In the words of one of the prayers of the Mass: "The joy of the Resurrection renews the whole world, while the choirs of heaven sing forever to your glory" (Easter Preface II). Glory also awaits us at the end of our life. It is the glory of eternal life with God, the glory of the Church united with her King. Ever since Jesus' time, Christians all over the world are convinced that nothing could be better, more blessed, or more joyful than union with God.

We have explored human origins and destiny in light of the Redemption. In the next chapter, we will see that Jesus shows us how to live day to day, through his teachings.

Describe What awaits us at the end of our lives?

Connect Why is Easter the most fitting time of the year to celebrate and renew our baptismal promises?

For now we see in a mirror, dimly, but then we will see face to face. Now I know only in part; then, I will know fully, even as I have been fully known.
—1 Corinthians 13:12

Paschal Candle

The use of candles has always played a role in the Catholic expression of faith. Perhaps no candle expresses our faith more than the Paschal Candle.

The tradition of the Paschal Candle most likely began in the fourth century as a way to represent Christ as the light and hope of the world. In fact, the candle's use at Easter is mentioned in a letter of Saint Jerome in 384. Use of the candle has changed over the centuries. It was at one time broken up after the Easter Vigil and given to the congregation, but since the tenth century it has remained intact. The custom of inscribing the candle started in the twelfth century.

> From Easter until Pentecost, the Paschal Candle remains lit on the altar until Pentecost, when it is extinguished and removed to the baptistery. It is then used during Baptisms and funerals as a symbol of Christ's Resurrection.

> The small candles received by the newly baptized are lit from the Paschal Candle during the baptismal service.

> At a funeral the candle is placed next to the casket.

The lighting of the Paschal Candle is an essential part of the Easter Vigil, which is celebrated on Holy Saturday evening and which marks the beginning of Easter. At this celebration, a new fire is lit outside the church and blessed by the priest. The priest prepares the Paschal Candle, traditionally made from pure white beeswax to signify Christ's purity. He decorates the candle with a cross, the Greek symbols *Alpha* and *Omega* (meaning that Christ is the beginning and the end), and the numerals depicting the current year. He then inserts five grains of incense in the cross to symbolize the five wounds of Christ. It is then lit from the new fire and processed into the darkened church as the deacon or priest sings "Christ our Light" *(Lumen Christi)* and the congregation replies "Thanks be to God" *(Deo gratias)*. The members of the assembly then light their individual candles from the Paschal Candle.

>> How often do you find that church candles help you express your faith?

What does the use of candles to express faith tell you about Catholicism?

What Catholic symbol is your favorite expression of faith? Explain.

QUICK REVIEW

1a. Define What is Baptism?

b. Recall How does Baptism change a person?

c. Analyze Why is it appropriate to renew our baptismal promises at Easter?

2a. List What five things make up the Paschal Mystery?

b. Analyze Who benefits from almsgiving?

3a. Interpret Explain how "the joy of the Resurrection renews the whole world."

b. Recall What is *glory*?

c. Explain Why do Christians aspire to go to Heaven?

ACT

Work with a group to answer the following:

○ List some things that you would expect to encounter in Heaven.

○ Explain why your greatest expectations are only part of what will be found there.

Pray Compose a short prayer about being more Christ-like.

SELF-ASSESS

Which statement best reflects where you are now?

☐ I'm confident enough about the material in this section to be able to explain it to someone else.

☐ I have a good grasp of the material in this section, but I could use more review.

☐ I'm lost. I need help catching up before moving on.

PRAYER

God our Father,

you make everything new.
We pray for new opportunities each day:
to live a new day,
to relate to new people,
to attempt to do the "usual" in a fresh way.
Send us your Holy Spirit to help us love as you love,
    to forgive as you forgive
and to serve as you served.
We do believe that nothing is ever too old
or too unchangeable or
too dead to be transformed by you.
It is you O God that makes all things new.
We believe O God in the promise of new life,
and in the promise of a day
on this Earth when there will be no more death,
no more grief, no more crying or pain!
We do believe that you, our God, will make all things new.
We ask this through Christ, our Lord.
Amen.

TERMS

Write a sentence for each word or phrase demonstrating what each term means.

creation	conversion
Redemption	holiness
disordered affections	Christian anthropology
grace	steward
salvation	soul
justification	particular judgment
sanctification	Paschal Mystery
almsgiving	

PEOPLE

Identify why each person is significant using information from the chapter.

1. Saint Irenaeus of Lyon

2. Saint Augustine

3. Thomas Merton

4. Anne Frank

5. Pope John Paul II

6. John Donne

7. Pope Benedict XVI

8. Blaise Pascal

9. Flannery O'Connor

UNDERSTANDING

Answer each question and complete each exercise.

SECTION 1

1. **Elaborate** What did Saint Irenaeus mean by "The glory of God is man fully alive"?

2. **Explain** How do Jesus' teachings expand our ideas about the significance of our lives?

3. **Elaborate** At what point do the desires to be liked or to succeed become disordered affections?

4. **Recall** Who offers and who receives the Good News of salvation?

SECTION 2

5. **Recall** What was the cost of human Redemption?

6. **Contrast** What is the difference between justification and sanctification?

7. **Interpret** What is the reason for Catholic Lenten practices?

8. **Describe** What is holiness, and how do we achieve it?

SECTION 3

9. **Analyze** Why should our faith be constant, even through our difficulties?

10. **Explain** What gives humans dignity?

11. **Contrast** Why do we honor creation, but we worship God?

12. **Explain** What is the soul, and why is it integral to who we are?

13. **Describe** How did Flannery O'Connor's Catholicism influence her writing?

14. **Analyze** Why is Baptism important?

15. **Explain** Why is Baptism ideally celebrated during Easter?

16. **Assess** Is reaching Heaven an end or a beginning? Explain your answer.

CONNECTING

Visual This photograph shows an infant being baptized.

What does this image say about Baptism? What does it say about God's action in the Sacrament? What does it say about how we are continually renewed?

Question After working through this chapter, what advice would you give someone who does not believe that people have souls?

Imagine You are in charge of a stewardship program in your community. Your first job is to help people recognize that they have an obligation to take care of the environment. Design a campaign to increase awareness of this obligation.

○ What means could you use to reach the public?

○ What will you say in your publicity materials?

○ What information from this chapter could be included in your campaign?

Challenge You are texting when your friend asks a question.

> **Friend:** Are you free on Saturday night?
>
> **You:** Sorry, I'm going to the Easter Vigil. A friend of mine is being baptized then.
>
> **Friend:** Why do you have to be there?
>
> **You:** I don't have to be there. But I want to. I want to help welcome him into the Church. Besides, I kind of like the vigil service.
>
> **Friend:** Why do you like it?
>
> **You:** Because it's the biggest feast of the year.
>
> **Friend:** I thought that Christmas was.

○ What is your next reply?

○ Continue the conversation, including at least two more questions your friend might ask and how you would answer. Use information from the chapter to answer your friend.

SELF-ASSESS

On Your Own Make a list of the most important things you learned from this chapter. Select three things that represent your growth in understanding as you worked through this chapter. Write a paragraph explaining your choices.

With a Partner List what you found most helpful or interesting in this chapter, as well as any other questions that have surfaced.

How might this photo relate to the Kingdom of God? What opportunities or risks do bridges offer? Explain.

CHAPTER **6**

Following His Way

DO

○ Name several teachings from the Sermon on the Mount.

○ Link the Beatitudes to the promises to Abraham.

○ Understand the relationship between the Ten Commandments, the Law of the Gospel, and Jesus' New Commandment.

○ Compare God's Law and human laws.

○ Examine the concept of the Kingdom of God in Jesus' teaching.

○ Explore the image of Jesus the Good Shepherd.

DEFINE

discernment
Mosaic Law
covenant
natural law
Sermon on the Mount
Law of the Gospel
Golden Rule
Beatitudes
Kingdom of God
detachment

A young celebrity is being interviewed on a late night talk show. When the host asks, "How do you know which films, deals, or projects to say yes to?" The celebrity smiles and says: "I'm a spiritual person. Faith's always been important to me. So I just ask God, 'What do you want me to do?'" The host responds, "So God tells you what to do?" "Yeah. Sorta," the celebrity answers. "God says, 'Do whatever will make you happy.'"

A popular TV preacher tells his audience: "God's will is for you to prosper and be happy. God wants you to enjoy the blessings of this life. Offer God your heart and he will take care of your material needs. Need a better job? He'll get you one. Need a better car? He'll get you one of those, too. God's riches have no end. And he wants to bless his people with them."

HOW DO YOU RESPOND?

Your friend is in an unhealthy dating relationship. After he/she is disrespected once again, you tell your friend to end it. Your friend replies, "Forgive and forget. Jesus said turn the other cheek, right?"

Where Are You?				
Choose the response that best reflects where you are right now.				
I know the Ten Commandments.	☐ Quite a bit	☐ Somewhat	☐ A little	☐ Not at all
I see how the Ten Commandments point the way.	☐ Quite a bit	☐ Somewhat	☐ A little	☐ Not at all
I know the difference between the Law of the Old Testament and the Law of the New Testament.	☐ Quite a bit	☐ Somewhat	☐ A little	☐ Not at all
I can explain the Great Commandment.	☐ Quite a bit	☐ Somewhat	☐ A little	☐ Not at all
I practice "Thou shall not judge."	☐ Quite a bit	☐ Somewhat	☐ A little	☐ Not at all
I understand what true happiness is.	☐ Quite a bit	☐ Somewhat	☐ A little	☐ Not at all

A World Without Road Signs

What's the difference between what the Old and New Testaments teach?

If we make the decision to become disciples, what happens next?

What's the difference between God's Law and human laws?

How do we get to the Kingdom of God?

How do the teachings of Jesus change our values and ideas about what is important?

How can the commandments in the Old Testament and the commandments of Jesus help with decisions I face?

The process of deciding what God is calling us to do—both in specific circumstances as well as in the big picture of our lives—is called **discernment**. The path of discipleship involves many daily decisions. Discerning God's will in the myriad of possibilities is a spiritual activity that may sometimes be crystal clear. At other times it may be difficult, but it is always essential.

Saying "yes" to discipleship implies that you are heading toward a specific destination—the Kingdom of God. Here's an example: If you had your license, a car, and permission to travel, and you decided to take a road trip, it would be a good idea to have a GPS device, a map downloaded from the Internet, or some other form of directions. So if the Kingdom of God is the destination, then discernment is in the process of figuring out the directions.

How does discernment work? To be honest, some adults still struggle with discernment. It definitely takes time, maturity, experience, and wisdom to do it well. But the process of discernment begins by simply looking and listening for signs of God's will. Let's look at a real world example of how we need signs to point in the right direction.

The former Soviet Union was determined to control the nation of Czechoslovakia in 1968. Just before the Soviet army invaded, the Czechoslovakian resistance radioed instructions to its people, and road signs and street numbers "mysteriously" disappeared. People shrugged their shoulders when Soviet soldiers asked directions.

The Czechoslovakian people were resisting an occupying power that had invaded their country. But imagine if somebody took down all the signs in our neighborhoods today and instead put up misleading signs. Such signs might say things like "This way to Main Street" with an arrow pointing in the wrong direction. It would be chaos. Traffic would paralyze the city. Business would bog down. People would get lost, frustrated, and angry.

discernment process—through prayer, study, Scripture reflections and discussions—of determining what God is calling us to do, both in a specific circumstance as well as in the big picture of our lives

143

Discern

○ What do you think is the most important thing to keep in mind when trying to practice discernment?

○ Write about a time when you were able to discern well. After describing the situation, see if you can identify what, if anything, was the key.

Do not let this soul be misled, or turn aside from the path it has taken. Give it your light, to see that its well-being depends on continuing along that path.

—Saint Teresa of Ávila

Mosaic Law the Law, most importantly the Ten Commandments, that God gave to Moses on Mount Sinai to guide the lives of the Israelites

covenant a solemn agreement between human beings or between God and his People involving mutual commitments or guarantees

Suppose the same kind of thing happened on the Internet? Instead of one click opening up the next screen, it might take you to a completely different site. Your misdirection would take you further and further away from the page you were viewing; each prompt, each direction deliberately misleading you.

The commandments of God are like road signs and directions. In the process of discernment, they help us to find our way. They help us to get our bearings, even in unfamiliar places, and they help to keep us from getting lost and frustrated. And when the weather in life gets stormy, they can lead you to the right place, like a spiritual GPS.

Spiritually speaking, a lot of messages from advertising, entertainment, and society can point us in the wrong direction. Every day, for example, we are encouraged in subtle and not-so-subtle ways to buy what other people have. These messages start when we are little children, inciting us to want the latest toys, clothes, and games. We can be shaped in such a way that our happiness is affected by whether we have the right things and how many things we end up with. Think about how quickly your cell phone seemed obsolete when new features were introduced that your phone didn't have. How does it feel to have "an old phone"? What causes us to feel that way?

The Tenth Commandment tells us not to covet our neighbor's goods. Why? Because our desire to have what our neighbor has becomes unreasonable. When we commit this capital sin, when we envy our neighbor's goods, it takes us down a path where we end up feeling unhappy, angry, and maybe even depressed all because we don't have certain "material things."

Guides for Life

The Ten Commandments that Moses received from God on Mount Sinai served as directions for living as God's people. The Israelites viewed the commandments as a gift, a way to know how to live. They were part of the **Mosaic Law**. The Israelite community enjoyed good order, stability, and fruitfulness when they followed the commandments.

The commandments themselves are well organized. The first three concern the love of God, and the rest deal with love of neighbor. The Israelites showed their **covenant** relationship with God by following the commandments. So does everyone who follows these same commandments today.

God's Law consists of:

- the Mosaic Law given to the Chosen People

- the law of the New Testament revealed by Jesus, which we will discuss in this section

These laws are only known because God revealed them. Many, like the Ten Commandments, could also be reached through human reason. God chose to reveal

List

We are governed by laws and rules in society, at school, at home, and at work, but what about the rules between friends?

○ Make a set of ten rules for friendship that need to be obeyed in order for a friendship to go well.

○ What happens when any of the rules between friends are not followed?

GO TO THE SOURCE

The psalmist sings gratefully for God's Law. Read Psalm 19 in its entirety.

○ What two things are being praised?

○ According to the psalmist, if you follow the Law, where will it take you?

them to us, however, to ensure that we accept them and understand them well. God is the authority of all law. This is because God, who created us, placed **natural law**—which humankind can reach through reason—in our nature. The many systems of human law, then, have some level of natural law, given to us by God. The Ten Commandments are a privileged expression of natural law.

All through the Old Testament, we see people expressing thanks for God's Law. These are not the words of people who find God's Law oppressive or limiting. They express confidence that God's commandments illuminate the path to happiness and living forever with him. As Moses says in the Book of Deuteronomy, "See, I have set before you today life and prosperity, death and adversity." He tells the people that they will survive and become numerous if they obey and live God's commandments. "And the Lord your God will bless you in the land that you are entering to possess . . . Choose life so that you and your descendants may live" (Deuteronomy 30:15-16, 19).

It is easy to see why the Gospel according to Matthew presents Jesus as the "new lawgiver." Matthew shows us that, like Moses on Mount Sinai, Jesus presented his followers with trustworthy and divine commandments, such as the New Commandment to love each other as Jesus loved us (see *Catechism of the Catholic Church*, 782). This should not be confused with the Great Commandment, which is to love God with all your heart, mind, and soul. The Great Commandment is not new, as it echoes the Old Law. Jesus' divine commandments, however, make up the New Law. They helped Jesus' first followers find their way and receive God's blessings even more abundantly than they had under the Old Law.

Jesus does not abolish the Old Law of Moses, which was the first stage of God's revealed Law. Instead he releases the hidden potential

natural law God's fatherly instruction that is written on the human heart and accessed by human reason

The Ten Commandments

1. I am the Lord your God; you shall not have strange gods before me.

2. You shall not take the name of the Lord your God in vain.

3. Remember to keep holy the Lord's Day.

4. Honor your father and your mother.

5. You shall not kill.

6. You shall not commit adultery.

7. You shall not steal.

8. You shall not bear false witness against your neighbor.

9. You shall not covet your neighbor's wife.

10. You shall not covet your neighbor's goods.

SOURCE: *Catechism of the Catholic Church*, Second Edition.

I am the Lord your God; you shall not have strange gods before me.

You shall not take the name of the Lord your God in vain.

Remember to keep holy the Lord's Day

Honor your father and your mother.

You shall not kill.

You shall not commit adultery.

You shall not steal.

You shall not bear false witness against your neighbor.

You shall not covet your neighbor's wife.

You shall not covet your neighbor's goods.

Apply

○ Read through the Ten Commandments in the accompanying chart.

○ Answer this question with each one: If a person chooses to go against this commandment, where does that path end up? Be specific.

of the Old Law. He fulfills the Mosaic Law, which sums up its moral lessons in the Ten Commandments. Thus the Ten Commandments still direct us today, with new demands arising from them. The Gospels, through the grace of the Holy Spirit, bring the Old Law to fullness in the New Law. Jesus best expresses the New Law in the Beatitudes. In short, Jesus shows us how to live and act.

The **Sermon on the Mount** is where Jesus puts into words the New Law, also called the **Law of the Gospel**. This Law, summarized in Jesus' New Commandment to love one another as he has loved us, is the perfection of the divine law here on Earth (see CCC, 1965). The Law of the Gospel requires people to practice the words of God summed up in the **Golden Rule** to treat others as you want to be treated yourself. "In everything do to others as you would have them do to you. For this is the law and the prophets" (Matthew 7:12). The Law of the Gospel is summed up in the Golden Rule.

Memorize List the Ten Commandments in order without looking them up.

Elaborate What does the New Law of Jesus do to the Old Law?

Sermon on the Mount the summary of key teachings of Jesus found in the Gospel according to Matthew

Law of the Gospel also called the New Law, it is summarized in Jesus' New Commandment to "love one another as I have loved you" (John 15:12)

Golden Rule in everything, do to others what you would have them do to you

Apply

The Golden Rule is taught to many people at a young age. Working with a partner or a group, brainstorm about what the meaning of this teaching might be at the following ages:

○ five years old
○ fifteen years old
○ thirty years old

SECTION 1 REVIEW

QUICK REVIEW

1a. Discuss How are God's commandments like road signs?

b. Recall What was the Israelites' attitude toward the Law of God?

2a. Recall Who received the Ten Commandments, where, and when?

b. Explain How did the Israelites view the commandments?

c. Explain Why was it important to the Israelites to carry out the commandments?

d. Interpret What is promised in Deuteronomy to those who follow the commandments?

3a. Analyze Why does the Gospel according to Matthew present Jesus as the new lawgiver?

b. Recall How did Jesus express the New Law?

Listen and Discuss Discuss these questions with classmates:

○ If one knows God's commandments, how could that knowledge affect that person's life?

○ Discuss the implications for your life that comes from one of the commandments.

Pray Compose a short prayer that does one of the following:

○ thanks God for the guidance you receive from the commandments

○ praises God for the Law in the style of the psalmist in Psalm 19

SELF-ASSESS

Which statement best reflects where you are now?

☐ I'm confident enough about the material in this section to be able to explain it to someone else.

☐ I have a good grasp of the material in this section, but I could use more review.

☐ I'm lost. I need help catching up before moving on.

Jesus Proclaims the Law of Love

Jesus repeatedly summed up the Law of the Gospel. The Gospel according to John puts it this way in the New Commandment of Jesus: "This is my commandment, that you love one another as I have loved you" (John 15:12). "The Law of the Gospel fine tunes the Old Law because it 'fulfills,' refines, surpasses, and leads the Old Law to its perfection" (CCC, 1967). The difference between the Old and New Testament law is this: When we allow the Holy Spirit to lead us, and we follow the Law of the Gospel, we become capable of acting out of love, not fear.

Another summation by Jesus that we mentioned comes to us as the Two Great Commandments, which echo the teachings found in the Old Testament books of Deuteronomy and Leviticus:

Jesus answered: "The first is, 'Hear, O Israel . . . you shall love the Lord your God with all your heart, and with all your soul, and with all your mind, and with all your strength.' The second is this, 'You shall love your neighbor as yourself.' There is no other commandment greater than these."

—Mark 12:29-31

Compare and Contrast
○ What is the difference between God's Law and human laws?
○ In what ways are they similar?

Jesus' whole life was a continual teaching. To understand what it means to love as Jesus did, we must look at what he taught in the Sermon on the Mount. This teaching is found in Chapters 5 to 7 in the Gospel according to Matthew. The beginning of Chapter 5 says Jesus went up the mountain, sat down, and began to teach the great crowds of people who followed him. His words astounded them. The end of Chapter 7 says they were amazed at his teaching. Keep in mind that when the New Testament uses the term "Law" it usually refers to the Law of Moses or the Law in the Old Testament.

Scripture scholars tell us that the Sermon on the Mount was not really a single sermon preached by Jesus all at one sitting. It is more likely an assortment of important and memorable sayings of Jesus that his early followers recalled and collected. The Gospel according to Matthew presents them all in one place, using this mountain setting, in order to make the point that in the teachings of Jesus we see a New Law being presented. The Old Law prepared us to hear this New Law, yet the New Law is a distinctive revelation through Jesus. It is the Law of Love.

The Sisters of Charity teach children in Tijuana.

147

What do you think happens to your soul when you die? Could the first words Jesus speaks in the Gospel according to Mark be especially helpful? Check it out. Write out the words of Jesus in Mark 1:15.

What does Jesus mean when he says the Kingdom of God is at hand? Is the Kingdom of God something we only experience in the afterlife? An entire branch of theology is devoted to the study of end times. It is called eschatology (es•kuh•TO•lo•gy), and we will discuss it more in Chapter 8.

Theologian Jürgen Moltmann popularized the theological idea that Christians should not only hope for eternal life in Heaven, but also work to bring about the Kingdom of God on Earth. He used the phrase "already, not yet" to help us understand that God's Kingdom can already be experienced here and now, yet will only be fully realized in Heaven.

>> **Write examples of how the Kingdom of God is already present on Earth.**

➤ Go to the student site at
hs.osvcurriculum.com

Beatitudes the teachings of Jesus in the Sermon on the Mount, addressing how to respond to the desire for happiness that God has given each of us

Kingdom of God also called the reign or rule of God, or the Kingdom of Heaven, it is the state of righteousness and joy in the Holy Spirit that the ministry of Jesus announced and inaugurated and which is mysteriously present in the Church today, most especially in the Eucharist

What did Jesus say that so impressed the crowds? First, he proclaimed the **Beatitudes**, which are Jesus' teachings from the Sermon on the Mount that address how to respond to the desire for happiness that God has given each of us (see page 236 for a complete list of the Beatitudes). These teachings are at the heart of Jesus' preaching. They deal with the meaning of and the way to true happiness. They are also revolutionary. Why? Each Beatitude begins with the words, "Blessed are the . . ." His first listeners would have been very well aware of how God promised blessings of land and countless descendants to Abraham, the great ancestor of the Chosen People.

When Jesus proclaims the Beatitudes, however, he is telling people that the way to inherit the blessings promised to Abraham is to set their hearts on the justice of his words. Living according to the Beatitudes will bring the Law to its fullness. Those guided by the Beatitudes will gain much more than the land promised to Abraham; they will gain the **Kingdom of God**, which is at hand. They will gain the vision of God, a participation in divine nature as God's sons and daughters, and eternal life and rest. We, the People of God, then, are called to transform this world, so that the Kingdom of God can be fulfilled "on earth as it is in heaven."

GO TO **THE SOURCE**

Read through Chapters 5 to 7 of the Gospel according to Matthew.

○ Jot down any items that surprise you or seem puzzling.

○ Now make a list of the items that seem consoling or encouraging.

○ Would you agree with the crowds' assessment at the end of Chapter 7:29? Why or why not?

The Beatitudes do not focus on possessing anything or on having a successful family and clan. The Kingdom of God, instead, is granted freely to those whom the world regards as most unfortunate—those who are poor, who mourn, who are meek, who are persecuted, and so on. This teaching turns our expectations upside down. To be merciful and pure in heart is more important than to be successful or wealthy.

Jesus affirmed that the directions for human behavior set by the Law of Moses must be observed. We must not murder, slander, commit adultery, or do any of the other things the Ten Commandments prohibit. In addition, we must not hate or despise or hold a grudge, or even look lustfully at another person. These are serious obligations. The way of life that Jesus teaches begins in the heart, with mercy, forgiveness, and love. Blessed are the pure in heart, he said. Good behavior must be authentic, coming from within, and not merely an outward show.

Identify How does the Law of the Gospel perfect the Old Law?

Integrate What clues do the Beatitudes give us about discipleship?

The Road Less Traveled

Jesus went on to teach the crowds not to swear (see Matthew 5:33) and not to retaliate when someone does us harm (see Luke 5:38). He even taught love of enemies (see Luke 5:43). It becomes clear that Jesus is describing a way to break out of the cycle of violence that leads people to take revenge and to perpetuate conflicts or fights. Such teaching can be hard to follow. It may take a long time with

Research
Independently research a contemporary story of either revenge and feuding or forgiveness and nonviolence. Then, in groups, compare the stories.

○ What do the revenge stories have in common?

○ What do the forgiveness stories have in common?

○ What insights did you gain from Jesus' teaching of love for enemies?

gradual conversion to get it right. But getting it right with that gradual conversion is the goal. Knowing that God always gives us grace to do what he wants helps us to stay on the path.

Jesus also counseled his followers to have **detachment** from material possessions. We are not to be overly concerned about material goods. The true treasures we possess are spiritual. If our focus is on our material goods, we will ultimately be disappointed, Jesus tells us. Like all the teachings of Jesus, this one demands a choice. We cannot serve both God and wealth (Matthew 6:24). And while we must put the Kingdom of God first, this does not mean we can forget about our material needs and responsibilities.

Serving the Kingdom of God also means creating the right relationships in all things. This includes personal and social relationships. It includes advocating and being an

detachment an attitude of spiritual freedom, which allows one to use material goods without becoming enslaved by them

Identify
○ What is your understanding of what it means to "be blessed"?

○ Is your own understanding more aligned with that of the ancient Israelites or with Jesus' description in the Beatitudes?

○ Identify the blessings you have in your own life.

By this everyone will know that you are my disciples, if you have love for one another.

—John 13:35

"Do unto others as you would have them do to you." Christians know this as the Golden Rule. Other religions and cultures have similar convictions. Ancient Greeks said: "Do not do to others what would anger you if done to you by others." Hindus would say: "One should never do that to another which one regards as injurious to one's own self." Muslims offer: "Hurt no one so that no one may hurt you," while Jews referring to the Old Testament would say: "You shall love your neighbor as yourself" (Leviticus 19:18). The secular world calls this the ethic of reciprocity.

○ In what ways do you see the world living out these philosophies?

○ When have you personally seen these demonstrated recently in your family, friendships, or school?

○ List two current obstacles that make these simple philosophies so difficult for the world to follow.

○ How can we start to live the way Jesus asked us to do, which is to love one another?

○ Extend the Golden Rule by creating two additional directions, beginning with "Love your neighbor as yourself *and . . .*"

↗ Go to the student site at **hs.osvcurriculum.com**

Apply

We are often told not to get too attached to material possessions, but many of the things we have help us learn, communicate, and create. Consider your own possessions and how much you are attached to them.

○ With which are you able to practice detachment?

○ With which do you struggle in the practice of detachment? Which are you overly dependent on?

agent of justice in the groups with which you are associated. Because the Kingdom of God is characterized by "joy," try to act out of the possibility of what can be accomplished, rather than doing nothing out of "despair" because the obstacles are too big. When it comes to serving the Kingdom of God, and discerning the path of discipleship, the Holy Spirit guides those actions and attitudes rooted in a right relationship with God. When Jesus is the beginning and end—the Alpha and Omega—of your desires, it is easier to be faithful to yourself, your family, and your friends.

Service in the Kingdom of God requires the pursuit of the common good—the Christian principle that society should be organized so that, as much as possible, both individuals and the entire community are equally thriving. It starts with the fundamental truth that the equality of all people involves their human dignity and the rights that come from it. We do this by considering other people as ourselves, and we treat them that way. On a global level, we look for ways to reduce social and economic inequalities, and there is an urgency to get rid of sins that produce these inequalities, such as unfair labor practices. We strive to do these things because everyone on the planet is given equal dignity from God.

Another quality that Jesus taught is humility in exercising our religious observances. He condemns the desire to "show off" our religious devotion. We should not seek approval from others when we give to the poor, pray, or fast. We should do these things because it benefits those who need help and because, in so doing, we act as Jesus' disciples. It also benefits our relationship with God the Father, who sees and blesses such actions.

GO TO THE SOURCE

Jesus uses a metaphor to explain why we ought to begin by judging ourselves, not others.

Go back and read Matthew 7:3-5.

○ What name does Jesus give to people who judge others while remaining sinners themselves?

○ What is something you complain about with friends and family that you do yourself?

Everyday life challenges you to think about right and wrong, to sort out the good from the bad, and to inform and form your conscience. Here's an example . . .

}

"Oh yeah. Everybody uses them. Be crazy not to" is how people justify the "shortcuts."

But teachers have been issuing specific rules against using these Internet resources and plagiarizing. "Do the research. Read the book. Quit cheating," the teachers say.

Students at all levels are facing tough choices.

Everybody IS doing it.

It IS cheating. You just cut and paste stuff somebody else wrote.

If I don't do it, I'll get a worse grade than they will.

If it's not cheating, then how come people are sneaky about it?

Not hurting anyone. So nothing is wrong.

No time to do all that reading. Impossible. No choice.

How do you respond?

Going Moral

Jesus also warns that we are not to judge each other. "For with the judgment you make you will be judged, and the measure you give will be the measure you get" (Matthew 7:2). He offered the Golden Rule, discussed earlier, as a simple rule for dealing with people.

Jesus knew that the way of life he was proposing was not easy. "For the gate is wide and the road is easy that leads to destruction" (Matthew 7:13). Only a narrow gate and a difficult road lead to eternal life, and few find the way, Jesus adds. This is another example of how Jesus' teachings are "counter cultural." Our society seems to believe that it is easy to travel the path that leads to eternal life. But Jesus knew it was going to be a challenge for people to live this way.

Name Which of Jesus' teachings speak of actions that help break the cycle of violence?

Infer Why is a teaching that can end conflicts and fights so hard to follow?

GO TO THE SOURCE

Even people who call on God often during their lives may not enter Heaven, Jesus tells us in the Gospel according to Matthew.

Read Matthew 7:21-23.

○ Why might those who say they act in God's name not be welcomed into Heaven?

○ Jesus says only those who do the Father's will can enter the Kingdom of Heaven. Make a list of ten things that might be examples of doing God's will.

SECTION 2 REVIEW

QUICK REVIEW

1a. Recall What are the Beatitudes and what do they promise?

b. Analyze How would you apply Jesus' teachings on the Kingdom to today's world?

c. Name According to the Beatitudes, who will be part of the Kingdom of God?

2a. Explain Do the Beatitudes contradict the Law of Moses?

b. List Besides the Beatitudes, what else did the Sermon on the Mount teach?

c. Predict What would happen if everyone took to heart the message of the Kingdom?

3a. Predict What will happen if we are too attached to material goods?

b. Interpret What does Jesus say in reference to the "narrow gate"?

c. Identify How are Jesus' teachings "countercultural"?

ACT

Reread the Beatitudes. Then answer these questions privately.

○ Which Beatitude expresses best how you would like to live?

○ What is the blessing associated with that Beatitude?

○ What can you do today to be worthy of that blessing?

SELF-ASSESS

Which statement best reflects where you are now?

☐ I'm confident enough about the material in this section to be able to explain it to someone else.

☐ I have a good grasp of the material in this section, but I could use more review.

☐ I'm lost. I need help catching up before moving on.

How to Enter the Kingdom

Many people who met Jesus asked him questions. Sometimes these ques tioners were hostile, sometimes they were sincere, and sometimes they were interested in their own agenda. According to the synoptic Gospels, three different people asked Jesus one particular question: Which commandment of the Old Law is the greatest? The person who asks the question in each Gospel has a different motive.

- In Matthew 22:34-40, a Pharisee asks the question as a test.

- In Luke 10:25-28, the question comes from a lawyer who wants to justify himself.

- In Mark 12:28-34, a scribe asks the question in a friendly way, sincerely wanting to know Jesus' answer to the question.

These accounts show that the commandments are essential. But just knowing the commandments is not enough. The scribe's response shows that we must have the right attitude to enter the Kingdom of God. Our hearts must be open to the words of Jesus. It is then that we can "answer wisely" and with understanding.

Identify Which of the three people who ask Jesus which is the greatest commandment does so in a friendly way?

Infer What does Jesus' answer say about how we should treat ourselves?

The Most Important Thing

There is an old proverb that reads: "All that is not given is lost." In the Gospels, Jesus encounters a rich young man who wanted to know what he should do to gain eternal life. He was a good person, and when questioned it became clear that he had observed the Law of Moses and obeyed the commandments. But Jesus advised him that if he wanted to be perfect, he should sell all his possessions, give the money to the poor, and follow Jesus. The young man "went away grieving, for he had many possessions" (Matthew 19:22).

Create

Design a table titled Hard Choices with four columns and fill them in with the following in mind:

○ First column: List five situations or moral dilemmas people your age regularly encounter.

○ Second column: What is the popular response or action to take in each situation?

○ Third column: What is the right choice, based on our Catholic teachings, to make in each situation?

○ Fourth column: What is the cost of doing each of the things in the third column?

GO TO **THE SOURCE**

Let's look at the three passages in which people ask Jesus which commandment is the greatest.

Read Matthew 22:34-40, Luke 10:25-28, Mark 12:28-34.

○ What answer does Jesus give each time?

○ Which of the three people "got it"?

○ Make up a new question you wish someone had asked Jesus in the Gospels.

PRIMARY SOURCES

Visit hs.osvcurriculum.com for a link to "A Common Word Between Us and You" and read the summary and abridgement of the statement. Here is a portion of the beginning:

Today's world has seen numerous conflicts that seem to be based in religion, yet many people of faith on all sides believe God wants peace. In 2007, a group of one hundred thirty-eight Muslim scholars and religious leaders wrote a statement addressed to Christians everywhere, calling for peacemaking based on the "common word" of the two Great Commandments. Their statement, "A Common Word Between Us and You," has sparked new efforts, including a dialogue with the Vatican.

➜ Go to the student site at **hs.osvcurriculum.com**

Muslims and Christians together make up well over half of the world's population. Without peace and justice between these two religious communities, there can be no meaningful peace in the world. The future of the world depends on peace between Muslims and Christians.

The basis for this peace and understanding already exists. It is part of the very foundational principles of both faiths: love of the One God, and love of the neighbour. These principles are found over and over again in the sacred texts of Islam and Christianity. The Unity of God, the necessity of love for Him, and the necessity of love of the neighbour is thus the common ground between Islam and Christianity.

>> Why is it essential for Muslims and Christians to be at peace, according to the statement?

Why do you think the writers chose the sacred texts of the Bible and the Qur'an as a basis for common ground, rather than secular documents?

According to this response, what concern is a "strong and liberating current" that runs through the statement?

Faith & Culture

There have always been people in the Church who embrace Jesus' call to rid themselves of possessions in service to God's Kingdom.

○ Saint Francis of Assisi is an outstanding example of someone who actually loved and sought out poverty as a way to walk the path of discipleship.

○ You may know that Francis grew up as the son of a wealthy cloth businessman in Assisi. Gradually he embraced poverty and became a role model for untold millions since the thirteenth century.

○ Francis is often credited with the creation of the first Christmas crèche. Churches bear his name and movies have depicted his life. He founded the Franciscan Order of priests and brothers. He assisted Saint Clare of Assisi to found Franciscan women religious orders.

Many gardens have statues of Saint Francis, known for his love of animals.

The call to give up everything in order to gain the Kingdom is mentioned in several places in the New Testament. In the parable of the pearl, the merchant sells everything he has in order to buy one perfect pearl (see Matthew 13:45-46). Likewise in a separate parable, a man finds a treasure buried in a field. He sells all he has in order to buy the field (see Matthew 13:44). The Kingdom of God is like the perfect pearl and the field of treasure.

These passages all make the same point: God's Kingdom is worth more than anything. The spiritual task is to set your life around it. Why is it so difficult for a rich person to enter the Kingdom? One reason is that the more material possessions one has, the harder it is to practice detachment and focus on the Kingdom. Being rich isn't the problem. Many people use their wealth for the benefit of others. It is the excessive attachment to material possessions that can blur our view of the Kingdom of God. And, it's not only those considered wealthy who have excessive attachments to material possessions, such as cars, jewelry, clothes, or electronics. Everyone must struggle to keep this in balance and perspective.

Jesus also showed that discipleship does come with a cost. He gave up home and family and all worldly ambitions in order to announce the Kingdom of God and bring it about. As he said to those who wanted to follow him, "Foxes have holes, and birds of the air have nests; but the Son of Man has nowhere to lay his head" (Luke 9:58). Throughout the Gospel, he was not afraid to call his followers to make hard choices in order to enter the Kingdom of God.

Saint Paul also found that the Kingdom was only to be gained by putting it first in his life. He believed it was worth it. In his letter to the Philippians, he writes: "I regard everything as loss because of the surpassing value of knowing Christ Jesus my Lord. For his sake I have suffered the loss of all things, and I regard them as rubbish, in order that I may gain Christ and be found in him" (Philippians 3:8-9).

Discernment, discipleship, and service to the Kingdom of God is really a matter of setting our priorities a certain way. When we consider all the things and decisions in our lives, we should ask ourselves whether or not they lead us closer to the Kingdom.

Yet, this call to set our priorities a certain way is not just for saints or members of religious communities. All of us, once we are consecrated in Baptism, are called to "strive first for the kingdom of God and his righteousness" (Matthew 6:33) and to hold it more dearly than any earthly possession. This inner attitude brings us freedom, and is based on trust that God will care for us. It shows itself in our outward behavior, too, such as faithfulness in our friendships, kindness to family, the making of moral decisions, sacrificing for others, giving to the poor, and participating in the Eucharist.

Recall Why did the rich young man (Matthew 19:16-22) go away grieving?

Distinguish How can we determine what is most important in life?

Imagine

The rich young man runs into Peter and John at the village cafe three days later. Over tea and pita bread, he asks them what they thought of his conversation with Jesus. Create a conversation that might have taken place among them.

○ How does the rich young man feel about what Jesus told him?

○ Does the rich young man still have questions?

○ What insights might the two Apostles add to the whole situation?

Research

○ Go through one of the four Gospels and develop a list of choices Jesus asks his disciples to make, the requirements he points out, and other costs and expectations.

SECTION 3 REVIEW

QUICK REVIEW

1a. Summarize What is the greatest commandment? The second greatest?

b. Analyze What does Mark's story about the greatest commandments teach us?

2a. Explain What is the mission of the "A Common Word" movement?

b. Analyze Why is Jesus' advice to the rich young man disturbing?

3a. Recall Which parables show the value of the Kingdom of God?

b. Analyze How did Saint Francis of Assisi show that he understood Jesus' teachings?

c. Evaluate What is the relationship between our priorities and our spiritual health?

ACT

Try giving up a material good, such as a cell phone or a favorite article of clothing, for a week.

○ Keep a small journal on your reflections on this exercise.

○ Did you gradually become detached from the thing you gave up? Why or why not?

Pray Write a short prayer related to something in this section, such as the Two Great Commandments, or the cost of discipleship. Put it where you will remember to pray it once a day.

SELF-ASSESS

Which statement best reflects where you are now?

☐ I'm confident enough about the material in this section to be able to explain it to someone else.

☐ I have a good grasp of the material in this section, but I could use more review.

☐ I'm lost. I need help catching up before moving on.

The Good Shepherd

Many people are familiar with the twenty-third Psalm: "The Lord is my shepherd, I shall not want" (Psalm 23:1). Jesus had a lot to say about the many ways he cares for us. He urged us not to be anxious or worried. He taught everyone to rely on God completely. Jesus himself exercised great care for his disciples, even to the point of being their servant and washing their feet. He called himself the Good Shepherd.

An actual shepherd who is good at his job cares for his sheep and keeps them safe. He provides for them, and he even saves them from themselves when they wander off and get lost. We can see the analogy with Jesus, who offers guidance through his teaching and by his continual presence with us in the Church. We may also go astray by making poor choices, but Jesus seeks us out and calls us home. The challenge when we go off the spiritual path is to remain open to hearing his voice—and letting it guide you back.

GO TO **THE SOURCE**

Jesus compares himself to a Good Shepherd in the Gospel according to John.

Read John 10:1-21.

- What is Jesus saying about himself by using this image?
- What image can you come up with that describes how Jesus has related to you and others you know?

Sometimes people have an image of God as a stern judge or a ruler who is distant from his subjects. When we think of the image of the Good Shepherd, however, we see a much different face of Jesus—one that is caring, near to us, and who takes delight in our well-being. On the other hand, some people overemphasize his unconditional love and make Jesus into someone who allows them to do whatever they want.

Discuss

What are some ways in which people can perceive Jesus incorrectly?

How Do We Find Happiness?

The desire for happiness is built into human nature. God has placed that longing in the human heart. The whole witness of Sacred Scripture, from creation onward, shows that God wants us to be happy. However, the kind of happiness that God desires for us is deep, lasting fulfillment, not immediate gratification. It would be fair to say that God's vision of happiness for us includes having true, meaningful friendships and finding a fulfilling career, but it probably does not include whether we get all the items on our Christmas wish list.

Some psychologists tell us that happiness is a feeling that comes when we are in "flow" moments. These are moments when we are completely caught up in a meaningful action such as a conversation in which we momentarily forget where we are and time seems to

Catholic Volunteers in Florida

Service to the Kingdom of God has been mentioned a lot in this chapter. And for Catholics, service is truly an expression of faith.

Catholic Volunteers in Florida (CVIF) "attempt to live a simple lifestyle while being more attentive of their daily actions in challenge to our society's growing consumerism."

CVIF serve for at least one year and come from all over the United States. They are placed throughout the state in positions that fit their backgrounds and skills. The program pays each Volunteer a living stipend and transportation and meal allowance each month and provides health insurance and housing. They also receive an Americorps educational award at the end of their service. This can be used to pay student loans or pursue further education. The Volunteers often live together in a community where they support each other spiritually. CVIF offer twenty days of retreats across the state each year.

The CVIF lifestyle is one of spirituality, simple living, community service, and living Gospel values every day.

Founded in 1983 by Augustinian Father Patrick O'Neill, then president of St. Thomas University in Miami Gardens, Florida, CVIF address poverty in Florida and encourage adults over twenty years old to dedicate one year to serve the poor, the sick, the elderly, and migrant workers; those with the greatest needs.

The Volunteers follow Catholic social teachings and work at non-profit organizations that seek to empower those suffering from injustice or powerlessness in today's society.

Such assignments can include work with at-risk elementary school students, Big Brothers Big Sisters, migrant farm workers, the homeless, or in food banks, health clinics, and youth shelters.

>> **What are the benefits of joining with other Catholics to take an organized approach to service?**

How does such service teach us about human dignity?

Which kind of service do you prefer?

slow down. Examples may be an athletic event in which you are performing difficult plays, or the sights and sounds you take in as you stand near the stage at a sold-out concert.

Others say that happiness comes mainly from our favorite physical activity. And still others say happiness comes mainly from our social lives, having positive interactions with the people we care about the most. Despite the psychological, physical, or social factors, Jesus tells us that happiness comes from attending to our spiritual longings for God's love. Because we have souls, our deepest longing is for a right relationship with the One who made us.

We share in Jesus' joy and remain in his love when we keep the Law of the Gospel. "As the Father has loved me," Jesus said, "so I have loved you; abide in my love. If you keep my commandments, you will abide in my love, just as I have kept my Father's commandments and abide in his love. I have said these things to you so that my joy may be in you, and that your joy may be complete" (John 15:9-11).

In this there is a spiritual secret. Spiritual happiness—what we also call "true joy"—comes when you serve someone and something greater than yourself: the Kingdom of God. This is what Jesus taught us: Serve the Kingdom of God and you will meet your soul's deepest desire for happiness and joy.

> For those who want to save their life will lose it, and those who lose their life for my sake will save it.
>
> —Luke 9:24

There is also a spiritual myth that if we serve the Kingdom of God, all will be good. Our problems will vanish. Life will be easy. The Law of the Gospel never makes that guarantee. The truth is that we will still experience life's pains and struggles, heartaches and disappointments. Jesus tells us, "If any want to become my followers, let them deny themselves and take up their cross daily and follow me" (Luke 9:23). We can rely on the grace of God to support us.

Explain

○ Fill in the blanks of the following sentence pairs. Create several versions of each. In the first sentence pair, try to define what happiness really is and how one gets it. In the second sentence pair, fill in the blanks in ways that describe several misconceptions about happiness.

Happiness is _____ and comes from _____ .

Happiness is _____ and comes from _____ .

Happiness is not _____ and you can't get it by/from _____ .

Happiness is not _____ and you can't get it by/from _____ .

○ What has been your experience of happiness? Briefly write about what has brought you real happiness, or what turned out to be false happiness. Describe it in a paragraph or two and conclude by sharing how this relates to the true happiness for which God created us and that Jesus taught us.

When it is your turn to carry a cross, the Good Shepherd will always find you. This is why Paul could write so confidently to the community at Philippi even though he was in prison at the time.

> Rejoice in the Lord always; again I will say, Rejoice. Let your gentleness be known to everyone. The Lord is near. Do not worry about anything, but in everything by prayer and supplication with thanksgiving let your requests be made known to God. And the peace of God, which surpasses all understanding, will guard your hearts and your minds in Christ Jesus.
>
> —Philippians 4:4-7

Discipleship is not meant to be carried out alone. The Church, as a community of disciples, can bring us joy as well. In the next chapter, we will see how.

Describe How do we remain in God's love?

Predict What will happen if all of our actions are governed by the question, "What will I get in return?"

Sofia Cavalletti
AND THE CATECHESIS OF THE GOOD SHEPHERD

Ever wonder how little children can best develop their spirituality?

Ever wonder what might be a good way to help children learn about God?

Ever wonder what image of Jesus seems to help children most?

An Italian woman named Sofia Cavalletti spent her whole life trying to answer these types of questions. She was influenced by the insights of the educator Maria Montessori, who developed the Montessori method of early childhood education by observing and respecting children in all stages of their development.

Cavalletti applied these same insights to catechesis and created something unique for young children. The goal of her method, which begins with children as young as age three, is to help

them have "a living encounter with the living God." She called her method the Catechesis of the Good Shepherd, named for the parable of the Good Shepherd.

In a specially prepared room, called an atrium, the children are introduced to the scriptural story, and given time to explore it for themselves, using wooden figures of the shepherd and the sheep. They are introduced to various elements of the world of the Bible and the liturgy, too. Cavalletti and others concluded by observing the responses of the children that this parable corresponded to their deepest nature and interests. The catechetical process is followed by using different kinds of Scripture stories in addition to the parable of the Good Shepherd.

Adults who use this method receive extensive training. They are taught how to present the story and then allow children to explore the concept. God and the child do the rest.

The Catechesis of the Good Shepherd has spread to thirty-two countries on five continents. Most of those churches that sponsor this style of catechesis are Catholic or Episcopal, although some other Christian traditions have also adopted her approach.

Cavalletti is content to remain in the background herself. She places the spotlight on young children and their innate ability to enjoy a spontaneous and joyful relationship with God. "We are dealing with a joy that puts the child in peace, that makes him serene and calm," she wrote in her book, *The Religious Potential of the Child.*

Think About It What do you think it is about the Good Shepherd that can make children joyful and bring them peace? When do you experience spiritual joy?

Go to the student site at **hs.osvcurriculum.com**

MY FAITH

At this point in your life, what have you found to be essential when it comes to satisfying your soul's desire to be in a relationship with God?

The Commandments. The Beatitudes. The Law of the Gospel. The Good Shepherd. The Kingdom of God. Discipleship.

What's your map to a strong relationship with God?

What do you think contains the best directions to a true, deepening relationship with God?

In this chapter you have reviewed many of these concepts. They point us toward God and a strong relationship with him. And a true, deep relationship with God is the soul's deepest longing.

Which, if any, of the spiritual sources discussed in this chapter provide you with the best set of directions?

Take some time to think about this. Feel free to write a couple of different summaries until you think you have found the best way to explain your experience and convictions. Remember that you may choose to include this as part of the report you give at the end of the course.

_____
_____
_____
_____
_____
_____
_____
_____
_____
_____
_____
_____
_____
_____
_____
_____
_____
_____
_____

Go to the student site at
hs.osvcurriculum.com

Discipleship . . . within the Body of Christ . . .
for the glory of God and the good of the world

SECTION 4 REVIEW

QUICK REVIEW

1a. Recall What does God have to do with happiness and human nature?

b. Analyze Why is the Good Shepherd an appropriate metaphor for Jesus?

c. Speculate What misconceptions or myths does our culture promote regarding happiness?

2a. Tell Fill in the following quote: If you keep my commandments, . . .

b. Summarize What is the key to true happiness?

c. Explain Which of Jesus' quotations discussed in this chapter was most helpful or challenging to you? Why?

Listen and Discuss Talk with a small group about these questions.

○ What "cross" have you seen a person of faith have to carry?

○ What thoughts, questions, or truths did you get from observing this?

SELF-ASSESS
Which statement best reflects where you are now?

☐ I'm confident enough about the material in this section to be able to explain it to someone else.

☐ I have a good grasp of the material in this section, but I could use more review.

☐ I'm lost. I need help catching up before moving on.

PRAYER

Lord Jesus, you said, "Blessed are the poor in spirit, for theirs is the kingdom of heaven."

Keep us from being preoccupied with money and worldly goods, and with trying to increase them at the expense of justice.

Lord Jesus, you said, "Blessed are the gentle, for they shall inherit the earth."

Help us not to be ruthless with one another, and to eliminate the discord and violence that exists in the world around us.

Lord Jesus, you said, "Blessed are those who mourn, for they shall be comforted."

Let us not be impatient under our own burdens and unconcerned about the burdens of others.

Lord Jesus, you said, "Blessed are those who hunger and thirst for justice, for they shall be filled."

Help us be uncomfortable until those who are in need are taken care of.

Lord Jesus, you said, "Blessed are the merciful, for they shall receive mercy."

Grant that we may be quick to forgive and slow to condemn.

Lord Jesus, you said, "Blessed are the clean of heart, for they shall see God."

Free us from our senses and our evil desires, and fix our eyes on you.

Lord Jesus, you said, "Blessed are the peacemakers, for they shall be called children of God."

Help us to make peace and to forgive those who have made mistakes.

Lord Jesus, you said, "Blessed are those who are persecuted for the sake of justice, for the kingdom of heaven in theirs."

Give us the courage to suffer for the sake of right rather than to practice injustice; and do not let us discriminate against our neighbors regardless of their religion, race, or differences.

TERMS

Use each of the following terms in a sentence that shows you know what the term means. You may include more than one term in a sentence.

discernment

Mosaic Law

covenant

Sermon on the Mount

Law of the Gospel

Golden Rule

Beatitudes

Kingdom of God

detachment

PEOPLE

Use information from the chapter to tell why each person or term is significant.

1. Moses

2. A scribe in the Gospel according to Mark

3. Rich young man in the Gospel according to Matthew

4. Saint Francis of Assisi

5. The Good Shepherd

6. Sofia Cavalletti

UNDERSTANDING

Answer each question and complete each exercise.

SECTION 1

1. **Evaluate** Think about two or three of the commandments. How does society pressure us to disobey them or help to support them?

2. **Summarize** Explain the attitude that the Israelites, as a whole, had toward the commandments.

3. **Explain** What part did the Ten Commandments play in the covenant between the God and the Israelites?

SECTION 2

4. **Analyze** What did the Beatitudes change?

5. **Explain** How should we feel about material goods? Explain your answer.

6. **Explain** What did Jesus teach about religious observances?

SECTION 3

7. **Recall** What are the two great commandments?

8. **Analyze** How are these commandments a summary of the Ten Commandments?

9. **Name** List some people who exemplified Jesus' advice for entering the Kingdom of God.

10. **Apply** What can you do in your everyday life to serve God's Kingdom?

SECTION 4

11. **Recall** What is the origin of the image of Jesus as the Good Shepherd?

12. **Analyze** How do we know that God wants us to be happy?

13. **Name** What sort of happiness does following Jesus bring us?

14. **Explain** Why is the Catechesis of the Good Shepherd successful?

CONNECTING

Visual Jesus the Teacher is shown here in this image from the book *At the Name of Jesus*. He is holding the symbols of the ways Scripture has been taught over the centuries.

How does this picture fit with your vision of Jesus? How many of the different ways that Scripture has been taught can you identify from the picture? How many of these methods have you used, which do you use the most, and why?

Challenge You are riding the bus with a friend who notices something different about you.

Friend: Did you lose your MP3 player?

You: No, I left it at home.

Friend: Is it messed up?

You: No, it was just getting to be too important for me.

Friend: What do you mean?

You: I felt like I needed to have it with me all the time.

Friend: So you left it at home on purpose?

O What would you say next?

O Continue the conversation. Include at least two more questions your friend might ask and how you would answer. Use information from the chapter to answer your friend.

Question After working through this chapter, what advice would you give someone who is having trouble understanding the meaning of Jesus' teaching to love our enemies?

Imagine You know that advertisers try to make us want something. Make a reverse ad for something that many people want, but they don't really need. A reverse ad discourages people from excessive consumption. Here are some ideas for your reverse ad:

O Point out negative aspects of owning the item. This could include upkeep expenses or its impact on the environment.

O Point out what would change for the better if people didn't feel that they had to have the item.

O Suggest substitutions for the item that would be more economical, increase friendships, or add to other skills.

SELF-ASSESS

On Your Own Make a list of the most important things you learned from this chapter.

Select three things that represent your growth in understanding as you worked through this chapter. Write a paragraph explaining your choices.

With a Partner Share two things from your list. See what is similar or different on your partner's list as well as any other insights or questions that have surfaced for you from this chapter.

Why are these people gathered together? Describe what you think their connection to the Church might be.

Jesus Continues His Mission

Go to the student site at
hs.osvcurriculum.com

DO

- Explain the missionary mandate of the Church.

- Describe the link between Jesus and Church teaching today.

- Make the connection between Jesus and the Church's concern for the poor.

- Explore the Communion of Saints.

- Research a mission that appeals to you.

- Identify the source of the Church's unity.

- Explain what Mary tells us about Jesus Christ, discipleship, and the mystery of the Church.

DEFINE

Great Commission

evangelize

witnesses

missionary mandate

mystical Body
 of Christ

hierarchy

sanctify

laity

Sacrament of
 Holy Orders

Communion of Saints

merit

intercession or
 intercessory prayer

unity

ecumenism

ecumenical dialogue

Immaculate
 Conception

Assumption

As the relationship deepens between the two main characters in a movie, they start telling each other about their childhoods. One tells of growing up in a very religious family. "Church was important in my house . . . " The speaker waits, but gets no reply from the other. "What?" the speaker finally asks. Then the other character responds: "Not at mine. If Jesus were alive today, I wonder what he would say about that."

An elderly Catholic widow has made a prayer altar on a small table in her house. On it, she has pictures of close family members, a few small statues of saints, her favorite crucifix, and some holy water. She tries to keep a candle lit all the time. "Here I get my strength, praying to God with the saints, the angels, and the Madonna."

WHAT DO YOU SAY?

Where Are You?				
Choose the response that best reflects where you are right now.				
I understand the Great Commission.	☐ Quite a bit	☐ Somewhat	☐ A little	☐ Not at all
I'm involved as a member of the Church.	☐ Quite a bit	☐ Somewhat	☐ A little	☐ Not at all
I think everyone should be part of a faith community.	☐ Quite a bit	☐ Somewhat	☐ A little	☐ Not at all
I understand "apostolic succession."	☐ Quite a bit	☐ Somewhat	☐ A little	☐ Not at all
I understand the correct Catholic practice of praying with Mary and the saints.	☐ Quite a bit	☐ Somewhat	☐ A little	☐ Not at all

The Church of Jesus

How is each of us called to participate in the life of the Church?

How did the Church get started?

How do we know what the Church teaches comes from God?

What is the purpose of the Church?

How did we arrive at the Church as we know it?

Jesus founded the Catholic Church. He did this by calling believers together, sharing his life with and teaching them, and calling them to serve others. His Apostles and other disciples heard him preach about the Kingdom of God. They saw him perform many signs and wonders. They witnessed his death, and spent forty days with him after his Resurrection. But it wasn't until the Risen Jesus was ready to ascend into Heaven that he gave the Apostles their mission, or what we call the **Great Commission**.

> *Go therefore and make disciples of all nations, baptizing them in the name of the Father and of the Son and of the Holy Spirit, and teaching them to obey everything that I have commanded you.*
>
> —Matthew 28:19-20a

GO TO THE SOURCE

The Gospel according to Matthew records two different responses to the Risen Jesus.

Read Matthew 28:16-20.

- What are the two responses?
- Why do you think the Evangelist kept both responses in the story?
- Look at the very last verse of the Gospel according to Matthew, and compare it with Matthew 1:23. What do these two verses reveal about who Jesus is for us?

Summarize

You have been hearing about the Good News since you were a child, but have you ever had to summarize it succinctly and accurately?

- Explain it in no more than three sentences—or compose a text in even fewer words. What is the Good News?

Then and now, the followers of Christ are called to **evangelize** by proclaiming their belief in Christ and his Gospel with their words and actions. Evangelization is about sharing one's excitement and passion for the life-giving experience of Christ. This Good News that God sent his Son to accomplish his plan of salvation would change the lives of those who received it. Christ inaugurated the Church by preaching the Good News (see *Catechism of the Catholic Church*, 714).

Jesus told his disciples: "You will receive power when the Holy Spirit has come upon you; and you will be my **witnesses** in Jerusalem, in all Judea and Samaria, and to the ends of the earth" (Acts 1:8). From that moment on, the Holy Spirit would lead, direct, bring life to, and make holy the Church. If you witness an incident, it means that you saw what happened. To be a witness in the way that Jesus calls his followers means to share the truth that one has come to know about Christ, and to offer evidence of this truth in one's own life.

Great Commission the final command Jesus gave to all of his followers, to spread the Good News of God's plan for salvation to the whole world

evangelize to share the Good News of Christ and the experience of Christ and his Gospel in the things we say and do

witnesses sharers of the truth that we have come to know about Christ, and offer evidence of this truth in our own lives

Jesus' Ascension into Heaven did not end his mission. Instead it began a new time in which the mission would flourish and grow, through the life of the Church. The Apostles were in awe as they watched the Ascension. The Acts of the Apostles tells us that two men in white appeared immediately after Jesus ascended into Heaven, and challenged the followers of Jesus: "Men of Galilee, why do you stand looking up toward heaven?" (Acts 1:11). The Apostles were so absorbed in the moment that they needed help returning to reality.

Jesus' Apostles clearly felt that they had to go out and share their stories about and experiences of Jesus. Not only were they "sent to proclaim the faith," but they were also "given a share in Christ's mission." We have to remind ourselves that the followers of Jesus did this with delight. They had witnessed power over death. The Messiah who had been promised throughout Jewish history had come. And the Holy Spirit was now here to guide them, support them, and help them grow in wisdom as a group. It is in this way that we understand that the Holy Spirit is the "principal agent" of the Church's mission (CCC, 852). We can say with conviction

missionary mandate the command to the whole Church to further the mission of Jesus Christ, including spreading the Good News in word and deed, loving one another, and working for peace and justice as we participate in bringing about the Kingdom of God

Analyze

In 2009, Trinity College in Hartford, Connecticut, released the results of a national survey reporting that the number of those who say they have no religion at all has risen in each state. Overall responses rose from 8.2 percent in 1980 to 14.2 percent in 1990 to 15 percent in 2008.

○ What do you think are three reasons that 15 percent of the people in the United States say they have no religion at all?

○ How do you think Jesus would want his Church to respond?

○ What are the reasons for your membership in Christ's Church?

that the saving mission of Jesus and the Holy Spirit is completed in the Church (see CCC, 737).

> *As a community, the Church must [practice] love. Love thus needs to be organized if it is to be an ordered service to the community.*
>
> —Pope Benedict XVI, *Deus Caritas Est*, 20

The whole Church shares in the apostolic mission of the first disciples. The Church has a **missionary mandate** from Christ, her founder, to work for the salvation of all people. It is because of God's love for all that the Church's mission extends to all. This involves spreading the Good News in word and deed, loving one another as Jesus loved us, and working for peace and justice as we participate in bringing about the Kingdom of God on Earth. The unity of the human race also demands that all be invited into the Kingdom of God.

Explain What role does the Holy Spirit play in the Church?

Evaluate Has the Gospel message reached "to the ends of the earth" (Acts 1:8) as Jesus commanded?

REFLECT

>> Describe a time when either people or events unexpectedly helped you grow in faith.

Describe a time when you were in awe of something or someone.

Making CHANGES

A spiritual practice for the life of discipleship

Change is a natural part of life. Seasons change naturally. So do your interests. And life in high school is a big change from life in middle school. Some changes you make are for the better. Some are not.

In this course you are reminded that Jesus was always inviting people to make changes. Making changes is a spiritual practice focused on living the way God intended. It's a spiritual practice that requires honesty, openness, courage, and sometimes strength.

Sometimes you are forced into making changes:

• your parents decide to move to another state

• your new coach has a different philosophy

• a friend goes in a different direction

And sometimes you are invited to change by the voice of God within you and the voices of those who love you.

Either way, when you practice making changes for spiritual reasons, you are taking control of the kind of person you want to be:

1. Victor instead of victim.

2. Awake instead of asleep.

3. Disciple as well as a believer.

4. Doing good instead of doing no harm.

5. Participant instead of spectator.

6. _____

7. _____

Making changes can apply to big issues or small. The size of the change doesn't matter. The reason for the change does matter. Making changes for spiritual reasons is exactly what will set you free from things that hold power over you.

So when you begin the practice of making changes for the right reasons, it helps to:

• **Name it.** When you are asked to be part of something you have decided to change, calmly and quietly tell someone, "I'm making changes." It will send the signal that you have given your decision thought and that you are doing it on purpose. People will understand.

• **Rearrange.** Don't keep all the same routines, friends, environment, or schedules. If everything in your outside world remains exactly the same, the spiritual changes you want to make will be harder.

• **Pray for real.** Change is hard. Ask for God's grace and the Gifts of the Holy Spirit to guide you.

• **Bounce back.** Get back up if you slip up. Don't give up.

>> Write out some of what you have learned from your own experience of making changes.

Write down something specific that "the voice of God within" is telling you about making changes these days.

When it comes to making changes, is the Holy Spirit's voice more like an occasional whisper or is it more like a constant reminder?

Community Ordered to Its Purpose

Each Christian has a role to play in carrying out the mission of the Church, but the mission is not given only to one or another individual exclusively. It is given to the Church collectively, to all of us, as a community of disciples.

Recall the word *convocation* (an assembly of people). The very word *church* means convocation. It is an assembly of people called together to study God's Word and be

mystical Body of Christ the Church, united with Christ

Research

There are many charities, volunteer organizations, and movements that work to make the world a better place.

○ Find out more about one organization whose mission particularly appeals to you.

○ How does the organization's work promote Jesus' teaching on love of God and neighbor and the equality of all people?

○ How can people like you contribute to the organization's efforts?

GO TO THE SOURCE

Read the entire chapter of 1 Corinthians 12, paying attention to Saint Paul's metaphor describing the unity of gifts that people have in the Church.

○ What is the point Paul is making about Church membership?

○ Think of three or four different people you know who have accepted the Great Commission. Make a list of the gifts that they bring to the world.

○ Make a list of the gifts you bring to the world.

nourished by the Eucharist, so that it becomes the Body of Christ. The Church is called the **mystical Body of Christ** because people come into contact with Christ himself through the Church. This mysterious union between Christ and his Church—the union of the divine and the human—is a mystery which only faith can accept.

The Church is both a visible and a spiritual reality. She has visible structures, a history, and a presence in the world that can be perceived by anyone, including those who do not believe. But by calling the Church a "spiritual reality," we mean that she was brought into being and is sustained by the Holy Spirit. There are worthy causes for justice and peace that secular organizations such as Habitat for Humanity fulfill, but the Church intentionally brings with it a spiritual dynamic: discipleship in Christ.

Explain What does it mean to say the Church is both a visible and a spiritual reality?

Predict How do you see yourself carrying out the mission of the Church as an adult? Explain the reasoning behind your answer. Is it due to certain gifts you have? Is it related to your interests? Or is it about situations needing help?

QUICK REVIEW

1a. List What actions did Jesus take in founding the Church?

b. Explain What was the Great Commission?

c. Recount What did Jesus' followers witness and what did they do about it?

2a. Discuss Explain why the Holy Spirit is the "principal agent of the Church's mission."

b. Analyze Why does the Church have a missionary mandate?

3a. Interpret How is love a service?

b. Connect What God-given gift could you use for the mission of the Church?

ACT

Make an art piece, a poster, a wall hanging, or a visual representation of the mystical Body of Christ.

○ You may want to investigate how earlier artists represented this theme.

○ Consider using a variety of colors and fabrics to represent different cultures or areas within the Body.

Pray Compose a short prayer about your role in the mystical Body of Christ.

SELF-ASSESS

Which statement best reflects where you are now?

☐ I'm confident enough about the material in this section to be able to explain it to someone else.

☐ I have a good grasp of the material in this section, but I could use more review.

☐ I'm lost. I need help catching up before moving on.

Handing on Christ's Message

It has always been understood that as a spiritual reality, Christ guides and directs the Church. As a visible reality, Christ handed the authority and responsibility to lead the Church over to the Apostles. He appointed Peter as the Church's first Pope. Peter was the first bishop of Rome, the first Pope and pastor of the whole Church. Peter and his successors down to our current Pope serve as head of the college of bishops, the Vicar of Christ, and pastor of the universal Church.

hierarchy the Apostles and their successors, the bishops, to whom Christ gave the authority to teach, sanctify, and govern the Church

The Church is led by a **hierarchy** of bishops in union with the Pope. As successors to the Apostles, the hierarchy has a special responsibility to teach, govern, and **sanctify**, meaning to bring people to holiness through the Sacraments. Christ, by sending the Holy Spirit to the Church, entrusted the power to sanctify to the Apostles and their successors. Ordained priests and deacons share in this work in service to the Church and call us together to celebrate the Sacraments.

sanctify to bring people to holiness through the Sacraments; this begins with Christ sending the sanctifying Holy Spirit to Church members who respond to God's grace

All of us, through our various callings and labors, family life, and other experiences, are members of the Body of Christ serving the world. All members of the Church, including the hierarchy, priests, religious, and **laity**, live from Christ, in Christ, and for Christ.

laity or **lay persons** refers to all members of the Church who are not ordained as bishops, priests, or deacons

- We live *from* Christ because he brought us to new life through Baptism. We are strengthened in Confirmation and nourished with the Eucharist.

- We live *in* Christ because he has shown us the way to live day by day.

- We live *for* Christ because we continue his mission to build the Kingdom, especially by serving those in need.

GO TO THE SOURCE

Jesus asks his disciples who they think he is. Peter's answer reveals him as the first leader of the Church. Read the account in Matthew 16:13-20.

- How is Peter's answer different from how others described Jesus?
- How did Peter know what to answer?
- Describe the power that Jesus will give to Peter.

One concrete way in which we continue Christ's mission is in our care for the poor. Jesus identified with the poor. He announced his mission in the synagogue at Nazareth: "The Spirit of the Lord is upon me, because he has anointed me to bring good news to the poor" (Luke 4:18). Jesus also made it clear that anyone who wanted to enter the Kingdom had to practice active love for the poor (see Matthew 25:31-40). It is therefore a mark of the Church's faithfulness that she is always concerned for the poor and the humble. As Blessed Pope John Paul II once said: "The poor are those to whom the mission is first addressed, and their evangelization is *par excellence* the sign and proof of the mission of Jesus" (*Redemptoris Missio*, 60).

One way schools and parishes encourage us to participate in Christ's mission is by prompting care for the poor through service. Does your school or parish have a service program? Did you (or will you) perform service as part of your preparation for Confirmation? Is performing service part of your experience in a Catholic high school? How can we bring Jesus' message to those we serve?

PRIMARY SOURCES

Read article 13 of the Vatican II document *Lumen Gentium*, the "Dogmatic Constitution on the Church," which speaks of the importance of unity amid diversity. The first paragraph of the article is reprinted here, and you will find the entire article on the student site. Several times in article 13, the authors use the word catholicity, with a lowercase "c." The word means universal.

➚ Go to the student site at
hs.osvcurriculum.com

13. All men are called to belong to the new people of God. Wherefore this people, while remaining one and only one, is to be spread throughout the whole world and must exist in all ages, so that the decree of God's will may be fulfilled. In the beginning God made human nature one and decreed that all His children, scattered as they were, would finally be gathered together as one.(117) It was for this purpose that God sent His Son, whom He appointed heir of all things,(118) that be might be teacher, king and priest of all, the head of the new and universal people of the sons of God. For this too God sent the Spirit of His Son as Lord and Life-giver. He it is who brings together the whole Church and each and every one of those who believe, and who is the well-spring of their unity in the teaching of the apostles and in fellowship, in the breaking of bread and in prayers.(119)

>> List the reasons article 13 offers to explain why the unity of the human race compels the Church to be a "catholic" community.

Explain in your own words why unity compels the Church to be a "catholic" community.

Do unity and catholicity require people and parishes to be uniform or all alike? Why or why not?

WITH THE POOR IN BRAZIL:

Dom Hélder Pessoa Câmara

(1909–1999)

Dom Hélder Câmara, an archbishop from Brazil's impoverished northeast, was legendary for his spiritual character and for the way he championed the cause of the poor. Flávio Rocha, a lay missioner in Brazil, heard him speak in 1994 to a packed crowd in a gymnasium in his town.

"I was taken aback when I first saw him. This was the famous prophet and government critic? He looked so tiny, so fragile. Scarcely over five feet tall, he was accompanied to the speakers' table by two taller men who supported his arms. But then he began to speak. 'My brothers and sisters,' he said in a strong voice that belied his diminutive appearance, 'do you want God to hear your voice?' He paused before the mute audience. 'Well,' he demanded, 'do you?' The crowd broke its silence with a thunderous *yes*. 'Then

lend your voice to the voiceless poor, because God hears their cry.' He then pleaded the cause of those he called 'the miserables'—the millions of homeless and hungry in Brazil. We must show solidarity with them by demonstrating for justice, jobs, housing, and health care. But we were to do this as Jesus taught: prayerfully, lovingly, nonviolently. 'We need to "act out" our prayers,' he said."

Dom Hélder lived what he preached. He held the high rank of an archbishop, but he wore simple clothes and a wooden cross. He had no car, no housekeeper. He lived like the poor. He ate his meals in a small corner restaurant frequented by workers. The sacristy of an old chapel was his home, and the door was always open.

He was an absolutely fearless advocate of human rights. A coup in 1964 resulted in military rule that brought with it repressions and assassinations (a situation that was to last for twenty-one years). Dom Hélder protested vigorously and consistently. The government retaliated by forbidding him to speak publicly for more than ten years. No mention of his name was permitted in the news media. His life was threatened, but he would not turn away from his mission. He died at age 90. In the words of Cardinal Evaristo Arns of São Paulo, he was "the greatest man in the history of the Church in Brazil."

Think About It What do you think Dom Hélder meant when he said, "We need to 'act out' our prayers"?
Identify the ways in which you "act out" your prayers.
What Scripture passage does this story remind you of?
What does Dom Hélder's example teach us about the Church?

Go to the student site at
hs.osvcurriculum.com

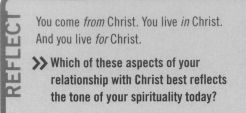

REFLECT

You come *from* Christ. You live *in* Christ. And you live *for* Christ.

>> **Which of these aspects of your relationship with Christ best reflects the tone of your spirituality today?**

From the Apostles to the Church

Peter and the other Apostles, who witnessed the life, death, Resurrection, and Ascension of Jesus, passed on what they received— the teachings, the understanding, the wisdom, and the gift of spiritual healing and wholeness. They faithfully communicated the truth about Jesus. Their successors, the Popes and the bishops, in turn passed that Revelation down throughout the centuries. In this way, the apostolic Tradition, or teaching that comes to us from the Apostles, has been carefully kept and maintained.

> *About Jesus Christ and the Church, I simply know that they're just one thing, and we shouldn't complicate the matter.*
>
> —Saint Joan of Arc

Our history shows that while the decisions and actions of the hierarchy have not always been perfect, the authentic teachings and practices of the Apostles have always been preserved. The celebration of the **Sacrament of Holy Orders**, in which only a baptized man, found by the Church to be suitable for ministry is ordained as a deacon, priest, or bishop, contains a ritual action that illustrates this continuity. A bishop lays his hands on the head of the priest or deacon

Sacrament of Holy Orders
the Sacrament in which only a baptized man, found by the Church to be suitable for the ministry is ordained as a deacon, priest, or bishop who continues the mission that Christ gave to the Apostles

being ordained. The essential rite of ordination is the consecratory prayer, meaning the man is consecrated, or made holy.

Every bishop is consecrated by another bishop, who was consecrated by an earlier bishop, and so on. If all the information and records were available for inspection, you could trace the apostolic succession of any Roman Catholic bishop all the way back to the Apostles. Bishops stand in a direct line reaching back to the Apostles, who received the Revelation of the Gospel from Jesus Christ himself. Bishops, priests, and deacons are irreplaceable components of the Church.

It is important to remember, though, the full meaning of the laying on of hands. It is a gesture that has always, from as far back as New Testament times, been associated with the work of the Holy Spirit. Although laying on of hands is a human action, it is quite unlike other human actions and gestures that designate the monumental occurrence of something special. For example, when public officials take an oath of office, we recognize the meaning of the words and gestures involved. The laying on of hands does not merely evoke meaning and significance for the participants and the witnesses; it is a ritual in which the Holy Spirit is called upon. The presence and grace of God are actively working in, through, and with this ritual.

In Catholic Tradition, the Holy Spirit, through apostolic succession, is the ultimate guarantor of the faith we have received. This knowledge recognizes that it is God—specifically the Holy Spirit—who is the source of our faith. It is the Holy Spirit, not any human or institution, which keeps our faith alive today.

GO TO THE SOURCE

The laying on of hands is a gesture that arises from the apostolic Church. Saint Paul's Second Letter to Timothy mentions the laying on of hands.

Read 2 Timothy 1:3-14.

○ Who are the people in Timothy's family that Saint Paul talks about?

○ What treasure does Saint Paul ask Timothy to guard? Who will help him?

JUSTICE AND DISCIPLESHIP

Jesus tells us that discipleship involves praying to the Father, studying his teachings and following his example, participating in the Eucharist, and living the virtues. He also calls us to act for justice.

POVERTY IS A WORD THAT GETS THROWN AROUND a lot. Jesus was poor. In the Gospels we hear him say, "Blessed are the poor in spirit" (Matthew 5:3, see Luke 6:20). Some priests, members of religious communities, and lay people take a vow of poverty. Yet, poverty is the root cause of many injustices (such as homelessness, hunger, and lack of health care and deprives people of the chance to flourish, as God's children). So how can poverty be a good thing and a bad thing?

Poverty is an economic reality involving a shortage of basic necessities (food, clothing, shelter, safe drinking water), and it is definitely not a good thing. In *Economic Justice for All*, the U.S. Conference of Catholic Bishops goes so far as to call poverty "a social and moral scandal that we cannot ignore," especially since it means being deprived of the things that most of us take for granted.

> *In the United States, thirty-four million people live below the official poverty line . . . If all these people lived in one state, its population would be larger than the combined current populations of Colorado, Utah, Wyoming, Nevada, New Mexico, Oklahoma, Nebraska, South Dakota, North Dakota, Idaho, Iowa and Arizona.*
>
> —USCCB, *A Place at the Table*, page 6

As a matter of justice, you have the choice to act.

Learn Find out more about the root causes of poverty and how people are finding success in ending it. Read more about the dignity of life and why the Church teaches us to respect everyone.

Act Help increase awareness of poverty in America. Volunteer with an organization that works to help the poor. Advocate for change in your community by writing a letter to your government representatives. Pray for moderation and prudence of individuals and nations.

Give Financially support organizations such as the Catholic Campaign for Human Development, which helps people get out of poverty.

↗ Go to the student site at **hs.osvcurriculum.com**

What about Saint Francis and those who choose to live in poverty? Rather than being deprived of basic necessities, voluntary poverty is an active choice to live simply. Again, the U.S. Conference of Catholic Bishops tells us:

> *Each of us should carefully consider our choices and lifestyles. We live in a culture that prizes the consumption of material goods. While the poor often have too little, many of us can be easily caught up in a frenzy of wanting more and more—a bigger home, a larger car, etc. Even though energy resources literally fuel our economy and provide a good quality of life, we need to ask about ways we can conserve energy, prevent pollution, and live more simply.*
>
> —USCCB, *Global Climate Change*, 15

You can be for justice without being a disciple, but you cannot be a disciple without being for justice.

Identify

○ What new and complicated moral issues facing the world do you see the Church currently addressing?

○ How do you see the Holy Spirit at work in the Church as it pertains to these issues?

○ Which issues need more attention from the Church?

The Spirit not only enables the Church to preserve intact what was handed down from the beginning, but also helps the Church to rise to new challenges. The Holy Spirit has guided the Church through the centuries whenever disputes arose about the Trinity, about who Jesus is, or about what the Gospel really means or requires of us. And the Holy Spirit guides the Church today as it addresses the new, and complicated, moral issues facing the world today.

The foundation on which the Church rests is made up of the Apostles chosen by Christ and their successors, namely the Pope and the bishops in union with him. This foundation will last until the end of time, when Christ comes again in glory. The Holy Spirit upholds the Church and urges her to remain faithful to Jesus Christ, to read "the signs of the times," and to respond to the issues facing the world.

Recall The Pope and bishops are successors of what group of people?

Explain How does apostolic Tradition work?

SECTION 2 REVIEW

QUICK REVIEW

1a. Summarize What is the role of the lay faithful in the Church?

b. Explain How do we live *from*, *in*, and *for* Christ?

2a. Explain How does apostolic succession work?

b. Elaborate What is the significance of the laying on of hands in the Sacrament of Holy Orders?

3a. Explain Who was Dom Hélder Câmara?

b. Summarize How does the Church address modern issues facing the world?

Listen and Discuss Talk about these questions in a small group.

○ What effect did Dom Hélder Câmara have on the faithful who followed him?

○ Would he have been more effective if he had tried to get along with the government?

Pray Compose a short prayer regarding the Holy Spirit's guidance or presence in the Church.

SELF-ASSESS

Which statement best reflects where you are now?

☐ I'm confident enough about the material in this section to be able to explain it to someone else.

☐ I have a good grasp of the material in this section, but I could use more review.

☐ I'm lost. I need help catching up before moving on.

The Communion of Saints

When we think about who Jesus Christ is, we have to include the **Communion of Saints**. What comes to mind when you hear the phrase "Communion of Saints"? For one thing, the Communion of Saints, in fact the whole history of the People of God right up to today, helps answer how we know that God exists. You may think of all the saints in Heaven enjoying the eternal presence of God. Or you might think of the saints you or some of your ancestors prayed with for help. There are actually two meanings to the phrase.

"Communion of Saints" refers to the community of redeemed people, among the living *and* the dead, who are united with Christ. In other words, the term refers to all Christians on their earthly pilgrimage, the souls being purified in Purgatory, and the saints in Heaven (see CCC, 962).

We pray for the living and the dead because they share in the Communion of Saints. We pray for them, and they pray for us. The unity or communion that exists among people in Christ also means that we can benefit each other through what we call **merit**. Whatever anyone does or suffers for Christ is good for the whole community. Catholics also pray and ask Mary and the saints to intercede with God on behalf of themselves and others.

The Communion of Saints also refers to the holy things which believers hold in common. These are the things that help identify Church members as followers of Christ. For example, the Sacraments are holy things that unite the Church and form her into one community. This is especially true of the Sacrament of the Eucharist, which is the best sign of our oneness in Christ.

We affirm our belief in the Communion of Saints when we recite the Apostles' Creed. We believe in the bond that exists among the living and the dead who share Christ's life. God is a community of three Persons in relationship. Scripture constantly demonstrates the value and importance given to the experience of community. Catholics recognize this and understand that the Communion of Saints is a community that extends through time and space, across the globe, and through the ages. Christ is our connection.

Saints, in the Catholic understanding, are ordinary people who lived with extraordinary love for God and others. Some saints made extraordinary changes in their lives. Some made extraordinary commitments to prayer and some made extraordinary efforts to serve others.

As Catholics, we have always held up saints as strong examples of the spiritual life. And we also consider them friends we can ask to pray with us when we make our petitions to God. Saints have no power; only God does. But, we are not alone when we strive to live a holy life. When we pray for others and for the souls of those who have died, we do so in union with the saints.

Communion of Saints those united with Christ, both living and dead, on the Earth, in Purgatory, and in Heaven; also refers to the holy things, such as Sacraments (especially the Eucharist), that unite the Church and the community of holy people

merit the reward which God promises and gives to those who love him, and who by his grace perform good works (see CCC, 2008)

Research
Prepare a brief report on three saints, summarizing their lives, what was interesting or unique about them, and how they lived a life of virtue. Be sure to share your thoughts on how they modeled holiness. Include the saint you may have been named after, a lesser-known saint, someone recently canonized, or saints associated with specific professions. Is there a saint for teachers? Parents? Students? Politicians? Soldiers? Musicians?

Litany OF THE Saints

The Litany of the Saints is a sacred prayer of the Catholic Church. There are traditional and contemporary versions, but the litany starts by asking for mercy from God the Father, the Son, and the Holy Spirit. In the traditional prayer, the prayer then asks Jesus as our mediator with the Father to hear us. That is followed by requests from each member of the Trinity for mercy. Participants then ask for the intercession of the friends of God, the saints who have lived holy lives and who now rest in eternity with God.

> First among these friends is Mary, the Mother of God; followed by the angels; the patriarchs and prophets, including John the Baptist;

> the martyrs, beginning with Stephen the protomartyr; bishops; Doctors of the Church; priests and religious as well as laity.

> Jesus' foster father Saint Joseph; the Apostles, including Peter and Paul;

> The traditional litany is used most prominently at the Easter Vigil Mass and the Sacrament of Holy Orders.

Elizabeth Barakah Hodges/Getty Images

Black Madonna V Icon by Elizabeth Barakah Hodges, mixed media and collage

A cantor will chant or sing the saints' names, followed by a chant of "pray for us" from the congregation. The traditional litany ends with a plea to the Son of God to hear the prayers and two prayers for mercy and protection.

Here is an excerpt from *The Catholic Source Book.*

... **Holy Mary,**
Pray for us. **(after each invocation)**
Holy Virgin of Virgins
Saint Michael
Saint Gabriel
Saint Raphael
All holy angels and archangels
All holy orders of blessed spirits
Saint John the Baptist
Saint Joseph

All holy patriarchs and prophets
Saint Peter
Saint Paul
Saint Andrew ...

>> What does the Litany of the Saints express? Symbolize?

What stands out for you?

If you could make your own personal Litany of the Saints, who would you put in it?

Would you memorize it or write it out and read it? How often would you pray it?

In Catholic Tradition, we call this **intercessory prayer**.

Restate What are the interrelated meanings of the expression "Communion of Saints"?

Recall What are the holy things that unite the Church, and which ones stand above the rest?

One in Christ

The Church possesses the great gift of **unity**. In fact, being *one* is one of the four marks or identifying characteristics of the Church. The other three marks are that the Church is holy, catholic, and apostolic. The Catholic Church preserves these gifts, given to Peter and the Apostles.

"The Church . . . is . . . holy. This is because Christ, the Son of God, who with the Father and the Spirit is hailed as 'alone holy', loved the Church as his Bride, giving himself up for her so as to sanctify her. . . . The Church then, is 'the holy People of God . . .'" (CCC, 823).

The Church is made holy because of her union with Christ; in turn, she makes others holy. She disseminates through her ministries the graces won by Jesus on the cross that make us holy. The Church, then, is holy in her members.

The Church is catholic in two ways. "First, the Church is catholic because Christ is present in her. . . . Secondly, the Church is catholic because she has been sent out by Christ on a mission to the whole human race" (CCC, 830).

Jesus dwells in the Catholic Church. Through his Holy Spirit he energized the Church to live and act in his name. The Church is for all people, everywhere. We are called to share the Good News by what we say and how we act. The Church's missionary work continues today, as the Holy Spirit guides her to go "to the ends of the earth" to preach, baptize, and minister in Jesus' name.

And the Catholic community is apostolic because we can trace our roots back to Peter and the Apostles and those who came after them. We are the sole Church led and united by the Pope and bishops, and ministered to by the ordained ministry of bishops, priests

GO TO **THE SOURCE**

To see the unity that Jesus prayed for, read John 17.

- Who is Jesus praying to and whom is he praying for?
- Why do you think Jesus' prayer sounds so urgent?
- How does Jesus expand his prayer in John 17:20?
- What verses seem to summarize the kind of spiritual unity for which he is praying?
- What are some obstacles to this unity? What can we do to help create unity?

intercession or **intercessory prayer** praying to God on behalf of, or for the needs of someone else

unity the members of the Church are united under the Pope and bishops, profess the same faith, and join in common worship

and deacons. The Church will last forever on its foundation, the twelve Apostles of Jesus, and their successors through whom Christ governs.

While there are expressions of holiness and truth that exist outside the Church, these are among the characteristics that make us who we are.

Getting back to us being one in Christ, the Church "acknowledges one Lord, confesses one faith, is born of one Baptism, forms only one Body, is given life by the one Spirit, for the sake of one hope, at whole fulfillment all divisions will be overcome" (CCC, 866).

This unity should not be confused with uniformity. Unity does not mean that we are all the same, nor does it mean that we will always agree on everything.

Identify those family members (or close friends) with whom you have a "deep and lasting bond."

>> **What qualities or characteristics would you use to describe your relationships? How do you know you share a "deep and lasting bond"?**

Have you ever attended a retreat, mission trip, or other experience during which you felt a "deep and lasting bond" to the other members of the group?

What would it take to achieve "unity" with all Christians?

REFLECT

> "Do you not know that your body is a temple of the Holy Spirit within you, which you have from God, and that you are not your own? ... Therefore glorify God in your body."
> —(1 Corinthians 6:19-20)

Whole Body

THE INCARNATION DEEPENS our understanding of human dignity and reminds us of the goodness of the human body. Our bodies are amazing creations. They reflect the image and likeness of God that resides in every man and woman. In our body language and communication, then, God's image and likeness "shines forth in the communion of persons, in the likeness of the unity of the divine persons among themselves" (CCC, 1702). Spend some time meditating on the capabilities of our whole body as resembling the Trinity.

> *Happiness is being rooted in love.*
> —Blessed Pope John Paul II, *Theology of the Body*, 16:2

So often we take the physical functioning of our bodies for granted. That is, until something goes wrong. We tend not to think about breathing until we have a cold. A person with a broken toe may tell us about its importance in the balance required for walking.

Genuine spiritual wholeness can be found in contemplating the gift of God's life pulsing through our bodies and the communion of persons we are able to form.

Take a moment and intentionally focus attention on breathing. Think about the ways in which our bodies automatically take care of us. Science refers to involuntary reflexes: the lungs breathe, the eyes blink, the heart beats, the blood flows, all without thought or choice. What does that tell us about God and how he created us?

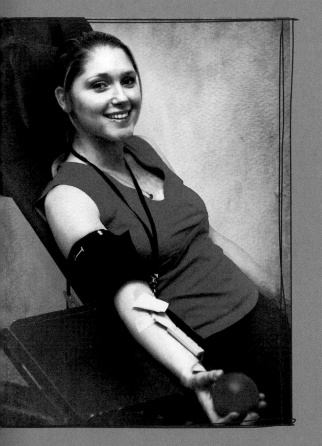

Moreover when our minds work in union with our bodies, our ability to refine our skills is awe-inspiring. Athletes, musicians, and artists are keenly aware of the way in which the body can steadily learn to perform with more and more precision through practice. What once may have seemed improbable becomes possible. What does that tell us about God and the need to practice Christian virtues?

This works the same way with moral virtues—namely the cardinal virtues of prudence, temperance, fortitude, and justice. We acquire these through repeatedly practicing them, but it's not easy. When we fail to consider consequences or abstain from things we know are bad for us, we also know we have the gift of God's grace to renew our efforts to make the right choices. This practice stems from Blessed Pope John Paul II's point that the giving of ourselves—in this case through practicing moral virtues—takes place most completely between married couples, but also happens at some level with the many other significant people in our lives. This is part of the communication the Pope has referred to as the language of the body.

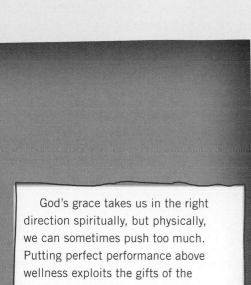

God's grace takes us in the right direction spiritually, but physically, we can sometimes push too much. Putting perfect performance above wellness exploits the gifts of the body. Our bodies need proper rest and nourishment or they become compromised and can break. Injury occurs when we disregard bodily limits. Our creative spirit as well as the communion of persons can be crushed by abuse and overuse of the body.

Our bodies are not performance machines; rather they are creations that reflect the image and likeness of God. Our bodies are animated by our spiritual soul, which makes us particularly human. This human body and soul then are intended by God to become a temple of his Holy Spirit. Our bodies make it possible for us to thank God, serve our neighbor, and eventually be happy with God forever.

>> Describe a physical skill that you have developed to the point where your body is now able to perform it instinctively. What insights do you gain from reflecting on this ability?

What does this tell you about the importance of growing spiritually through cultivating the moral virtues, like prudence and temperance and the importance of regular Mass attendance and prayer?

In what ways can meditating on the physical capabilities of the whole body deepen spirituality and your relationship with God?

Unity in the Church reflects three things: we are all united under one hierarchical leadership (the Pope and bishops), we all profess the same faith, and we all join in a common worship.

This unity goes deeper than sharing a common purpose. While tensions may exist in the Church as they would in a family, Church unity is more involved than simply getting along with one another. It is the sort of unity that belongs to a family, with all its faithfulness and tensions. Spiritually speaking, the Church's unity reflects the divine unity that exists in the three Persons of the Blessed Trinity. When we say that we are "united in Christ," we are referring to this kind of deep and lasting family bond. The Holy Spirit, sent by Christ, gives life to the Church, and one of the ways the Spirit does that is through the unity the Church enjoys in diversity.

As he was preparing for his crucifixion, Jesus prayed that his disciples would also have this spiritual unity with the Trinity.

Unity is a gift from God and part of the nature of the Church. Disunity, conflict, and division, however, have marred the long history of the Church. The very fact that there are a multitude of Christian denominations represents division, not unity in Christ, for Christ, and with Christ.

> *By this everyone will know that you are my disciples, if you have love for one another.*
>
> —John 13:35

Since the Second Vatican Council (1962–1965), the Church has been involved in **ecumenism**, which seeks to unite Christians throughout the world. Ecumenism is the desire to have all Christians focus on their shared faith again. Through prayer, study, and **ecumenical dialogue**, or conversations between the different denominations, the hope is restoration of Christian unity. We are reminded that this is exactly what Jesus prayed for.

Not only have Christian communities been divided from one another historically, but there are also painful conflicts and divisions within existing communities today.

ecumenism the desire to restore the unity of Christians throughout the world, which is a gift from Christ to the Church

ecumenical dialogue conversations between different Christian denominations, working toward Christian unity

MY FAITH

With whom are you personally connected in the Communion of Saints?

Who are the holy friends who have given you guidance . . . or prayed for you . . . or have accompanied you in the past?

And who are the holy friends who occasionally guide, pray, or accompany you now?

Remember that you may choose to include this when you share what's been particularly helpful to your spiritual growth at the end of this course.

The Communion of Saints is one of the doctrines that make Catholicism unique. Holy friends help guide us, pray for us, and accompany us on our journey of faith. These holy friends include those living here on the Earth and the saints in Heaven.

Use this time now to:

○ *recognize* your past and present holy friends who have provided spiritual support for you.

○ *actually make a list.* They can be ancestors, peers, family, saints, or even people with whom you have only had limited but significant interactions.

○ *remember their spiritual wisdom.* You can even try to write down what each person provided you.

○ *give thanks* to these holy friends who have supported you spiritually.

○ *stay in touch* with them.

Use this space to write down your list and the spiritual wisdom that these people have shared with you.

➜ Go to the student site at
hs.osvcurriculum.com

Discipleship . . . within the Body of Christ . . . for the glory of God and the good of the world

Divisions in the Church compromise our witness and weaken our common life, just as conflicts within families can destroy the harmony of family life.

> *I ask not only on behalf of these, but also on behalf of those who will believe in me through [my disciples'] word, that they may all be one. As you, Father, are in me and I am in you, may they also be in us, so that the world may believe that you have sent me.*
>
> —John 17:20-21

Analyze
Write an essay about what you see as obstacles to unity and keys to maintaining the unity for which Christ prayed.

As humans, we come into the world made in the image of God and wounded by Original Sin. Don't let divisions in the Church discourage you. You can still model and promote the unity for which Christ prayed.

Name What are the three things that the Church's unity reflects?

Recall In his prayer for unity, who was Jesus praying for?

GLOBAL PERSPECTIVES

The great cathedrals founded after the Roman Emperor Constantine became Christian were given names of those who died for the Church. That custom continued with the Communion of Saints. Saints are acknowledged as intercessors for those still living on Earth. You may know that the patron saint of North America is Our Lady of Guadalupe, but what about other countries and regions around the world?

Here are a few examples: Belgium—Saint Joseph; Canada—Saints Anne and George; Germany—Saint Michael; South America—Saint Rose of Lima; United States—Our Lady of the Immaculate Conception; Norway—Saint Olaf; Congo—Our Lady of the Immaculate Conception; Ireland—Saint Patrick; Borneo—Saint Francis Xavier.

○ Look up a saint and country of your choice and summarize the connection between that saint and nation. See if you can include a photo of a cathedral named after that saint.

Go to the student site at **hs.osvcurriculum.com**

SECTION 3 REVIEW

QUICK REVIEW

1a. Compare What are the two meanings of the term "Communion of Saints"?

b. Analyze What is our place in the Communion of Saints?

c. Define What is the role of the saints in the Church?

2a. Infer Why would Jesus pray for unity?

b. Infer How do you think disunity can hurt the Church?

c. Evaluate What can we learn by reconciling differences?

Listen and Discuss This section addresses how groups must work together to succeed.

○ When has a group you belonged to needed to be unified?

○ How did the group achieve unity?

○ What was the result of that unity?

Pray Compose a personalized litany of the saints, incorporating some traditional saints as well as some ancestors and even contemporary figures who have been saints to you.

SELF-ASSESS

Which statement best reflects where you are now?

☐ I'm confident enough about the material in this section to be able to explain it to someone else.

☐ I have a good grasp of the material in this section, but I could use more review.

☐ I'm lost. I need help catching up before moving on.

The Unique Role of Mary

Immaculate Conception
from the moment of her own conception and by grace from God and the virtue of the merits of Jesus Christ, Mary was preserved from Original Sin

Mary, the Mother of Jesus, holds a special place within the Communion of Saints. Her role in bringing Jesus into the world was unique from the moment of her own conception in her mother's womb. After centuries of Tradition, Pope Pius IX made the following proclamation in 1854: "The most Blessed Virgin Mary was, from the first moment of her conception, by a singular grace and privilege of almighty God and by virtue of the merits of Jesus Christ, . . . preserved immune from all stain of original sin"[135] (CCC, 491).

Heaven, stars, earth, waters, day, night, and all that serves humankind has been raised up and newly graced in you, our Lady.

—Saint Anselm, Discourse 52

We call this the **Immaculate Conception**. The angel Gabriel then appeared to Mary as told in the Infancy Narratives. Gabriel hailed Mary as one who is especially favored by God (see Luke 1:28). She remained sinless and a virgin throughout her life. Mary is the true Mother of God (Theotokos).

Mary was an adolescent when the angel Gabriel announced to her that she would bear a son. Although she questioned how it would be possible that she could conceive a child because she was a virgin, she also said she was willing to do whatever God asked. Her wholehearted "yes" to God is a perfect model for everyone today, young and old.

Although Jesus was the Son of God, he was Mary's child. She and her husband Joseph raised Jesus in the Jewish religion (see Luke 2:22-24). They cared for him as he grew up just as any Jewish parents did with their children (see Luke 2:41-52). Jesus was Mary's only child, and she remained a virgin throughout her life (see CCC, 499). The Bible mentions the brothers and sisters of Jesus, but the Catholic Church has always understood these passages to refer to cousins and other close relatives and not to other children of Mary.

Mary's role did not end with caring for Jesus at home. It was a Jewish custom in those days for the mother to be the child's principal religion teacher. It was likely Mary, then, who assumed responsibility to see that Jesus was brought up with a thorough knowledge of the Jewish faith.

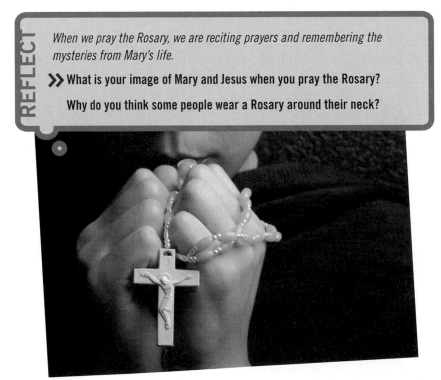

REFLECT

When we pray the Rosary, we are reciting prayers and remembering the mysteries from Mary's life.

>> **What is your image of Mary and Jesus when you pray the Rosary?**

Why do you think some people wear a Rosary around their neck?

Our Lady of Guadalupe

The story of Our Lady of Guadalupe began on December 9, 1531. Juan Diego, a poor Aztec Indian who had recently become Catholic, was walking to Mass in honor of Our Lady. As he walked by the Tepeyac hill country in central Mexico, he heard the melodious sounds of birds singing. A beautiful woman dressed like an Aztec princess appeared in a cloud. She told him in his own language that she was the "Mother of the true God from whom all life has come" and asked him to go to the bishop of Mexico to tell him to build a chapel on that hill so that she could be present to the suffering Aztec people.

Juan relayed the message to the bishop who was unsure about the story Juan was telling. The bishop had been praying for Mary's intercession because at that time the Spaniards had conquered the Aztecs and were treating them badly. He told Juan to return to the lady to get a sign.

Our Lady met Juan as he returned to the hill and told him to look for flowers that were growing there. Despite the fact that it was a cold winter day, Juan found abundant Castilian roses growing there. He wrapped them in his *tilma* (cactus fiber cloak) and took them to the bishop. When he unfolded his cloak, the roses fell out and an image of Our Lady dressed as an Aztec princess appeared on the inside of the cloak.

The bishop had the church built as Our Lady had requested. In the seven years following her appearance to Juan Diego, millions of Aztecs were baptized and many miracles were reported. The image of Our Lady of Guadalupe can be seen today in the Basilica of Our Lady of Guadalupe in Mexico City.

Go to the student site at
hs.osvcurriculum.com

Blessed Pope John Paul II canonized Juan Diego on July 31, 2002, and said, "he facilitated the fruitful meeting of two worlds and became the catalyst for the new Mexican identity, closely united to Our Lady of Guadalupe, whose mestizo [mixed European and American Indian ancestry] face expresses her spiritual motherhood which embraces all Mexicans."

Our Lady of Guadalupe's feast is held on December 12 in the United States, and she is known as the patroness of the Americas.

A man prays before an image of Our Lady of Guadalupe.

>> What expressions of faith are found in the tradition of the Lady of Guadalupe?

What are some reasons you think it is so important to so many Catholics?

Assumption the teaching affirming that at the end of her life, Mary was taken up, body and soul, into Heaven

Mary is fittingly considered a disciple. She is revered as the first of the disciples, because she was the first to receive Jesus in this world and to cooperate with God's plan of Redemption in sending Christ to be our Savior. By giving birth to Jesus, the second Person of the Holy Trinity, Mary became the Mother of God and the Mother of the Church.

She was with Jesus as he performed his first miracle (see John 2:1-11). She was also present at his crucifixion, standing near the cross (see John 19:25). After his Resurrection, Mary was among the disciples "constantly devoting themselves to prayer" (Acts 1:14). On the day of Pentecost, Mary is included in the description: "they were all together in one place" (Acts 2:1) as the Holy Spirit came to rest on them.

According to the accounts of the early Church, at the end of her life Mary was taken up, body and soul, into Heaven where she shares in the glory of Jesus' Resurrection. The **Assumption** of Mary into Heaven is "a singular participation in her Son's Resurrection and an anticipation of the resurrection of other Christians" (CCC, 966). The Catholic Church continues to uphold these two Marian doctrines of the Immaculate Conception and the Assumption.

Mary intercedes for us in Heaven. Catholics ask her to pray for us and to intercede with God on our behalf. Mary and the saints present our prayers to God. Only God can answer prayer, but Mary enjoys a special closeness to her Son and can present our needs to him.

Name To whom does the expression "Immaculate Conception" apply?

Elaborate What was Mary's role in Jesus' life?

Mary's Life as a Disciple

Contemplate the seven characteristics of Mary displayed in the accompanying chart.

○ For each characteristic, list three examples of the ways in which you can express that quality.

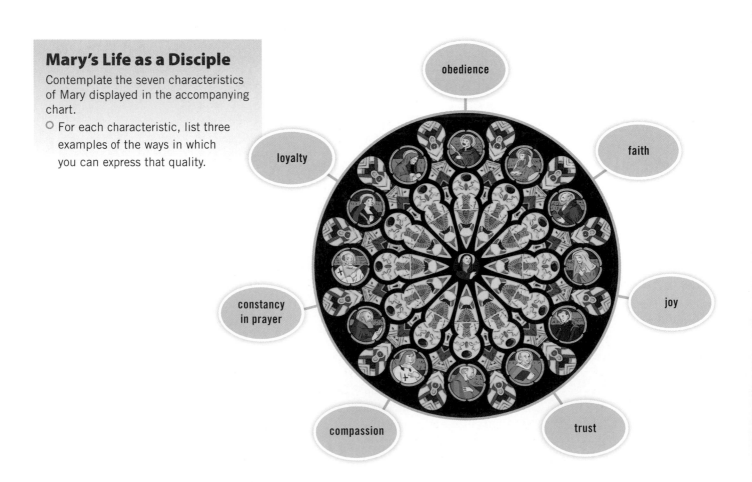

obedience

faith

loyalty

joy

constancy in prayer

trust

compassion

GO TO THE SOURCE

Jesus sees his Mother and one of his Apostles as he hangs on the cross.

Read John 19:26-27.

○ What pictures does the account paint of Mary's role in the early Church?

The Life of Mary

As the *Catechism* points out: "What the Catholic faith believes about Mary is based on what it believes about Christ, and what it teaches about Mary illumines in turn its faith in Christ" (CCC, 487).

There are many examples of how our beliefs about Jesus and Mary mutually support and reinforce one another. That Mary was sinless, for example, is reinforced by our conviction that Jesus was never tainted by Original Sin. We call Mary the Mother of God because Jesus is the Son of God. Because of the bodily Resurrection of Jesus and his Ascension into Heaven, we can know about Mary's Assumption. These are just three examples of many.

What we know about Mary also enriches our understanding of what it means to be a disciple. Mary speaks little in the New Testament, but everything she says is worth reflecting on. Her "yes" to God at the Annunciation is a model of faithfulness. Her song of joy, the Magnificat (see Luke 1:46-55), is a testimony to her knowledge of God's faithfulness to humanity.

> *My soul magnifies the Lord, and my spirit rejoices in God my Savior, for he has looked with favor on the lowliness of his servant.*
>
> —Luke 1:46-48

Mary shows her complete trust in Jesus at the wedding feast at Cana when she says to the servants: "Do whatever he tells you" (John 2:5). She shows us loyalty by standing with Jesus through his beating and crucifixion. She models the willingness to pray constantly after the Resurrection and Ascension.

All of her qualities—obedience, faith, joy, trust, loyalty, compassion, and constancy in prayer—are characteristics that disciples of Jesus can emulate.

In this chapter, we have seen that the Church Jesus founded is a mystery of love. We have also seen that Mary is important in working out the plan Jesus had for the Church. In the next chapter, we will see that Jesus stands at the end of life as the Lord of History, and how he judges all people with justice and mercy.

Describe Give an example of how the Church's beliefs about Jesus and Mary mutually support and reinforce one another.

Reflect Which of Mary's qualities do you most identify with and why?

SECTION 4 REVIEW

QUICK REVIEW

1a. Define What does the term *Immaculate Conception* refer to?

b. Explain How does the Catholic Church understand the Bible's mentioning Jesus' brothers and sisters if he was an only child?

c. Analyze How did Mary show her support of Jesus' ministry?

2a. Specify What is the correct Catholic approach to praying to Mary?

b. Demonstrate How do beliefs about Jesus reinforce our beliefs about Mary?

c. Name What are the characteristics Mary teaches us about discipleship?

ACT

Find a way to honor Mary in a traditional way.

○ Find out if there are any special devotions to Mary that you can participate in.

○ Pray the Rosary privately.

SELF-ASSESS

Which statement best reflects where you are now?

☐ I'm confident enough about the material in this section to be able to explain it to someone else.

☐ I have a good grasp of the material in this section, but I could use more review.

☐ I'm lost. I need help catching up before moving on.

PRAYER

Prayer to Mary, Help of Christians

Most Holy and Immaculate Virgin, Help of Christians,
we place ourselves under your motherly protection.
Throughout the Church's history you have helped Christians
in times of trial, temptation, and danger. Time and time
again, you have proven to be the Refuge of sinners, the
Hope of the hopeless, the Consoler of the afflicted, and the
Comforter of the dying. We promise to be faithful disciples
of Jesus Christ, your Son, to proclaim His Good News of
God's love for all people, and to work for peace and justice
in our world. With faith in your intercession, we pray for the
Church, for our family and friends, for the poor and
abandoned, and all the dying. Grant, O Mary, Help of
Christians, the graces of which we stand in need. *(Mention
your intentions.)* May we serve Jesus with fidelity and love
until death. Help us, and our loved ones, to attain the
boundless joy of being forever with our Father in Heaven.
Amen.
Mary, Help of Christians, pray for us!

TERMS

Use each of the following terms in a sentence that shows you know what the term means. You may include more than one term in a sentence.

Great Commission	Communion of Saints
evangelize	merit
witnesses	intercession or intercessory prayer
missionary mandate	
mystical Body of Christ	unity
hierarchy	ecumenism
sanctify	ecumenical dialogue
laity	Immaculate Conception
Sacrament of Holy Orders	Assumption

PEOPLE

Use information from the chapter to tell why each of the names below is significant.

1. Holy Spirit
2. Dom Hélder Câmara
3. Saints
4. Archangel Gabriel
5. The first disciple

UNDERSTANDING

Answer each question and complete each exercise.

SECTION 1

1. **Summarize** How did Jesus' followers take up the challenge of the two men who spoke to them after the Ascension?

2. **Extend** How does the entire Church share in the missionary mandate?

3. **Analyze** How is the Church both a visual and a spiritual reality?

4. **Explain** Why is the Church called the mystical Body of Christ?

SECTION 2

5. **Describe** What roles do the Church hierarchy and the lay faithful have within the Church?

6. **Connect** Why does Jesus have a special link to the poor?

7. **Explain** Describe the importance of the laying on of hands.

8. **Analyze** What continuing role does the Holy Spirit have in the Church?

SECTION 3

9. **Define** What is the Communion of Saints?

10. **List** How do saints help us?

11. **Infer** What is ecumenism? What is its goal and how is it promoted?

12. **Speculate** How might disunity and reconciliation strengthen relationships?

SECTION 4

13. **Analyze** Why was Mary taken body and soul into Heaven?

14. **Explain** How is Mary a model for us?

15. **Interpret** What does the Magnificat say about Mary's relationship with the People of God?

CONNECTING

Visual This image is a detail of a statue of Jesus and Mary.

What point in their lives does this depict? What does the image say about their relationship? What does the image teach you about them? Explain your answer.

Challenge A non-Catholic friend sees a statue of the Blessed Mother in your home.

> **Friend:** So why do Catholics pray to statues?
>
> **You:** That's not what we do. We ask the saints to pray to God for us.
>
> **Friend:** So you pray to saints? Doesn't God get mad about that?

○ What do you say next?

○ Continue the conversation with two questions your friend might ask and how you would answer. If you find it too difficult to relate to "You," the Catholic Believer, then switch roles and imagine you are the friend. Identify what the Catholic Believer would say. One way or the other, be sure to use information from the chapter in the dialogue.

Question What would you say to someone who wants to know about the roots and traditions of the Catholic Church?

Imagine Discuss the following scenarios.

○ You have fifteen minutes to talk with Saint Joseph, the foster father of Jesus. What would you ask Saint Joseph? And what would his responses be?

○ Saints Peter and Paul show up at the freshman retreat to talk about the apostolic Church. What would they say in describing it?

SELF-ASSESS

With a Partner List what you found most helpful or interesting in this chapter, as well as any other questions that have surfaced.

What does this photo
say about God?
What does eternal life
mean to you?

CHAPTER **8**

Jesus with Us Always

DO

○ Explore the significance of the "I am" statements in the Gospel according to John.

○ Identify where prayer comes from and to whom it is directed.

○ Analyze the Lord's Prayer.

○ Describe several different kinds of prayer.

○ Identify Catholic teaching about divine judgment and the fate of souls.

○ Discuss how our choices have consequences for our eternal life.

○ Evaluate the Church's vision of Jesus Christ as Lord of the living and the dead.

DEFINE

prayer	active religious
"I am" statements	Pharisees
solitude	Sadducees
hypocrite	eschatology
perseverance	Heaven
the Lord's Prayer	Purgatory
domestic church	Hell
contemplative	beatific vision
religious	the elect
cloistered	final judgment

The religion department at a Catholic high school asked students:

"If you could meet Jesus face to face, what would you ask him?"

Student responses included:

What will Heaven be like? Will I see my relatives there?

Did you ever doubt God's plan?

Why is there suffering in the world?

Mural depicting Jesus Giving Blessing, created c. 1951–1975; photographed c. Sept. 1994–Feb. 1996. (Highland Park in Los Angeles, CA)

When is the world going to end?

Why was I put on the Earth; what's my purpose?

Is the DaVinci Code real?

What is going to happen when the judgment comes?

How am I doing on my way to Heaven?

Could you please tell the Israelis and Palestinians to stop fighting?

How can I repay you?

Why are there bad people on the Earth?

If you had the same chance, would you die for us again?

WHAT WOULD YOU ASK?

Where Are You?

Choose the response that best reflects where you are right now.

I know the different ways Jesus describes himself.	☐ Quite a bit	☐ Somewhat	☐ A little	☐ Not at all
I am aware of the different ways Jesus taught us to pray.	☐ Quite a bit	☐ Somewhat	☐ A little	☐ Not at all
I'm satisfied with my prayer life.	☐ Quite a bit	☐ Somewhat	☐ A little	☐ Not at all
I understand the Catholic view of life after death, Heaven, Hell, judgment, and so on.	☐ Quite a bit	☐ Somewhat	☐ A little	☐ Not at all
I realize that God will judge me.	☐ Quite a bit	☐ Somewhat	☐ A little	☐ Not at all

I Will Be There

What if we don't get what we pray for?

If God is all-knowing, what difference do our prayers make?

Does God hear our prayers?

Does it matter to God that we pray persistently?

What happens after death—particularly to people who do really bad things?

What about the mercy of God?

What exactly is prayer? In the most simplistic sense, it is communicating with God. Yet it is much more than that. **Prayer** is the raising of one's mind and heart to God, in which we enter into a conscious, loving communion. It is our belief in the mystery of our faith, celebrating that mystery, and living it out "in a vital and personal relationship with the living and true God" (*Catechism of the Catholic Church*, 2558).

Sometimes we might wonder how prayer works, but we can understand it better when we look more closely at who God is.

Moses & the burning bush, by Hans Feibusch

GO TO THE SOURCE

Moses was hesitant when God first called him to undertake the mission of freeing the Israelite slaves.

Read Exodus 3:1-15.

○ What is Moses' first question?

○ Why do you think he was alarmed?

○ What is reassuring about God's reply?

○ Imagine you were a bystander, personally witnessing this scene. What surprises you most about what you see? Why?

Recall the Old Testament story of Moses. When he encountered God in the burning bush, he asked God his name. The answer God gave was puzzling, yet revealing: "I AM WHO I AM," sometimes translated as "the One who is." God said to Moses: "Thus you shall say to the Israelites, I AM has sent me to you" (Exodus 3:14).

This was a crucial moment in salvation history. God had never before revealed the divine name. He drew closer to the people than ever before. In biblical times, giving someone your name was like giving someone permission to become your friend, establish a relationship with you or ask you for help. I AM brought hope to a community

prayer the raising of one's mind and heart to God, in which we enter into a conscious, loving communion

in a desperate situation (slavery in Egypt). This required trust. God was not pinning himself down to any one particular course of action. But he was letting his People know how to address him in prayer and that he could be trusted to be there for them. By giving Moses his name, God was telling people that he was willing to be in a relationship with them.

This name, I AM, reveals God's being in its fullness. His name indicates his nature as the One who is the Word. His name reveals that he is a self-existent being, who is the source of everything that is. The Word reflects God's presence and faithfulness.

In the New Testament the phrase "I am" is used many times in connection with Jesus. It is an unusual and noteworthy feature of the Gospel according to John. When the Gospel was written, the author recorded Jesus himself saying "I am" forty-five times. Twenty-four of these are "emphatic," which means insistent or strongly expressive. Scholars consider these emphatic because they also specifically use the pronoun "I"—something that is not necessary in the Greek language. The author of John intended to convey something special about Jesus through the frequent use of these **"I am" statements**.

When people other than Jesus use the phrase "I am" in the Gospel according to John, often they are saying "I am *not*" one thing or another.

- John the Baptist says, "I am not the Messiah" (John 1:20).

- When questioned about whether he is a follower of Jesus, Peter replies, "I am not" (John 18:17 and 18:18-25).

- In answer to a question from Jesus, Pontius Pilate asks, "I am not a Jew, am I?" (John 18:35).

But when Jesus says "I am," he is sharing something about who he is. Because of the

Old Testament background, in which "I am" is the name of God, these statements are affirmations of the divinity of Christ.

Sometimes an "I am" statement stands alone, as it does in John 8:58, when Jesus says, "Before Abraham was, I am." Notice the Gospel does not say "I was," but "I am." This statement enraged the crowd. They instantly perceived that Jesus was identifying himself with God—which, if untrue, would have been a terrible blasphemy. Another example can be found in John 4:26, when Jesus speaks to the Samaritan woman at the well. She voices her hope for the coming of the Messiah. When Jesus replies to her: "I am he, the one who is speaking to you," he identifies himself as the Messiah.

In a number of instances the "I am" statement is followed by a metaphor. These are some of the most well-known and best-loved statements about Jesus in the Gospels. They help us understand who Jesus is himself, and they call attention especially to who he is for us. "I am the bread of life" and "I am the living bread that came down from heaven" (John 6:48, 6:51) are two such examples.

GO TO **THE SOURCE**

In the Gospel according to John, Jesus uses "I am" to explain his mission and purpose in several different ways. Inside these simple "I am" statements, you will find a lot of truth about who Jesus is.

Look up the following verses. After each one, explain "the truth" Jesus is revealing about himself.

- John 6:35
- John 8:12
- John 10:7
- John 10:11
- John 11:25
- John 14:6
- John 15:1

"I am" statements direct statements by Jesus in the Gospel according to John concerning who he is

Even though God is greater than anyone or anything we can imagine, he has chosen to reveal himself in Christ. So, unlike Moses and the Israelites, we know to whom we are praying: the One who will always be there and who provides us with what we need. He is the shepherd, the light, the bread, the vine, and the way.

Recall How many times does the Gospel according to John record Jesus saying "I am" statements, and of these, how many are emphatic, meaning they specifically use the pronoun "I"?

Elaborate Name two people other than Jesus who used "I am" statements and explain how their statements were different from those of Jesus.

SECTION 1 REVIEW

QUICK REVIEW

1a. Analyze How did knowing God's name bring his People closer to God?

b. Recall What does the name I AM reveal about God?

2a. Compare When people other than Jesus say "I am" in the Gospel according to John, how does this compare to Jesus' use of the phrase?

b. Explain Why would Jesus' listeners be angry with him for saying, "Before Abraham was, I am"?

3a. Reflect Which metaphor for Jesus do you find most significant? Why?

b. Relate How do metaphors for Jesus help us relate to God?

ACT

Create a new metaphor for Jesus that reflects your personal experience.

○ Finish an "I am" statement of Jesus that is true to your relationship with him.

○ Create your own illustration of the metaphor or use art from a library resource or magazines.

○ Explain the truth about Jesus that your new "I am" statement holds for you.

Pray Compose a short litany using two or three metaphors for Jesus. For example: "Good Shepherd, guide me." "Light of the World, _____." "Bread of Life, _____."

SELF-ASSESS

Which statement best reflects where you are now?

☐ I'm confident enough about the material in this section to be able to explain it to someone else.

☐ I have a good grasp of the material in this section, but I could use more review.

☐ I'm lost. I need help catching up before moving on.

Jesus: Example and Teacher of Prayer

solitude the condition of being alone; in the spiritual life, separation from human company or being busy in order to be wholly present to and attentive to the mystery of God

hypocrite person who says one thing, but does another; person guilty of spiritual pride, particularly a person who does the right thing for the wrong reasons

perseverance steadfastness, holding to a course of action without giving way

The Gospels show us that Jesus prayed frequently. Often he prayed alone. He sought **solitude** in order to pray, and he recommended that his disciples do the same (see Matthew 6:6). Being alone with God the Father at certain times was essential to his prayer.

Jesus gave his disciples several teachings and parables about prayer. He cautioned them to pray sincerely and humbly (see Luke 18:9-14), and not with an attitude of superiority or arrogance. "And whenever you pray, do not be like the hypocrites; for they love to stand and pray in the synagogues and at the street corners, so that they may be seen by others. Truly I tell you, they have received their reward" (Matthew 6:5).

GO TO THE SOURCE

We see Jesus in intense prayer before and after some of the most important events of his life. Read each of the following and write down the circumstances he was dealing with in each.

- Matthew 14:23
- Mark 1:12-13
- Mark 1:29-38
- Luke 3:21
- Luke 9:16
- Luke 9:28-31
- Luke 22:39-46
- John 11:41-42
- John 17:1-26

In solitude we can listen to the voice of him who spoke to us before we could speak a word . . . and who loved us long before we could give love to anyone. It is in this solitude that we discover that being is more important than having, and that we are worth more than the result of our efforts.

—Henri J.M. Nouwen, *Out of Solitude*

Jesus was critical of **hypocrites**. We usually understand this term to refer to people who say one thing, but do another. In this context, Jesus was also condemning those who have spiritual pride, particularly those who do the right thing for the wrong reasons.

Jesus also taught his disciples to be persistent in prayer (see Luke 18:1-8). Their **perseverance**, or steadfastness in doing something despite difficulty or delay in achieving success, would be rewarded (see Luke 11:5-13). Jesus emphasized the importance of expecting good things from God. Prayer flourishes within an attitude of trust, and an expectation of blessings. He counseled his followers to trust God and humbly ask for what they need, just as a child would ask a parent for

Compare and Contrast
Jesus normally prayed a blessing before eating.

- Discuss the positive impact of saying grace before meals today: (a) at home, (b) when you are out at a restaurant.
- Recall a time when blessing before a meal was difficult. What made it so?

THINKING THEOLOGICALLY

Can you imagine Jesus calling a group of people "snakes"? Jesus used his harshest words when he condemned a group of religious leaders for their hypocrisy:

> Woe to you, scribes and Pharisees, hypocrites! For you are like whitewashed tombs, which on the outside look beautiful, but inside they are full of the bones of the dead and of all kinds of filth.
>
> —Matthew 23:27

The dictionary states that a hypocrite is a "person who puts on a false appearance of virtue or religion" or a "person who acts in contradiction to his or her stated beliefs or feelings." In the Gospel according to Matthew, Jesus is saying that hypocrites will not survive the judgment of God. It was this harsh criticism of the religious and political leaders that most likely led to Jesus' arrest and crucifixion.

>> Why do you think Jesus so harshly criticized hypocrites?

What does this criticism reveal about the nature of God?

---

food (see Luke 11:9-13). Prayer and the Christian life, then, are inseparable. It is always possible to pray. "So I say to you, Ask, and it will be given you; search, and you will find, knock, and the door will be opened for you" (Luke 11:9).

God always hears our prayers. Sometimes, however, the answers may not be what we want or expect. Sometimes we don't hear God through the loudness of our lives, or we don't listen the right way. When prayer is undertaken with sincerity and perseverance, however, it changes us for the better. Praying to God the Father, in the way Jesus taught us, helps us become more humble and trusting. We pray primarily to the Father, and we can call him Father because Jesus told us to do so. With heartfelt prayer, we not only surrender control over to God, but we are also reminded to be more like God—generous, kind, loving, and forgiving. Whoever prays daily discovers that the Kingdom of God is not only planted in the world around them,

GO TO THE SOURCE

Read the Parable of the Pharisee and the Tax Collector in Luke 18:9-14.

- What did the Pharisee do that was so wrong?
- Why do you think the tax collector behaved the way he did?
- Who was more sincere and humble in their prayer?
- Which character in this parable can you relate to, and why?

but it also develops inside. "The kingdom of God is among you," Jesus said (Luke 17:21).

Describe What did Jesus mean when he said that people who pray like hypocrites have already received their reward?

Connect Jesus taught his disciples to be persistent in prayer. What can people do to be persistent in prayer?

Teach Us to Pray

The disciples of Jesus asked him to teach them to pray. They were looking for a way of prayer, such as the disciples of John the Baptist had been given. They acknowledged his authority and special knowledge just by asking him how to communicate with God. The answer Jesus gave them has been passed on in the Church as the quintessential prayer of Christians, the **Lord's Prayer**. In the Scriptures, there are two versions of this prayer, one in Matthew (see Matthew 6:9-13) and one in Luke (see Luke 11:1-4).

The version in Matthew sounds more like the one we use at Mass, but the passage in Luke will sound familiar as well: "Father, hallowed be your name, Your kingdom come. Give us each day our daily bread. And forgive us our sins, for we ourselves forgive everyone indebted to us. And do not bring us to the time of trial" (Luke 11:4-5).

Notice that the Lord's Prayer is directed to "Our Father," and not "*My* Father." Jesus called God his Father, and here he invites us into a relationship of communion with the Father. God is our Father just as he is the Father of Jesus. The Lord's Prayer reminds us that God is the Father of all.

In the traditional wording of the Lord's Prayer, there are seven different prayers. The first three are petitions of praise, which speak to the glory of God the Father, the sanctification of his name, the coming of the Kingdom, and the fulfillment of his will. They express our love for God. Prayer in the way Jesus taught his disciples does not begin with our needs, but with praise for God. As it says in the *Catechism*, "In none of the three petitions do we mention ourselves; the burning desire, even anguish, of the beloved Son for his Father's glory seizes us" (CCC, 2804).

the **Lord's Prayer** the quintessential prayer of Christians given by Jesus to his followers (also called the "Our Father")

Faith & Culture

Imagine a hit song with lyrics composed completely from the words that Jesus taught us in the Lord's Prayer. That was the case in 1974, when Australian Sister Janet Mead's song titled "The Lord's Prayer" rose on Billboard's Hot 100 list and peaked at number four in the United States. The record went gold, selling more than one million copies. Sister Mead was also nominated for a Grammy in the Best Inspirational Performance (non-classical) category. On her album "With You I Am," Sister Mead said Christ was initiating the Kingdom of Heaven with his prayer. "What I think he meant was that he wanted us to share in his vision of drawing people together in happiness, joy and peace," she said.

○ What songs personally do this for you? Create your own playlist of these inspirational songs.

Music has all the qualities to help in this—it breaks down barriers, unites, makes us forget ourselves, makes us aware of others and is totally involving.

—Sister Mead

↗ Go to the student site at **hs.osvcurriculum.com**

Everyday life challenges you to think about right and wrong, to sort out the good from the bad, and to inform and form your conscience. Here's an example . . .

Friday night home game at the high school. A guy shows up with his sagging pants so low that the belt is actually underneath his rear end. His baby blue briefs are blowing in the wind—so to speak. A junior girl shows up in a low-cut top that's way too low. The teacher working the door refuses to let either one in, saying,

"Indecent. Inappropriate. Improper."

No law against it.

Teacher got it right.

It is immoral.

You can't discriminate against somebody because of how they dress.

Fashion's not a sin.

They're just trying to get attention.

How do you respond?

Going Moral

> "Do you not know that your body is a temple of the Holy Spirit within you, which you have from God, and that you are not your own? ... Therefore glorify God in your body."
>
> —(1 Corinthians 6:19-20)

Language of the Body

THROUGH JESUS, WE come to appreciate that God communicates with us not just through words, but also through how we are created. Our own bodies tell us something about God and his plan.

This language of the body takes place most completely between a married man and woman. When spouses are honest and faithful to one another, their physical relationship speaks a truth about who they are as a couple. It says, "We give ourselves completely to one another in love." Without this honesty and faithfulness, the physical relationship between man and woman can be deceitful. The language of the body, then, proclaims God's truth in the communion of husband and wife, and also speaks this truth to others in their life.

> It is obvious that the body as such does not "speak," but man speaks, rereading that which requires to be expressed precisely on the basis of the "body," of the masculinity and femininity of the personal subject, indeed, on the basis of what can be expressed by man only by means of the body.
>
> —Pope John Paul II, *Theology of the Body*, 107:1

Humans do not have two separate natures. We possess a single nature formed through the unity of matter, our body, and spirit, our soul. Our body, then, has a way of speaking. In a marriage, for example, the language of the body allows spouses to communicate through their bodies in physical and spiritual ways. In fact, God communicates to us through our body and soul.

Imagine

Think of some of the people you find it hard to love.

○ Visualize "Our Father, who art in heaven" watching them with interest and care every day, just as the Father watches your life with interest.

○ How does this visualization help you to "forgive their trespasses"? Do you "see" anything differently? Explain.

It is God's name, God's Kingdom, and God's will that we must think of first of all when we begin to pray. When we truthfully pray the words "thy will be done," we are asking God to help us align our will with his.

The late author C.S. Lewis offers the insight that ultimately there are two kinds of people: those who honestly say to God, "*Thy* will be done," and those who prefer to say, "*My* will be done." When Jesus taught us to pray these words, he helped all humankind with this struggle.

The final four prayers of the Lord's Prayer are petitions that place our needs before God and acknowledge God's ability to provide for us. We ask that our lives be nourished in our daily bread, forgiveness of sin, protection from temptation, and deliverance from evil.

In asking for deliverance from evil, we seek freedom from all evil, whether moral, physical, or spiritual. We also see, especially here, that the prayer directs our thoughts to the final judgment or the second coming of Christ. This is also called the final consummation of Christ's return. As it says in the *Catechism*:

> *In this final petition, the Church brings before the Father all the distress of the world. Along with deliverance from the evils that overwhelm humanity, she implores the precious gift of peace and the grace of perseverance in expectation of Christ's return.*
>
> —CCC, 2854

Jesus Christ is the one "who is and was and is to come" (Revelation 1:8). Thus the prayer he gave his disciples prepares us in this life

We often use the phrase "body language" to refer to all of our non-verbal communication with others—facial expressions, gestures, appearance, and so on. But we can also understand body language as more than communicating with others. Our bodies united with our spiritual soul have quite a lot to say to us. Often, in listening to our bodies, we can hear the voice of God.

Gut instincts, heartaches, butterflies in the stomach, a lump in the throat, goosebumps … these have a way of telling us something.

Our bodies have a way of detecting things and expressing them to us. It's important that we listen to and interpret the body's signals.

Sometimes we can get confused when we are trying to understand what our bodies are telling us. Our minds might seem to tell us one thing, while our bodies tells us something different. This is sometimes described as a body-mind conflict. But we have one, human nature, and our body, mind, and spirit are intertwined. They are designed to work in union with one another. When we seem to be getting mixed signals, it's important that we reflect on what God might have to say about the conflict we are experiencing. Seeking guidance through prayer, Scripture and spiritual direction from a priest or qualified layperson can assist us in finding the integration of body, mind, and spirit that God desires for us.

Sometimes we may get a bad feeling in the pit of our stomachs about doing something, but (regretfully) do it anyway. When we say, "I should have known better," we indicate that we neglected the "inner voice of God" (conscience) speaking through our body and soul. Such feelings, arising in the body, sometimes remind us that there are other ways of knowing.

>> What does your body language tell others?

Recall a time when you were glad you listened to your bodily language.

Have you ever had a body-mind conflict? How did you decide what to do?

How does God communicate to us through our bodies?

for the life to come. It connects the way we live on the Earth to our goal of eternal life, where God will be all in all.

The final two sections of this chapter will expand on this idea by focusing on prayer in the Church and our final judgment.

Identify Of the seven different prayers in the Lord's Prayer, how many are prayers of praise? How many are petitions?

Categorize What are the prayers of praise from the Lord's Prayer that focus on the glory of God and what are the petitions that bring our own needs to God?

SECTION 2 REVIEW

QUICK REVIEW

1a. Relate How does solitude help people pray?

b. Analyze Why would Jesus pray before and after important events in his life?

2a. Infer Why is perseverance in prayer important?

b. Explain How does praying to God help us develop characteristics of God?

c. Analyze How were Jesus' teachings on prayer consistent with his life?

3a. Analyze What is the significance of calling God "our Father" rather than "my Father"?

b. Analyze Explain the structure of the Lord's Prayer.

c. Explain How does the Lord's Prayer connect us to Heaven?

ACT

○ Which prayer do you like to say most often? Why?

○ Which type of prayer are you most comfortable with? Why?

SELF-ASSESS

Which statement best reflects where you are now?

☐ I'm confident enough about the material in this section to be able to explain it to someone else.

☐ I have a good grasp of the material in this section, but I could use more review.

☐ I'm lost. I need help catching up before moving on.

Prayer in the Era of the Church

How do we learn to pray today? First and foremost, we know that through our Tradition, the Holy Spirit helps us to pray, guiding us and teaching us how to do so throughout the Church's history to today. One important way the Holy Spirit does this is through his presence and work in the Church.

> *For me, prayer is . . . a simple look toward heaven, it is a cry of recognition and of love, embracing both trial and joy.*
>
> —Saint Thérèse of Lisieux

The Church has developed many traditions of prayer in response to the teaching and example of Jesus. In addition, the Church relies on families to be the **domestic church**, to provide for the physical and spiritual needs of young people. Parents have the initial responsibility to educate their children in faith, prayer, and virtues (see CCC, 2252). Families that encourage prayer are the first schools of prayer. Prayer groups can also be a source of spiritual renewal and a school of prayer. Group prayer, verbalized prayer,

domestic church the experience of learning and growing in faith, prayer, and virtues within one's family, particularly through prayer, love, and forgiveness (see CCC, 1657)

silence, and solitude are all elements of personal prayer. They anchor us in a deep way to God.

Church life is enhanced by what is known as popular piety, and there is a renewed interest in what we used to call "popular prayer devotions." Examples of these are adoration of the Blessed Sacrament, the Rosary, the Way of the Cross, and novenas, to name a few. There has been an increase in Small Christian Community groups, known as SCCs, and lay movements that have become very popular as lay people around the world find ways to join others to pray in words, rituals, and service. These devotions and movements reach out to others and express the wisdom of the faithful. That is why they enjoy support from the Church.

In liturgical prayer, we join with the Church at worship to raise our hearts, minds, and voices in prayer. The Mass includes all five forms of prayer.

- We offer prayers of contrition in the Penitential Act when we pray "Lord Have Mercy."

- Our prayers of petition are specifically offered in the Prayer of the Faithful, after the homily and Creed.

- Prayers of intercession are used when we pray to God on behalf of someone else. This happens during the Prayer of the Faithful and also during the Eucharistic Prayer.

- Prayers of thanksgiving and praise permeate the whole Eucharistic celebration, especially during the consecration of the Eucharist. We offer our liturgical prayer

MY✝FAITH

This is the last My Faith exercise of this course. You were praying before this course started and you will keep praying afterward, even if you don't remember all of the parts of the course. Prayer is food for the soul.

Take time to write down key parts of the story of your prayer so far.

○ What are some of your first memories of praying?

○ Who first taught you to pray?

○ What was your experience of prayer in your family while growing up?

○ What sort of prayers do you pray? Are they traditional prayers, such as the Lord's Prayer or Hail Mary, or do you make up your own prayers?

○ Do you prefer praying alone or in groups, and why?

Then outline the next chapter of the story of your prayer.

○ What part(s) of your prayer would you like to change, increase, decrease, do differently?

○ What prayer forms new to you most interest you?

○ What heartfelt hopes do you have for your future prayer?

Praying
What's the story with your prayer?

Go to the student site at
hs.osvcurriculum.com

Discipleship . . . within the Body of Christ . . .
for the glory of God and the good of the world

---

to the Father in union with Christ and through the Holy Spirit. The Communion of Saints on Earth and in Heaven join in celebrating the liturgy (see CCC, 1090). It is a taste of the heavenly Liturgy that is to come.

• There are prayers of blessing, which are used for people, objects, and often for food. The priest blesses us before sending us out to give glory to God.

Ordained ministers have accepted the call to lead us in liturgical prayer by presiding over liturgical ceremonies, preaching, praying the Liturgy of the Hours, and living a prayerful life.

Some ordained and lay faithful have chosen **contemplative religious** life. Hermits, monks, and nuns since the time of the ancient desert fathers have sought out lives of prayer and devotion. These men and women freely choose to be **cloistered**, or set apart from the world, in order to continually praise God and intercede for the needs of others. There are also various religious communities who choose *not* to live cloistered. These sisters and brothers in **active religious** communities are likewise prayerful and devout, but their practice of spirituality is appropriate for their calling and true to the spirit of their founders. They offer their lives as a prayer. Examples are religious who serve among the people as teachers, healthcare workers, or social workers and organize their daily prayer to complement their calling.

List Give four elements of personal prayer.

Elaborate Why does the Church rely on families?

cloistered set apart or shut off from others as in a convent or monastery

active religious prayerful and devout religious sisters and brothers who usually live in community and work among the people; their practice of spirituality is appropriate for their calling and true to the spirit of their founders

contemplative religious hermits, monks, and nuns who set themselves apart from the world, living cloistered lives of prayer and devotion

Jesus with Us Always **209**

Novena

The Novena was a popular expression of faith for Catholics in previous generations that is still used today.

A novena is a recitation of prayers or spiritual devotions with a specific request or intention that are performed nine times in a row, whether that is nine hours in a row, nine days in a row, nine week-days (such as nine Fridays), or nine days of the month (such as First Fridays or First Saturdays). These devotions can include fasting, almsgiving, or receiving Holy Communion as well as prayer.

The name *novena* comes from the Latin word for nine (*novem*, meaning "nine each") and is based on the nine days the Apostles and Mary spent in prayer between the Ascension of Jesus Christ into Heaven (forty days after Easter) and Pentecost (the coming of the Holy Spirit).

Novenas may be private devotion or public prayer. They often focus on a particular saint, Mary, image (such as the Sacred Heart of Jesus), or occasion (such as the Annunciation).

The Pentecost Novena in honor of the Holy Spirit is prayed nine days before Pentecost Sunday. It is based on Acts 1:14: "All these were constantly devoting themselves to prayer, together with certain women, including Mary the mother of Jesus, as well as his brothers."

The Christmas Novena starts nine days before Christmas and honors the mystery of Christ's birth.

The four types of novenas are: novenas of mourning (such as following the death of a loved one); novenas of preparation (such as Christmas or Easter novenas); novenas of prayer; and indulgenced novenas.

Pope Leo XIII, in 1897, directed that "throughout the whole Catholic Church, this year and in every subsequent year, a novena shall take place before Whit-Sunday (Pentecost), in all parish churches." The Pentecost Novena is the only novena officially prescribed by the Church.

The Rosary Novena, which originated in 1884 at the Sanctuary of Our Lady of the Rosary in Pompeii, takes fifty-four days to complete and involves praying nine complete Rosaries (of fifteen decades each) in petition and nine complete Rosaries in thanksgiving.

>> What aspects of faith does the novena express?

If possible, ask one of your grandparents to share their experience of novena.

What Makes a Prayer Good and Sincere?

Jesus cautioned his disciples not to just speak a lot of empty words in prayer.

> *When you are praying, do not heap up empty phrases as the Gentiles do; for they think that they will be heard because of their many words.*
>
> —Matthew 6:7

This can be difficult. We often have the benefit of memorizing prayers from the time we were little, and yet we can forget to listen to the meaning of the words we say. Actually, the words and gestures we use are a normal part of prayer, but they are not the only or even the most important aspect of prayer. Something *different* is at stake in prayer, something more basic than particular words or a set of gestures and postures. We must look at where prayer originates to understand what this "something different" is.

What makes a prayer good and sincere? See the chart below to examine what the example and teaching of Jesus on prayer shows us.

Research
- Choose a religious community that you would like to know more about and find out about the members' spirituality and habits of prayer. Note whether they pray alone, together, morning and evening, through their lives of service, liturgically, silently, etc.
- Identify the community as active or contemplative.
- How does their way of praying fit with their particular vocation and mission as a community?

We mentioned that prayer is directed primarily to God the Father, but sometimes prayer is directed to Jesus Christ and to the Holy Spirit. Whenever we pray, however, we are praying to the Trinity: One God in three Persons. Remember, our Triune God is always united and always present to us.

Recall What did Jesus caution his disciples about regarding prayer?

Summarize What does it mean to say that true prayer comes from the heart?

Jesus on Prayer

Here are four characteristics of prayer that come from the Gospels and the life and example of Jesus.

1. Prayer is a free gift. It comes from God, who calls each of us to this mysterious encounter with him. Saint Augustine observed that we would not seek God unless God first sought us. God initiates the encounter of prayer. Prayer originates as a response to the One who is, and who calls us to himself. He "thirsts" for a relationship with us. And when we respond, our own "thirst" is deeply satisfied.

2. Deep prayer comes from the whole person, and it often flows from the heart. "The heart" is not merely the seat of the emotions. Rather, it is the hidden center of the person, the core of his or her being. "The heart is the dwelling-place where I am, where I live" the *Catechism* tells us. "The heart is the place of decision, deeper than our psychic drives. It is the place of truth, where we choose life or death. It is the place of encounter . . . it is the place of covenant" (CCC, 2563).

3. Some people get anxious about what to say when they pray. We do not need to fear "doing it right" or "getting the words" down perfectly. We can turn to God just as we are. All that matters is that we are sincere, honest, and open.

4. Since prayer is communicating with God, we have to get in the habit of listening to what God might be trying to say to us. Too often we make prayer an experience of "one-way" communication. Deep prayer is a two-way communication.

Pray

One early Christian prayer which comes out of the Eastern (Orthodox) Christian tradition and has become more familiar to Catholics today is the Jesus Prayer. It is simple: "Lord Jesus Christ, Son of God, have mercy on me, a sinner." The Jesus Prayer—or an adopted version of it—can be said repeatedly during a time of quiet. It can be prayed with every breath you take. It can be said during the day, while doing other activities such as washing dishes, exercising, or traveling. It is a way to "pray constantly," as Paul urged the Christian community at Thessalonica (1 Thessalonians 5:17). It can also be prayed in time of need, to ward off temptations or anxiety.

Try it right now as a quiet prayer that accompanies your breathing.

After a few minutes, write down your feelings.

Pray it in some different circumstances during the week.

SECTION 3 REVIEW

QUICK REVIEW

1a. Interpret How can the Catholic family serve as the "first school of prayer"?

b. Explain What is liturgical prayer?

c. Infer Why might some people become cloistered?

d. Describe How do other religious communities "pray with their lives"?

e. List Name five types of prayer.

2a. Discuss Where does prayer come from?

b. Explain Why is prayer called a free gift?

c. Recall What are four basic points about prayer?

ACT

Deliberately try praying in a different way than usual. Try with your headphones, with the Bible, with a Rosary, or at a different time than you regularly pray.

Pray Compose a short prayer thanking God for those who first taught you to pray and believe in prayer.

SELF-ASSESS

Which statement best reflects where you are now?

☐ I'm confident enough about the material in this section to be able to explain it to someone else.

☐ I have a good grasp of the material in this section, but I could use more review.

☐ I'm lost. I need help catching up before moving on.

Death Is Transformed

Throughout this course, we have been reminded that it is easy to get distracted by "things of this world" and take our eyes off the things that matter in the Kingdom of God. Jesus pointed this out in his parable of the Rich Fool, to whom God said: "'You fool! This very night your life is being demanded of you. And the things you have prepared, whose will they be?' So it is with those who store up treasures for themselves but are not rich toward God" (Luke 12:20-21).

"Lord, take me by the hand and walk with me" (Kate E. Ritger).

So, how do we stay focused on the things of God? With God's grace, we work at the life Jesus modeled and the teachings he shared. With the Holy Spirit's help, we pray, and our community also helps us remain focused on God. We know that it's not just about the here and now. To be human is to long for that fulfillment that comes only from God.

To be human is also to know that we will die someday. The end of our earthly life is one of the facts of existence. Many of us have already experienced the death of a loved one. Our mortality gives urgency to the business of life. We do not have an infinite amount of time. The challenges of life must be embraced, as our relationship with God should be.

The meaning of death, for the Christian at least, is not negative. Jesus Christ transformed death; instead of it being the end, he taught us that it is the beginning of eternal life of happiness with God. We believe that when physical death comes and we die in God's grace, we will indeed remain united with the Triune God and share in Jesus' Resurrection (see CCC, 1010), which is assurance for our own resurrection.

God only gradually revealed to his people that there would be a resurrection from the dead. At the time of Jesus, there was an ongoing discussion about life after death, occurring between the two major schools of thought among the Jewish faithful: the **Pharisees** and the **Sadducees**. The Sadducees were the priestly class. They were part of the aristocracy closely linked to leadership of the Temple. Sadducees were known for being conservative and using a strict, literal interpretation of Scripture and the central role of Temple leaders. The Pharisees were less conservative. They believed that the Torah was the source of understanding the faith. In fact, the Pharisees were responsible for maintaining the oral tradition of

Pharisees leaders and teachers of Jewish faithful who held on to the Torah as the source of their understanding of faith

Sadducees the priestly class/aristocracy; closely linked to leadership of the Temple; known for being conservative and taking a strict, literal interpretation of Scripture

GO TO **THE SOURCE**

Although the Pharisees in Jesus' day believed in the resurrection of the dead, the Sadducees did not. Some of the Sadducees challenged Jesus by trying to create a puzzle he could not solve.

Read Mark 12:18-27.

○ What does Jesus say about God?

○ What does he say about the contrast between life on Earth and life in Heaven?

PRIMARY SOURCES

Saint Ignatius of Antioch wrote a letter to the Church in Rome while he was on his way to his martyrdom. Read the following excerpt from the letter:

Go to the student site at
hs.osvcurriculum.com

"The time for my birth is close at hand. Forgive me, my brothers. Do not stand in the way of my birth to real life; do not wish me stillborn. My desire is to belong to God. Do not, then, hand me back to the world. Do not try to tempt me with material things. Let me attain pure light. Only on my arrival there can I be fully a human being. Give me the privilege of imitating the passion of my God. If you have him in your heart, you will understand what I wish. You will sympathise with me because you will know what urges me on.

"The prince of this world is determined to lay hold of me and to undermine my will which is intent on God. Let none of you here help him; instead show yourselves on my side, which is also God's side. Do not talk about Jesus Christ as long as you love this world. Do not harbour envious thoughts. And supposing I should see you, if then I should beg you to intervene on my behalf, do not believe what I say. Believe instead what I am now writing to you. For though I am alive as I write to you, still my real desire is to die. My love of this life has been crucified, and there is no yearning in me for any earthly thing. Rather within me is the living water which says deep inside me: 'Come to the Father.' I no longer take pleasure in perishable food or in the delights of this world. I want only God's bread, which is the flesh of Jesus Christ, formed of the seed of David, and for drink I crave his blood, which is love that cannot perish.

"I am no longer willing to live a merely human life, and you can bring about my wish if you will. Please, then, do me this favour, so that you in turn may meet with equal kindness. Put briefly, this is my request: believe what I am saying to you. Jesus Christ himself will make it clear to you that I am saying the truth. Only truth can come from that mouth by which the Father has truly spoken. Pray for me that I may obtain my desire. I have not written to you as a mere man would, but as one who knows the mind of God. If I am condemned to suffer, I will take it that you wish me well. If my case is postponed, I can only think that you wish me harm."

>> What will martyrdom bring to Ignatius?

Who is the prince of this world?

How does this letter reflect the Christian view of death?

the Torah, and the actual writing of the Septuagint and of what we call the Vulgate.

The Pharisees and Sadducees disagreed about many tenets of Jewish life and faith. When it came to life after death, the Pharisees believed in the afterlife, while the Sadducees did not.

At one point in his ministry, Jesus was asked his own beliefs on the subject. Many of Jesus' contemporaries were more interested in whose side he was going to choose (the Pharisees or the Sadducees), than they were in what his actual answer would be.

Jesus taught that there is life after death. Yet he also did something more. He identified resurrection with himself, saying, "I am the resurrection and the life" (John 11:25). As Christians today, we understand that to accept Christ is to be united with him in his Resurrection, in a life that does not end.

Recall Our mortality gives what to the business of life?

Conclude When we die in God's grace, what happens?

Judgment of Souls

We believe in life after death, but what exactly happens, and how do we get to wherever we're going? The theological term for this topic is **eschatology**, which literally means the study of "last." It is the area of theology referring to death, judgment, resurrection of the body, Heaven and Hell, and the final coming of Jesus on the last day.

Each human soul will be judged immediately after death (see CCC, 1021). As we mentioned earlier, this is called the particular judgment. One's immortal soul will either go immediately to Heaven, to Purgatory for purification, or to Hell as the case may be.

At the end of time, Christ will judge those still living and the dead, each according to that person's deeds and acceptance or rejection of God's grace. Each will appear at Christ's tribunal in his or her own body. **Heaven** is the state of eternal blessedness. It is the happiness of being united forever with

the Triune God, with Mary, the angels, and with all the just, who belong to him. **Purgatory** is the state of being purified prior to entering Heaven. **Hell** is the state of eternal damnation. It involves being separated from God forever, completely isolated from God by choice.

One of the most common questions people asked regarding judgment is: "If God is all-loving and forgiving, how can there be anyone in Hell?" As we just mentioned: it is *our own choice.*

Throughout this whole course, we have discussed the fact that God loves us and wants us to choose a life of discipleship. However, where we spend eternity is ultimately our choice. It is a choice we make not by words alone, but in our thoughts, beliefs, attitudes, desires, and actions.

The way to Christ is the path of truth. In light of the truth—that is, our loving and forgiving Triune God—we need to take responsibility for our sinfulness. Earlier, it was noted that particular judgment occurs according to our faith and deeds. It is not as if all our deeds will be placed atop some cosmic scale and whichever way the scale tips determines our final destination.

Judgment is about coming to terms with our shortcomings and failures. If we have responded to God's gifts and if we have developed ourselves to take responsibility and seek forgiveness from God, then we have chosen Heaven. If people would rather believe their own versions of the truth regarding how God wants humans to live and rationalize away all their sinfulness, then they very well may end up being eternally separated from their Creator.

Heaven is the ultimate fulfillment of the deepest human longings (see CCC, 1024). It is the final communion with God, being completely and totally in the divine presence and seeing the face of God. Catholic Tradition calls this the **beatific vision**, seeing the face of God.

The wonder and glory of Heaven can hardly be imagined. The Scriptures are rich with images that inspire us with anticipation.

Purgatory a purification after death that prepares the soul to enter into Heaven

hell the state of eternal separation from God after death, through the free choice to reject God's offer of forgiveness and redemption

eschatology literally means the study of "last," and refers to the part of theology that studies topics related to the end of time: death, judgment, resurrection of the body, Heaven, Purgatory, and Hell, the coming of Jesus on the last day, etc.

Heaven the state of supreme happiness for those who have died in God's grace and friendship; being united forever with God the Father, Son, and Holy Spirit, the Virgin Mary, the angels, and the just after death

beatific vision being completely and totally in the divine presence and seeing the face of God

Heaven is compared to a wedding feast, a banquet, and paradise. It is described by words such as life, light, and peace. There is no precise description of Heaven, however, because it is beyond our power to conceive what it will be like. As Saint Paul wrote, "no eye has seen, nor ear heard, nor the human heart conceived, what God has prepared for those who love him" (1 Corinthians 2:9).

What we do know is that we will be ourselves and we will see God as he is. As the *Catechism* says: "To live in heaven is 'to be with Christ.' **The elect** live 'in Christ,' but they retain, or rather find, their true identity, their own name" (cf. Revelation 2:17) (CCC, 1025). Eternal life with God does not erase our individuality, but brings it to perfect fulfillment.

The elect in this case means God's chosen ones who because of their deeds and faith enter into Heaven with Christ. The term "the elect" can also refer to those found ready to be initiated into the Catholic Church during the Rite of Christian Initiation of Adults.

One concern many people have when contemplating judgment involves those who have not completely reconciled with God. To put it another way, perhaps they need more time to come to terms with the truth of their life; they need more time to think through the implications of their choice. When we

the elect God's chosen ones who persevere in faith and enter into glory with Christ in Heaven

final judgment the judgment of the hearts and works of all people and the definitive triumph of good over evil at the end of time. At the time, the material world will be transformed and Christ's Kingdom of justice and peace will be fully established.

understand this sort of human nature along with the depth of God's love and forgiveness available to us, it makes sense that our Catholic Tradition describes what we call Purgatory.

Purgatory is a purification. It reflects that a person lived in God's grace and friendship, but upon death, he or she still needs to prepare for the joy of Heaven (see CCC, 1030). Purgatory is not to be confused with the damnation of Hell; it is not a time of punishment, but rather a final purification.

One example of someone who would need purification might be a person who has lived a good and faithful life, but is unable to forgive those who have hurt him or her. In time this person will be able to forgive and be healed of his or her hurts and the veil will be lifted from this person's beatific vision.

The purification can be hastened for the souls in Purgatory by the prayer and good works of the faithful on Earth. Through the Communion of Saints, the Church offers prayers for the dead, especially at Mass. From the beginning, the Church has offered prayers for the dead, especially at Mass, to help them reach the beatific vision of God. Almsgiving, indulgences, and works of penance are three other practices a person can do on behalf of the dead.

God does not desire damnation for anyone. He wishes all people to be saved, and to live eternally in complete happiness with him. Yet people are capable of choosing otherwise.

As the *Catechism* says, "We cannot be united with God unless we freely choose to love him" (CCC, 1033). Those who have committed serious sin, and refuse to repent or to accept God's merciful forgiveness, exclude themselves from Heaven.

Everyone will experience what is known as the **final judgment** at the end of time. We distinguish an individual's particular judgment from the final judgment of all humankind.

The final judgment will occur at the end of the world, with the second coming. Christ, who reigns over all, will come to judge all people who have ever lived. This will be the

Imagine

You are sitting next to God the Father in a large IMAX theater. You begin to recognize that the scenes you see on the screen are from your own life. This is no ordinary movie; you are being shown the complete truth of your life.

Imagine God putting a divine arm around you, squeezing your shoulder and commending you for all the times in your life you loved others as Christ loved us.

Imagine what it feels like as you both watch all the times in your life in which you were hurtful, hateful, and sinful.

○ Would you be able to watch or would you have to turn away?

○ When your life movie ends, what would you say to the Father?

○ What might he say to you?

consummation of human history. Those judged as just will rule with Christ forever more. And the material world will be transformed and Christ's Kingdom of justice and peace will be fully established.

In our Creed, when we confess that we believe in "life everlasting," we affirm our belief that at the end of the world, the Kingdom of God will come in its fullness. The just will be glorified. They will reign with Christ forever. Body and soul will be reunited. The material universe, too, will be transfigured into a new and glorious place. We affirm this in the Lord's Prayer when we pray, "Thy kingdom come."

We do not know when the world will end. It had a beginning. And it will come to an end someday. The mysterious visions in the Book of Revelation suggest there will be a time of great turmoil, leading up to the triumph of God.

These visions are hard to understand. But they convey a truth: Jesus Christ will reign. He is the Lamb who was slain for our sins and who now receives "blessing and honor and glory and might for ever and ever!" (Revelation 5:13).

List Name three comparisons of Heaven made in Scripture.

Predict What happens to people who sin gravely and refuse to repent or to accept God's merciful forgiveness?

> >> **What gives you the most to think about in eschatology?**
>
> **What gives you hope? What gives you concern?**
>
> **What aspects of eschatology do you want to discuss further?**

REFLECT

Heaven in the Bible	
Look up the following biblical passages about Heaven, and describe the image of Heaven each offers in the chart:	
Passage	**Image of Heaven**
Psalm 23	
Matthew 22:1-14	
Ephesians 1:20-23	
John 14:1-4	
John 18:36	
Hebrews 9:11	
Hebrews 11:16	
1 Corinthians 15:50-56	
Revelation 4:1-6	
Revelation 21:9-14	

THE APOCALYPSE TAPESTRY

The largest tapestry in the world hangs in the chateau of Angers, France. It depicts scenes of the end of time and Christ's reign, as described in the Book of Revelation and imagined by the artist. This woven masterpiece measures 104 meters long (740 square yards), and contains seventy scenes (originally ninety, but some have been lost). Using drawings of another artist, Hennequin of Bruges (a city in what is now Belgium), Nicolas Bataille completed it in 1380.

This was the great age of tapestry-making. Tapestries expressed the ideals and values of those who commissioned them. They were prized possessions. This one belonged to Louis I of Angers, the brother of the Emperor Charles V, who was also a great admirer of the art of tapestry.

The Apocalypse tapestry shows fantastic skill, workmanship, and materials, and it also is an expression of faith. It represents themes from the Bible that provoke fear and wonder. They inspire and yet also are sobering. They invite the viewer to meditate on the final days and the coming reign of Christ, and to repent while there is still time.

In 1937 an artist named Jean Lurçat saw the Apocalypse tapestry for the first time. He was captivated by it, and wanted to produce his own modern response. But there was no tapestry-making industry any longer. It was a lost art.

Lurçat was not deterred. Over the next twenty years, he revived the art of tapestry-making in France. By 1957 he was ready to begin his own masterpiece. He called it "The Song of the World" (*Le Chant du Monde*). This monumental tapestry consists of ten panels in brilliant colors. The first four concern nuclear war and the destruction that comes from the atom bomb—his contemporary version of the apocalypse. The fifth depicts the human person "in the glory of peace." Another five panels celebrate the joys of life, human creativity, and hope. It was completed in 1966, one year after his death.

Thus, because of a medieval Christian masterpiece of the fourteenth century, an artistic tradition was revived in modern times. A new warning was given of the destructive potential of war. And the call to live in peace was voiced again in our troubled world—a call to change before it is too late.

Think About It Sometimes the things we make by hand, whether fine arts or handcrafts of a simple nature, can pass on the faith.
Do you have any handmade item that you consider an expression of faith? What is it? How did you come to have it?
When Jean Lurçat wanted to express the joys of life, he wove into his tapestry pictures to represent things such as champagne and poetry and the exploration of outer space. What items or experiences would you include?
What, in your view, are the things the world most needs to repent of today, in order to be ready to welcome Christ when he comes again?

↗ Go to the student site at
hs.osvcurriculum.com

We do not know when the world will end, but some parts of God's creation have been around for a long time. Some may still be here at the end of time. Officials in Seminole County, Florida, for example, like to tell visitors that the Senator, a 3,500-year-old Bald Cypress in Big Tree Park, was already growing when Moses led the Hebrews out of Egypt. *National Geographic* informs us that the world's oldest living plant is a Norway spruce that took root in Sweden about 9,550 years ago, just after the last ice age. Scientists describe the Grand Canyon as young, geologically speaking. The canyon began forming about six million years ago, but that is still young compared to the age geologists give to the Earth: 4.5 billion years old.

○ Describe your reaction when you see how extremely old parts of nature are.

○ What if we knew when the world would end? How do you think knowing would affect how people live their lives?

↗ Go to the student site at **hs.osvcurriculum.com**

SECTION 4 REVIEW

QUICK REVIEW

1a. Infer How does the idea of death help us focus on life?

b. Explain How did Jesus transform death?

c. Analyze As Christians, should we fear death? Why or why not?

d. Explain What did Jesus teach about death?

2a. Recall What is the difference between the particular judgment and the final judgment?

b. Infer What do we know about Heaven?

3. Recall What does the Book of Revelation tell us about the end of the world?

ACT

Find some artwork that shows the end of the world or the last judgment.

○ Analyze the images and emotions portrayed in the work.

○ What do the images and emotions tell you about the beliefs of the artist and the culture in which the artist lived?

○ Share your ideas about the artwork and the final judgment.

○ If you could ask the artist to add or remove something so that it would better reflect the last judgment, what would it be and why?

Pray Compose a short prayer regarding "the final things."

SELF-ASSESS

Which statement best reflects where you are now?

☐ I'm confident enough about the material in this section to be able to explain it to someone else.

☐ I have a good grasp of the material in this section, but I could use more review.

☐ I'm lost. I need help catching up before moving on.

PRAYER

Good and gracious God,
You provide us with food and clothing
and everything we could possibly need from day to day.
We are grateful for the assurance that you have offered to us
through Jesus Christ, our daily bread. Every day you give us so
much that we often forget to say thank you.
Remind us daily of our abundance.
Remind us also of the needs of others, so our abundance can
be shared with all.
In Jesus' name we pray.
Amen.

God our Father,
We thank you for the food your bounty has given us,
your gathered family.
Send us your Holy Spirit to help us freely give to others
what you have so generously given to us,
and that we may all share
in the banquet of Heaven.
We ask this through Christ our Lord.
Amen.

TERMS

Use each of the following terms in a sentence that shows you know what the term means. You may include more than one term in a sentence.

prayer	Pharisees
"I am" statements	Sadducees
solitude	eschatology
hypocrite	Heaven
perseverance	Purgatory
the Lord's Prayer	Hell
domestic church	beatific vision
contemplative religious	the elect
cloistered	final judgment
active religious	

PEOPLE AND GROUPS

Use information from the chapter to tell why each is significant.

1. Moses
2. domestic church
3. cloistered
4. contemplative religious communities
5. active religious communities
6. Saint Thérèse of Lisieux

UNDERSTANDING

Answer each question and complete each exercise.

SECTION **1**

1. **Analyze** What is the divine name, and why is its revelation to Moses important?
2. **Recall** Tell some of the "I am" statements from the Gospel according to John.
3. **Explain** How do "I am" statements help us understand Jesus' role in our lives?

SECTION **2**

4. **Summarize** Describe the times when Jesus prayed.
5. **Explain** How does praying change a person?
6. **Analyze** Why is the Lord's Prayer important?

SECTION **3**

7. **Explain** How do members of religious orders combine prayer and work in the world?
8. **Analyze** How does knowing that prayer is a gift from God help us pray?
9. **Infer** Why is prayer directed primarily to God the Father?
10. **Recall** What are four basic points about prayer?

SECTION **4**

11. **Explain** What do Catholics believe about physical death?
12. **Summarize** What happens to the immortal soul after death?
13. **Infer** What is our belief about Hell?
14. **Define** What will happen at the end of human history?

CONNECTING

Visual This altarpiece panel is called "The Ascent of the Blessed." It was painted by Hieronymus Bosch, a Dutch painter who lived from about 1450 to 1516.

What mood does this painting bring to mind? What do you think it intended to show about life after death?

Challenge You are talking with a friend about the death of one of your elderly relatives.

Friend: Sorry to hear about your grandmother.

You: Thanks. But she's in a better place. "On the side of the angels," as my parents say.

Friend: You think?

You: Yeah. She was a really good person. Prayed a lot. She used to always remind me about God. I just know that she was close to him.

Friend: The whole Heaven/Hell thing confuses me. You know, why would God send someone to Hell? And what gets you into Heaven? And what's up with Purgatory?

○ Continue the conversation and answer your friend's questions using information from this chapter.

Question After working through this chapter, how would you summarize Jesus' advice on prayer? Write a full paragraph or two.

Imagine You are a gallery owner who wants to make a multimedia presentation about the end of the world. Think about how you would design a gallery space to present this idea.

○ What colors would you use on walls and floors, and what kinds of images would you include?

○ Would the overall feeling be optimistic or pessimistic?

○ What music, scents, or other ways to appeal to the senses would you use to convey your ideas?

SELF-ASSESS

On Your Own Make a list of the most important things you learned from this chapter. Select three things that represent your growth in understanding as you worked through this chapter. Write a paragraph explaining your choices.

With a Partner List what you found most helpful or interesting in this chapter, as well as any other questions that have surfaced.

THE BODY OF CHRIST

And I tell you, you are Peter, and on this rock I will build my church, and the gates of Hades will not prevail against it. I will give you the keys of the kingdom of heaven, and whatever you bind on earth will be bound in heaven, and whatever you loose on earth will be loosed in heaven.

—Jesus in Matthew 16:18-19

As Catholics, we travel the journey that Jesus asked his disciples to follow. We do it as a community of believers. Jesus made it clear that discipleship was not something to be lived on one's own in a "me and Jesus" relationship. He established the Church based on the rock of Saint Peter and the Apostles, and entrusted to them the Good News of salvation, his mission, and saving work. In every generation, through their successors, the Pope and bishops in union with him, continue to lead the Church and uphold her in the truth. Inspired by the Holy Spirit, the Pope and bishops hand on the faith of the Apostles until Christ returns in glory.

With Peter as their first universal leader, the Bible says the disciples "devoted themselves to the Apostles' teaching and fellowship, the breaking of the bread and to the prayers" (Acts 2:42). The "breaking of the bread" and "the prayers" refers to the celebration of the Eucharist. In so doing, the Apostles and disciples followed Jesus' command to "do this in memory of me." Catholicism traces its roots to Peter and the Apostles. It is a historical fact.

The Catholic Church preserves the special gifts given to Peter, the Apostles, and the disciples. These make us who we are and are at the center of our Catholic identity. However, we know that many expressions of holiness and truth exist outside the Church. Catholics base their faith and beliefs on Jesus' revelation of the Trinity, his founding of the Church, the Sacraments, Scripture and Tradition, and other gifts listed below. We root our Catholic belief in the Paschal Mystery—Jesus' Passion, death, Resurrection, and Ascension.

The gifts, given by Jesus to the Church, are described here in terms of "special characteristics." Taken together, they form the core of Catholic belief and practice. In a sense, they make us Catholic. These characteristics are consistent in Catholic Tradition from the time of the Apostles. They have not and will not change, no matter what's happening in society and the world. In every generation the Church passes them on to the next and teaches why they are important to understanding ourselves and our calling in life.

As we mature in faith, we better understand our Catholic identity; that is, what it means to be Catholic. Our faith is a way of life that is meant to permeate everything we do. In religion courses over the next several years, we'll study in detail these characteristics of Catholicism. We'll probe into the Church's teachings about them, and experience firsthand how each one enriches our faith.

Characteristics of Catholicism

1. The Church is Trinitarian.	The great mystery of the Trinity—God the Father, God the Son, and God the Holy Spirit—permeates every aspect of Catholic belief, practice, and worship. Our understanding of Trinity is part of everything Catholics believe and do, including how we worship and pray. The Trinity is a unity of three equal, yet distinct, Persons, possessing the same divine nature. The Trinity is a divine community, from which all loving human communities take their origin. The communal nature of the Catholic Church is based in the Trinity.
	The Trinity is the central mystery of our faith. Trinitarian belief roots who Catholics are, what we believe, how we pray, and what we teach. The Church administers the Sacraments using the Trinitarian formula. In the Rite of Baptism, for example, the bishop, priest, or deacon baptizes in the name of the Father, and of the Son, and of the Holy Spirit. The priest invokes the Trinity in the Eucharistic Liturgy, the Sacraments, and the Divine Office. Catholics begin and end their prayers with the Sign of the Cross, a reminder of our Baptism and the Trinity.
	Every time the Church celebrates the Eucharist, we remember the reality of Trinitarian love, witnessed in Jesus' eternal sacrifice, which he offered to the Father through the Holy Spirit. In the Eucharist, we receive Jesus, really present, Body and Blood, soul and divinity. Church members are united to Christ and one another. Together we form the Mystical Body of Christ.

Characteristics of Catholicism

2. The Church is Christ-centered.

The Catholic faith centers on Jesus Christ " …the eternal Son of God made man" (*Catechism of the Catholic Church*, 423). Jesus is the Alpha and the Omega, the beginning and end of all things. Jesus is the heart and center of the Catholic faith. He is the way, the truth, and the life. He reveals deep mysteries of the Triune God, heads the Church, shows us the moral path to salvation, and gives us the Sacraments as means to salvation. He teaches us about his Father and sends the Holy Spirit to be with us always.

Because of his great love, Jesus died on the cross for our sins and rose from the dead. He left us a perpetual reminder of his sacrifice in the Mass, when he is present among us, Body and Blood, soul and divinity. Jesus invites us into an intimate relationship of friendship with him, encourages us to praise the Triune God, and tells us to ask God for help in our needs. He promises eternal life to his faithful followers.

3. The Church is a community.

Jesus gifted us with the love that the three Persons in the Trinity share with each other. He founded his Church on the divine love that the Trinity has for humankind. United in the Holy Spirit, this Pilgrim People lives in the world, as Jesus did, but aspires for a more fulfilling happiness than this world provides. The Church anticipates Jesus' coming again and our eternal reward in Heaven.

The Trinity, a communion of love, shares divine grace through the Church, which is the Sacrament of the Trinity's unity with the People of God. The Church gives us the age-old teachings and practices that keep us on the right path. These are Jesus' gifts to us. Indeed, Catholicism is lived out in community, following Jesus' way and inspired by the Holy Spirit that praises and honors the Father in appreciation for what we received.

Catholics on Earth are united in faith and love with the saints in Heaven and the souls in Purgatory. We call this the "Communion of Saints." Every Sunday at Mass, we pray in the Creed: "I believe in the communion of saints." After Mass, some Catholics remain and pray the Rosary or before a statue of a saint. Our grandparent, aunt, or uncle may have a prayer table at home with a picture of a deceased loved one and a candle. Because we on Earth are united with the saints in Heaven and the souls in Purgatory, we ask all our friends to pray for us—those living on Earth, those being purified in Purgatory, and those rejoicing forever in Heaven.

4. The Church is sacramental.

Jesus is the fundamental Sacrament and most fully reveals God to us. The Catholic Church is a sacramental people. She carries on Christ's work on Earth and communicates his message and way of life through her teaching, social ministries, and liturgy. The seven Sacraments of the Catholic Church continue to celebrate Jesus' Paschal Mystery, each one celebrating a special aspect of this Mystery. The Sacraments are holy signs of God's desire to be one with us. For example, Baptism gives us the new life of grace, as we are reborn as sons and daughters of God. Matrimony reflects God's desire to share his love in the love that a husband and wife have for each other. Every Sacrament celebrates God's love and invites us into a special relationship with Jesus through the Sacrament celebrated.

Sacramental belief is fundamental to who we are and what we do as Catholics. The Sacraments help us fulfill our spiritual needs and draw us into relationship with Christ and one another. Instituted by Christ to give us grace, the seven Sacraments are outward signs of this grace. They use rituals and symbols reflecting the holy presence of the divine.

As concrete actions rooted in the things that we use daily (water, bread, wine), Sacraments do two things: they point beyond themselves to something else—a sacred reality—and they bring about what they signify by making that reality present—new life, healing, forgiveness, membership, and so on. We know that Sacraments point to something else, but often we forget that they bring about or effect what they signify. For example, the Anointing of the Sick brings about spiritual and sometimes physical healing.

Catholic sacramentality goes beyond the seven Sacraments. Rooted in them, we celebrate other sacred signs of God's love, called sacramentals. They bear a certain resemblance to the Sacraments, but are given to us by the Church, not Christ. Catholics walk into a Catholic Church, dip their hand into holy water, and make the Sign of the Cross. We genuflect or bow to Jesus, present in the tabernacle, before entering the pew and kneeling down. Some Catholics focus on the life-sized crucifix hanging above the altar. During Advent, we see a wreath with four candles at the front of the church. During Easter, we see a large, white Paschal candle near the altar. If we attend a Baptism, we see oils and water. Catholics use colors, symbols, and actions that speak to us in ways that don't require words.

Characteristics of Catholicism

5. The Church is Eucharistic.	The root meaning of Eucharist in Greek means "thanksgiving." Our thanksgiving rests in the great sacrifice that Jesus offered for us on the cross, which we celebrate in the Eucharist.
	As a sacramental community, Catholics root everything in the Eucharist. All the other Sacraments lead to it and flow from it. The Eucharist is the source and summit of our lives. Catholics also call the celebration of the Eucharist "Mass." The Eucharist is not simply a symbolic reminder of Jesus' sacrifice. Christ is present in this celebration in special ways. He is present in the community gathered together, in the Word proclaimed, in the person of the priest-celebrant, and most especially in the consecrated Eucharistic species, Jesus' Body and Blood.
	By "Real Presence" we mean that the Eucharist is the real presence of Christ, whole and entire, under the appearances of bread and wine. While a memorial of Jesus' sacrifice on the cross, the Eucharist is more than just that. It is Christ's real presence.
	In a wide sense, Catholics realize that we can be "eucharist" to each other when we share God's love with others. Since God dwells within us, we give thanks for the blessings we received by sharing our gifts with our brothers and sisters.
6. The Church is biblically based.	The *Catechism* says, ". . . the Church has always venerated the Scriptures as she venerates the Lord's Body . . . . In Sacred Scripture, the Church constantly finds her nourishment and her strength, for she welcomes it not as a human word, 'but as what it really is, the word of God'" (CCC, 103–104). These words indicate the importance of Scripture for Catholics.
	The early Church saw the Old Testament as containing the revelation of God's plan of salvation for humankind. They recognized the unity of this plan in the Old and New Testaments, studied the prophecies of a coming messiah, and showed how Jesus fulfilled them. New Testament writers wrote down faithfully the teachings of Jesus and interpreted the Old Testament in light of his death and Resurrection (see CCC, 129).
	New Testament writers, under the inspiration of the Holy Spirit, testified to the faith of the early Christian community. The New Testament must be interpreted in light of this faith, passed down to us in the Church's Tradition. Scripture and Sacred Tradition are bound closely together, as two distinct modes of transmitting God's Revelation.
	Catholics cherish the Scripture, read it, and use it in their prayers. The Church's Liturgy of the Hours and the Sacraments, and especially the Mass, contain readings from both New and Old Testaments. The Church encourages Catholics to read and study the Scriptures as key sources of spiritual nourishment and growth.
7. The Church is one.	There are four marks of the Church, that is, essential identifying characteristics by which she is known—one, holy, catholic, and apostolic. The descriptions that follow, like all the summaries in this section, are overviews to give the general sense of each.
	"The Church is one because of her source: 'the highest exemplar and source of this mystery is the unity, in the Trinity of Persons, of one God, the Father and the Son in the Holy Spirit'" (CCC, 813).
	"The Church is one *because of her 'soul'*: 'It is the Holy Spirit, dwelling in those who believe and pervading and ruling over the entire Church, who brings about that wonderful communion of the faithful and joins them together so intimately in Christ that he is the principle of the Church's unity'" (CCC, 813).
	The Church is one Body in Christ, in faith, in the Sacraments, and in hope (see CCC, 866). The Church is formed and united through the work of the Holy Spirit and under the leadership of the bishops united with the bishop of Rome, the Pope.
8. The Church is holy.	"The Church . . . is . . . holy. This is because Christ, the Son of God, who with the Father and the Spirit is hailed as 'alone holy,' loved the Church as his Bride, giving himself up for her so as to sanctify her . . . . The Church, then, is 'the holy People of God . . . .'" (CCC, 823)
	The Church is made holy because of her union with Christ; in turn, she makes others holy. She disseminates through her ministries the graces won by Jesus on the cross that make us holy. The Church, then, is holy in her members.
9. The Church is catholic (universal).	The Church is catholic in two ways. "First, the Church is catholic because Christ is present in her . . . . Secondly, the Church is catholic because she has been sent out by Christ on a mission to the whole of the human race" (CCC, 830-831).
	Jesus dwells in the Catholic Church. Through his Holy Spirit he energized the Church to live and act in his name. The Church is for all people, everywhere. We are called to share the Good News by what we say and how we act. The Church's missionary work continues today, as the Holy Spirit guides her to go "to the ends of the earth" (Acts 1:8) to preach, baptize, and minister in Jesus' name.

	Characteristics of Catholicism
9. The Church is catholic (universal). *continued*	Wherever we go, Catholics profess the same beliefs and celebrate the same Sacraments, under the leadership of the Pope and bishops. When at Mass, no matter where we are, we can recognize it as the same Mass as the one in our parish. Its style, language, or music may differ, but it is the same Mass, because Jesus himself again offers his eternal sacrifice to the Father, through the ministry of the priest.

Catholicism accepts people from every place and walk of life. If we want to attend Mass every day, welcome to the Catholic Church. If we want to pray the Rosary, this is a great Catholic blessing. If we want to study the Bible, the Church encourages it on all levels. If we want to serve the poor, this is a prime commitment of the Catholic Church. The Church unites diverse spiritual traditions, interests, devotions, and practices under the essential teachings of our faith. |
| **10. The Church is apostolic.** | The Church is founded and built on Peter and the twelve Apostles. After his Ascension, Jesus led the Church through Peter and the other Apostles. When they died, his leadership continued through their successors, namely the Pope and the bishops acting in union with him. Pope Benedict XVI succeeded Blessed Pope John Paul II, who succeeded Pope John Paul I, who succeeded Pope Paul VI, who succeeded Pope John XXIII. This line of Popes can be traced historically all the way back to Saint Peter, the first Pope.

The Catholic community is apostolic because we can trace our roots back to Peter and the Apostles and those who came after them. We are the sole Church led and united by the Pope and bishops, and ministered to by the ordained ministry of bishops, priests, and deacons. We profess in the Creed that the Church is one, holy, catholic, and apostolic.

Consecrated brothers and sisters and the laity exercise other important kinds of leadership. Lay ministry today has a big impact on the Catholic Church in the United States. There are lay and consecrated religious diocesan chancellors, canon lawyers, pastoral administrators, pastoral team members, liturgists, musicians, catechists, servers, readers, and others.

National Catholic organizations, social agencies, hospitals, diocesan staffs, pastoral councils, finance councils, youth organizations, and more help to bring Jesus' message to all people. Catholicism has a clear leadership and organizational structure to which many different Church ministries contribute and share in the Church mission. |
| **11. The Church advocates justice for all.** | Many Catholic organizations serve those in need. Catholic Charities provides direct aid to people in need as a result of various circumstances or natural disasters. Catholic Relief Services works around the world as an advocate for change, empowering people to overcome such things as poverty and armed conflict. Bishops lead national discussions about stopping the nuclear arms race and opposing abortion and euthanasia. They speak out on matters of social justice. The Church encourages her members to perform works of mercy by reaching out to the needy in our midst. She also advocates acts of social justice that challenge unjust social structures that keep people impoverished.

The Catholic Church emphasizes seven principles of social justice. They are: 1) life and dignity of the human person; 2) the rights and responsibilities of humans; 3) call to family, community, and participation; 4) option for the poor and vulnerable; 5) dignity of work and the rights of workers; 6) solidarity of the human family; and 7) care for God's creation. |
| **12. The Church has a positive view of creation, the world, and human nature.** | The Original Sin of Adam and Eve wounded creation. We are born into a flawed and imperfect world. Catholics believe that this world is not totally corrupt. God is very much present, and we recognize his presence in creation's beauty, truth, and love. We are made in the image of God and enter life with both goodness and imperfection.

To be saved, we need God's grace won by Jesus' death on the cross. As we reflect on our true meaning on Earth, we rely on our faith and reason to know more about God and our eternal destiny. Through faith and reason we probe more deeply into the world and human nature. In so doing, we discover how the Spirit is leading us.

For Catholics, faith and reason are partners. Catholicism fully accepts the Bible as God's word and welcomes ongoing biblical study and discussion. Often new insights come by using our reason to probe into the mysteries revealed in Scripture.

Catholics have always affirmed the importance of both faith and reason. Both are central to us and interconnected. Although we can come to certain knowledge of God's existence through reason alone, knowledge of the divine mysteries requires both faith and reason. |

The Ecumenical (General) Councils

An ecumenical council is a gathering of the bishops of the world called together, usually by the Pope, to share the responsibility of teaching and guiding the Church. It has full authority over the entire Church. This authority cannot be exercised without the Pope's agreement (see *Catechism of the Catholic Church*, 337). There have been twenty-one such worldwide councils (see CCC, 884).

Council name	Date	Topic
1. **First Council of Nicea** in NW Asia Minor	325	Council of Nicea I condemned the heresy of Arius (a priest of Alexandria), who denied Jesus' divinity. It defined the consubstantiality of God the Son with God the Father. It declared Jesus, the Son of God, *homoousios* (coequal, consubstantial, and coeternal) with the Father; fixed the date for keeping Easter; and drafted the original form of the Nicene Creed.
2. **First Council of Constantinople** near Bosporus, a strait in today's Turkey	381	Council of Constantinople I confirmed the results of the Council of Nicea; affirmed the divinity of the Holy Spirit; added clauses referring to the Holy Spirit to the Nicene Creed; and condemned all forms of Arianism and Apollinarianism.
3. **Council of Ephesus** south of Smyrna in SW Asia Minor	431	The Council of Ephesus defined Jesus as one divine Person with two natures, divine and human. He is the second Person of the Trinity, true God and true man. This Council emphasized the unity of the divine and human in the one divine Person. The divine *logos*, while retaining his divine nature, assumed a human nature. The Council declared Mary the Mother of God (*theotokos*); declared Nestorianism a heresy; and condemned Pelagianism.
4. **Council of Chalcedon** north of Constantinople	451	The Council of Chalcedon condemned Monophysitism (which claimed that there existed only one nature [the divine] in Christ). It declared Christ's two natures unmixed, unchanged, undivided, and inseparable.
5. **Second Council of Constantinople**	553	Council of Constantinople II condemned the errors of Origen and certain writings ("The Three Chapters") of Theodore, bishop of Mopsuestia, Theodoret, and Ibas, bishop of Edessa. It further confirmed the first four general councils, especially that of Chalcedon, whose authority was contested by some heretics.
6. **Third Council of Constantinople**	680–681	Council of Constantinople III put an end to Monothelitism (*Mono* [one] *thelema* [will]) by defining two natures in Christ, the human and the divine, as well as two wills in Christ, the divine and the human, which two are in perfect accord in the one divine Person, Jesus. It denounced and excommunicated Sergius (the patriarch of Constantinople who originated Monothelitism), Pyrrhus, Paul, Macarius, and all their followers.
7. **Second Council of Nicea**	787	Nicea II condemned Iconoclasm and restored and regulated the veneration of holy images. (Interesting fact: These first seven, "The Seven Great Councils of the Early Church," are the only ones on which many Eastern and Western Churches agree; they are the only test of orthodoxy among the Eastern Churches separated from Rome.)
8. **Fourth Council of Constantinople**	869	Council of Constantinople IV rejected the Acts of an irregular council (*conciliabulum*) brought together by Photius against Pope Nicholas and Ignatius the legitimate Patriarch of Constantinople; it condemned Photius, who had unlawfully seized the patriarchal dignity. The Photian Schism, however, triumphed in the Greek Church, and no other general council took place in the East.
9. **First Lateran Council** The Basilica of Saint John Lateran, Rome	1123	Lateran Council I, the first held in Rome, was concerned with the reform of the Church. It abolished the arbitrary conferring of ecclesiastical benefices by lay people, reestablished freedom from secular domination in the election of bishops and abbots, separated secular and Church affairs, reaffirmed that spiritual authority rests only in the Church, and did away with the emperor's claim to a right to interfere in a Pope's election. This Council also concerned itself with the recovery of the Holy Land from the Moslems.

Council name	Date	Topic
10. Second Lateran Council Rome	1139	The object of Lateran Council II was to put an end to the errors of Arnold of Brescia, who contended that the Church was an "invisible body," not of this world, and should own no property. It also condemned the heresy of Peter Bruys (Bruis) and his Neo-Manicheans, who denounced the Mass as a "vain show," opposed the Eucharist, marriage, and the Baptism of children—all this leading to Albigensianism, which contended that all material things are evil in themselves. This Council established rules for ecclesiastical conduct, morals, and discipline.
11. Third Lateran Council Rome	1179	Lateran Council III condemned the Albigenses and Waldenses and issued numerous decrees for the restoration of ecclesiastical discipline. It established that the election of a Pope was to be conducted by the Cardinals.
12. Fourth Lateran Council Rome	1215	Lateran Council IV issued an enlarged creed (symbol) against the Albigenses; condemned the Trinitarian errors of Abbot Joachim; made official the use of the word, "Transubstantiation;" and published seventy important reformatory decrees. This is the most important council of the Middle Ages, and it marks the culminating point of ecclesiastical life and papal power.
13. First Council of Lyons France	1245	Council of Lyons I excommunicated and deposed Emperor Frederick II for his attempt to make the Church merely a department of the state and directed a new crusade (the sixth), under the command of King Saint Louis IX, against the Saracens and Mongols.
14. Second Council of Lyons	1274	Council of Lyons II attempted a temporary reunion of the Greek Church with Rome; the word *filioque* (which expresses the procession of the Holy Spirit from both Father and Son as one principle) was added to the symbol of Constantinople; and means were sought for recovering Palestine from the Turks. It also laid down rules for papal elections.
15. Council of Vienne France	1311–1313	The Council of Vienne suppressed the Knights Templars; condemned the Beghards and the Beguines, who so stressed "inner union with God" (Quietism) that prayer and fasting became unimportant; and dealt with projects of a new crusade, the reformation of the clergy, and the teaching of Asian languages in the universities.
16. The Council of Constance Germany	1414–1418	The Council of Constance was held during the great Schism of the West. Its object was to end the divisions in the Church. The council became legitimate only when Pope Gregory XI formally convoked it. Owing to this circumstance, it succeeded in putting an end to the schism by the election of Pope Martin V, which the Council of Pisa (1403) had failed to accomplish on account of its illegality. The rightful Pope confirmed the former decrees of the synod against Wyclif and Hus. This council is ecumenical only in its last sessions (42–45 inclusive) and with respect to the decrees of earlier sessions approved by Pope Martin V.

Council name	Date	Topic
17. **Council of Basle** (Switzerland)/ **Ferrara** (Italy)/**Florence** (Italy)	1431–1439	The Council of Basle met first in that town. Its object was the religious pacification of Bohemia. Because of quarrels with the Pope, the council was transferred first to Ferrara (1438), then to Florence (1439), where a short-lived union with the Greek Church was effected, the Greeks accepting the council's definition of controverted points. The Council of Basle is only ecumenical till the end of the twenty-fifth session. Pope Eugene IV approved only those decrees dealing with the elimination of heresy, the peace of Christendom, and the reform of the Church. Many Church historians and theologians do not recognize this Council in its entirety as an ecumenical council.
18. **Fifth Lateran Council**	1512–1517	The many decrees of Lateran Council V are disciplinary. A new crusade against the Turks was also advocated, but did not proceed because of the religious upheaval in Germany caused by Martin Luther.
19. **Council of Trent** Italy	1545–1563	The Council of Trent lasted eighteen years under five Popes and was convoked to examine and condemn the errors promulgated by Martin Luther and other reformers, and to reform the discipline of the Church. Of all prior councils it lasted the longest, issued the largest number of dogmatic and reformatory decrees, such as those on the Eucharist, the Mass, the Sacraments (notably Baptism and Holy Orders), and teachings on marriage, Purgatory, indulgences, and the use of images. The Church officially designated all the writings of the Septuagint, along with all the books of the New Testament, as Sacred Scripture.
20. **First Vatican Council**	1869–1870	Vatican Council I was called by Pope Pius IX in December 1869, and lasted until July 1870, when it was adjourned. Besides important canons relating to the faith and the constitution of the Church, the council decreed the infallibility of the Pope when speaking *ex cathedra* (the seat of Peter), i.e., when as shepherd and teacher of all Christians, he defines a doctrine concerning faith or morals to be held by the whole Church.
21. **Second Vatican Council**	1962–1965	Called by Pope John XXIII, the Vatican Council II had four principal aims: first, the Church must impart to herself and to the world a new awareness of her inner nature; second, there must be a renewal and reform of the Church; third, the Church should work to bring about Christian unity; and finally, the Church should be in dialogue with today's world.

Adapted from Catholic Encyclopedia online

CATHOLIC PRAYERS AND PRACTICES

"Prayer and Christian life are inseparable, for they concern the same love and the same renunciation, proceeding from love; the same filial and loving conformity with the Father's plan of love; the same transforming union in the Holy Spirit who conforms us more and more to Christ Jesus; the same love for all men, the love with which Jesus has loved us."

—Catechism of the Catholic Church, 2745

The following prayers and practices are based in Sacred Scripture and have evolved through the Tradition of the Church. Some of the wording of the Apostles' Creed and the Nicene Creed changed when the Third Edition of the *Roman Missal* was introduced in November 2011.

Apostles' Creed

The Apostles' Creed contains a summary of the faith of the Apostles. It was developed from an early baptismal creed, and has existed since the second century. It was modified by early Church councils.

I believe in God,
　the Father almighty,
　Creator of heaven and earth,
　and in Jesus Christ, his only Son, our Lord,

At the words that follow, up to and including the Virgin Mary, all bow.

　who was conceived by the Holy Spirit,
　born of the Virgin Mary,
　suffered under Pontius Pilate,
　was crucified, died and was buried;
　he descended into hell;
　on the third day he rose again from the dead;
　he ascended into heaven,
　and is seated at the right hand of God the Father almighty;
　from there he will come to judge the living and the dead.
I believe in the Holy Spirit,
　the holy catholic Church,
　the communion of saints,
　the forgiveness of sins,
　the resurrection of the body,
　and life everlasting. Amen.

Nicene Creed

The Nicene Creed was formed as a response to the Arian heresy, which denied the divinity of Christ. It takes its name from the city of Nicea, site of the First Council of Nicea in A.D. 325. The original creed underwent modifications at ecumenical councils in Constantinople in A.D. 381 and Chalcedon in A.D. 451.

I believe in one God,
　the Father almighty,
　maker of heaven and earth,
　of all things visible and invisible.
I believe in one Lord Jesus Christ,
　the Only Begotten Son of God,
　born of the Father before all ages.
　God from God, Light from Light,
　true God from true God,
　begotten, not made, consubstantial with the Father;
　through him all things were made.
For us men and for our salvation
　he came down from heaven,

At the words that follow up to and including and became man, all bow.

　and by the Holy Spirit was incarnate of the Virgin Mary,
　and became man.
For our sake he was crucified under Pontius Pilate,
　he suffered death and was buried,
　and rose again on the third day
　in accordance with the Scriptures.
He ascended into heaven
　and is seated at the right hand of the Father.
He will come again in glory to judge the living and the dead
　and his kingdom will have no end.
I believe in the Holy Spirit, the Lord, the giver of life,
　who proceeds from the Father and the Son,
　who with the Father and the Son is adored and glorified,
　who has spoken through the prophets.
I believe in one, holy, catholic and apostolic Church.
I confess one Baptism for the forgiveness of sins
　and I look forward to the resurrection of the dead
　and the life of the world to come. Amen.

Athanasian Creed

This creed embodies Athanasius' theology of the Trinity and was composed by Hilary, bishop of Arles, in the fifth century.

Whosoever will be saved, before all things it is necessary that he hold the Catholic Faith. Which Faith except everyone do keep whole and undefiled, without doubt he shall perish everlastingly.

And the Catholic Faith is this, that we worship one God in Trinity and Trinity in Unity. Neither confounding the Persons, nor dividing the Substance.

For there is one Person of the Father, another of the Son, and another of the Holy Ghost. But the Godhead of the Father, of the Son, and of the Holy Ghost is all One, the Glory Equal, the Majesty Co-Eternal.

Such as the Father is, such is the Son, and such is the Holy Ghost.

The Father Uncreate, the Son Uncreate, and the Holy Ghost Uncreate.

The Father Incomprehensible, the Son Incomprehensible, and the Holy Ghost Incomprehensible.

The Father Eternal, the Son Eternal, and the Holy Ghost Eternal and yet they are not Three Eternals but One Eternal.

As also there are not Three Uncreated, nor Three Incomprehensibles, but One Uncreated, and One Uncomprehensible.

So likewise the Father is Almighty, the Son Almighty, and the Holy Ghost Almighty. And yet they are not Three Almighties but One Almighty.

So the Father is God, the Son is God, and the Holy Ghost is God.

And yet they are not Three Gods, but One God. So likewise the Father is Lord, the Son Lord, and the Holy Ghost Lord.

And yet not Three Lords but One Lord. For, like as we are compelled by the Christian verity to acknowledge every Person by Himself to be God and Lord, so are we forbidden by the Catholic Religion to say, there be Three Gods or Three Lords.

The Father is made of none, neither created, nor begotten. The Son is of the Father alone; not made, nor created, but begotten.

The Holy Ghost is of the Father, and of the Son neither made, nor created, nor begotten, but proceeding.

So there is One Father, not Three Fathers; One Son, not Three Sons; One Holy Ghost, not Three Holy Ghosts.

And in this Trinity none is afore or after Other, None is greater or less than Another, but the whole Three Persons are Co-eternal together, and Co-equal.

So that in all things, as is aforesaid, the Unity is Trinity, and the Trinity is Unity is to be worshipped.

He therefore that will be saved, must thus think of the Trinity.

Furthermore, it is necessary to everlasting Salvation, that he also believe rightly the Incarnation of our Lord Jesus Christ.

For the right Faith is, that we believe and confess, that our Lord Jesus Christ, the Son of God, is God and Man.

God, of the substance of the Father, begotten before the worlds; and Man, of the substance of His mother, born into the world.

Perfect God and Perfect Man, of a reasonable Soul and human Flesh subsisting.

Equal to the Father as touching His Godhead, and inferior to the Father as touching His Manhood.

Who, although He be God and Man, yet He is not two, but One Christ.

One, not by conversion of the Godhead into Flesh, but by taking of the Manhood into God.

One altogether, not by confusion of substance, but by Unity of Person.

For as the reasonable soul and flesh is one Man, so God and Man is one Christ.

Who suffered for our salvation, descended into Hell, rose again the third day from the dead.

He ascended into Heaven, He sitteth on the right hand of the Father, God Almighty, from whence he shall come to judge the quick and the dead.

At whose coming all men shall rise again with their bodies, and shall give account for their own works.

And they that have done good shall go into life everlasting, and they that have done evil into everlasting fire.

This is the Catholic Faith, which except a man believe faithfully and firmly, he cannot be saved.

The Lord's Prayer

Jesus "was praying at a certain place, and when he ceased, one of his disciples said to him, 'Lord, teach us to pray, as John taught his disciples.'"[1] In response to this request the Lord entrusts to his disciples and to his Church the fundamental Christian prayer. St. Luke presents a brief text of five petitions,[2] while St. Matthew gives a more developed version of seven petitions.[3] The liturgical tradition of the Church has retained St. Matthew's text (CCC, 2759).

Our Father, who art in heaven,
hallowed be thy name;
thy kingdom come,
thy will be done on earth as it is in heaven.
Give us this day our daily bread;
and forgive us our trespasses
as we forgive those who trespass against us;
and lead us not into temptation,
but deliver us from evil.
Amen.

Pater Noster

Pater noster, qui es in caelis:
sanctificetur nomen tuum;
adveniat regnum tuum;
fiat voluntas tua, sicut in caelo, et in terra.
Panem nostrum quotidianum da nobis hodie;
et dimitte nobis debita nostra,
sicut et nos dimittimus debitoribus nostris;
et ne nos inducas in tentationem;
sed libera nos a malo.
Amen.

Glory to the Father

Glory to the Father,
and to the Son,
and to the Holy Spirit,
as it was in the beginning,
is now, and will be
forever.
Amen.

Gloria Patri

Glória Patri,
et Fílio
et Spíritui Sancto,
Sicut erat in princípio,
et nunc et semper
et in sáecula saeculórum.
Amen.

Prayer to the Holy Spirit

Come, Holy Spirit, fill the hearts of your faithful.
And kindle in them the fire of your love.
Send forth your Spirit and they shall be created.
And you shall renew the face of the earth.
Let us pray:
Lord, by the light of the Holy Spirit
you have taught the hearts of your faithful.
In the same Spirit, help us to choose what is right
and always rejoice in your consolation.
We ask this through Christ our Lord.
Amen.

Veni, Sancte Spiritus, reple tuorum corda fidelium,
et tui amoris in eis ignem accende.
Emitte Spiritum tuum et creabuntur;
Et renovabis faciem terrae.
Oremus:
Deus, qui corda fidelium Sancti Spiritus illustratione docuisti.
Da nobis in eodem Spiritu recta sapere,
et de eius semper consolatione gaudere.
Per Christum Dominum nostrum.
Amen.

The Hail Mary

Beginning with Mary's unique cooperation with the working of the Holy Spirit, the Churches developed their prayer to the holy Mother of God, centering it on the person of Christ manifested in his mysteries. In countless hymns and antiphons expressing this prayer, two movements usually alternate with one another: the first "magnifies" the Lord for the "great things" he did for his lowly servant and through her for all human beings;[29] the second entrusts the supplications and praises of the children of God to the Mother of Jesus, because she now knows the humanity which, in her, the Son of God espoused. This twofold movement of prayer to Mary has found a privileged expression in the Ave Maria *(CCC, 2675–76).*

Hail, Mary, full of grace,
The Lord is with thee.
Blessed art thou among women
and blessed is the fruit of thy womb, Jesus.
Holy Mary, Mother of God,
pray for us sinners,
now and at the hour of our death.
Amen.

Ave Maria

Ave María, grátia plena,
Dóminus tecum.
Benedícta tu in muliéribus,
et benedíctus fructus ventris tui, Jesus.
Sancta María, Mater Dei,
ora pro nobis peccatóribus,
nunc et in hora mortis nostrae.
Amen.

The Magnificat

The Magnificat (also called the Canticle of Mary) is recorded in the Gospel according to Luke (1:46-55) and is Mary's joyous prayer in response to her cousin Elizabeth's greeting (Luke 1:41-45). This prayer forms part of the Church's prayer in the Liturgy of the Hours.

My soul proclaims the greatness of the Lord,
and my spirit rejoices in God my Savior,
for he has looked with favor on his lowly servant.
From this day all generations will call me blessed:
the Almighty has done great things for me,
and holy is his Name.
He has mercy on those who fear him in every generation.
He has shown the strength of his arm;
he has scattered the proud in their conceit.
He has cast down the mighty from their thrones,
and has lifted up the lowly.
He has filled the hungry with good things,
and the rich he has sent away empty.
He has come to the help of his servant Israel
for he has remembered his promise of mercy,
the promise he made to our fathers,
to Abraham and his children forever.
Glory to the Father and to the Son
    and to the Holy Spirit,
as it was in the beginning, is now,
    and will be forever.
Amen.

Magníficat ánima mea Dóminum,
et exsultávit spíritus meus in Deo
    salvatóre meo,
quia respéxit humilitátem
    ancíllæ suæ.
Ecce enim ex hoc beátam me dicent
    omnes generatiónes,
quia fecit mihi magna, qui potens est,
et sanctum nomen eius,
et misericórdia eius in progénies et
    progénies timéntibus eum.

Fecit poténtiam in bráchio suo,
dispérsit supérbos mente cordis sui;
depósuit poténtes de sede
et exaltávit húmiles.
Esuriéntes implévit bonis
et dívites dimísit inánes.
Suscépit Ísrael púerum suum,
recordátus misericórdiæ,
sicut locútus est ad patres nostros,
Ábraham et sémini eius in sæcula.
Glória Patri et Fílio
et Spirítui Sancto.
Sicut erat in princípio, et nunc
    et semper,
et in sæcula sæculórum.
Amen.

Act of Contrition (traditional)

O my God, I am heartily sorry for having offended you, and I detest all my sins, because of your just punishments, but most of all because they offend you, my God, who are all good and deserving of all my love. I firmly resolve, with the help of your grace, to sin no more and to avoid the near occasion of sin.

Act of Contrition (contemporary)

My God, I am sorry for my sins with all my heart. In choosing to do wrong and failing to do good, I have sinned against you whom I should love above all things. I firmly intend, with your help, to do penance, to sin no more, and to avoid whatever leads me to sin. Our Savior Jesus Christ suffered and died for us. In his name, my God, have mercy.

Prayer for Justice

Father, you have given all peoples one common origin.
It is your will that they be gathered together
as one family in yourself.
Fill the hearts of mankind with the fire of your love
and with the desire to ensure justice for all.
By sharing the good things you give us,
may we secure an equality for all
our brothers and sisters throughout the world.
May there be an end to division, strife, and war.
May there be a dawning of a truly human society
built on love and peace.
We ask this in the name of Jesus, our Lord.
Amen.

The Rosary

The Rosary is called the Psalter of Mary *because all fifteen of its mysteries, with their one hundred and fifty* Aves, *correspond to the number of Psalms. Saint Dominic popularized the fifteen-decade Rosary. He is so connected with this form of the Rosary that often it is referred to as the Dominican Rosary. Pope John Paul II added five luminous mysteries to the previous fifteen glorious, joyful, and sorrowful mysteries. The Rosary is the most well-known and used form of chaplet (a devotion using beads; from a French word meaning "crown" or "wreath"). There are other chaplets, including Saint Bridget's Chaplet and the Chaplet of the Immaculate Conception.*

1. Sign of the Cross and Apostles' Creed
2. Lord's Prayer
3. Three Hail Marys
4. Glory to the Father
5. Announce mystery
6. Lord's Prayer
7. Ten Hail Marys
8. Glory to the Father

Repeat last four steps, meditating on the other mysteries of the Rosary.

The Mysteries of the Rosary and Recommended Scriptural Meditations

Joyful Mysteries
(Mondays and Saturdays)

1. The Annunciation (humility)
   Isaiah 7:10-14; Luke 1:26-38
2. The Visitation (charity)
   Isaiah 40:1-11; Luke 1:39-45; John 1:19-23
3. The Nativity (poverty)
   Micah 5:1-4; Matthew 2:1-12; Luke 2:1-20; Galatians 4:4
4. The Presentation (obedience)
   Luke 2:22-35; Hebrews 9:6-14
5. The Finding of Jesus in the Temple (piety)
   Luke 2:41-52; John 12:44-50; 1 Corinthians 2:6-16

Sorrowful Mysteries
(Tuesdays and Fridays)

1. The Agony in the Garden (repentance)
   Matthew 26:36-46; Mark 14:26-42; Luke 22:39-53; John 18:1-12
2. The Scourging at the Pillar (purity)
   Isaiah 50:5-9; Matthew 27:15-26; Mark 15:1-15
3. The Crowning with Thorns (courage)
   Isaiah 52:13–53:10; Matthew 16:24-28, 27:27-31; Mark 15:16-19; Luke 23:6-11; John 19:1-7
4. The Carrying of the Cross (patience)
   Mark 8:31-38; Matthew 16:20-25; Luke 23:26-32; John 19:17-22; Philippians 2:6-11
5. The Crucifixion (self-renunciation)
   Mark 15:33-39; Luke 23:33-46; John 19:23-37; Acts 22:22-24; Hebrews 9:11-14

Glorious Mysteries
(Sundays and Wednesdays)

1. The Resurrection (faith)
   Matthew 28:1-10; Mark 16:1-18; Luke 24:1-12; John 20:1-10; Romans 6:1-14; 1 Corinthians 15:1-11
2. The Ascension (hope)
   Matthew 28:16-20; Luke 24:44-53; Acts 1:1-11; Ephesians 2:4-7
3. The Descent of the Holy Spirit Upon the Apostles (love)
   John 14:15-21; Acts 2:1-11, 4:23-31, 11:15-18
4. The Assumption (eternal happiness)
   John 11:17-27; 1 Corinthians 15:20-28, 42-57; Revelation 21:1-6
5. The Coronation of Mary (Marian devotion)
   Matthew 5:1-12; 2 Peter 3:10; Revelation 7:1-4, 9-12, 21:1-6

Luminous Mysteries

(Thursdays)

1. Baptism in the Jordan (commitment)
   Matthew 3:13-17; Mark 1:9-11; Luke 3:21-22; John 1:29-34

2. The Wedding at Cana (fidelity)
   John 2:3-5, 7-10; John 13:14-15; Luke 6:27-28, 37; Luke 9:23; John 15:12

3. Proclamation of the Kingdom of God (conversion)
   Mark 1:14-15; Luke 4:18-19, 21; Matthew 5:38-39, 43-44; Matthew 6:19-21; Matthew 7:12; Matthew 10:8

4. The Transfiguration (promise)
   Matthew 5:14, 16; Matthew 17:1-2, 5, 7-8; Luke 9:30-33; John 1:4-5, 18; 2 Corinthians 3:18

5. Institution of the Eucharist (grace)
   John 13:1; Matthew 26:18; Luke 22:15-16, 19-20; Matthew 5:14, 19-20; 1 Corinthians 11:26; John 17:20-21; 1 Corinthians 12:13, 26-27

The Ten Commandments

The division and numbering of the commandments have varied in the course of history. The Catechism of the Catholic Church *follows the division established by Saint Augustine which has become the Catholic (and Lutheran) tradition. The first three concern love of God and the other seven love of neighbor. (see Exodus 20:1-17, Deuteronomy 5:1-21)*

1. I am the Lord your God: you shall not have strange gods before me.

2. You shall not take the name of the Lord your God in vain.

3. Remember to keep holy the Lord's day.

4. Honor your father and your mother.

5. You shall not kill.

6. You shall not commit adultery.

7. You shall not steal.

8. You shall not bear false witness against your neighbor.

9. You shall not covet your neighbor's wife.

10. You shall not covet your neighbor's goods.

The Eight Beatitudes

The Gospels according to Luke and Matthew contain the Beatitudes. They are statements of praise, stressing the joy of those who participate in the Kingdom of God. The Beatitudes also tell us about what it means to be a member of the Church. (See Matthew 5:3-11; Luke 6:20-26.)

1. Blessed are the poor in spirit, for theirs is the kingdom of heaven.

2. Blessed are those who mourn, for they will be comforted.

3. Blessed are the meek, for they will inherit the earth.

4. Blessed are those who hunger and thirst for righteousness, for they will be filled.

5. Blessed are the merciful, for they will receive mercy.

6. Blessed are the pure in heart, for they will see God.

7. Blessed are the peacemakers, for they will be called children of God.

8. Blessed are those who are persecuted for righteousness' sake, for theirs is the kingdom of heaven.

The Seven Corporal Works of Mercy

". . . Just as you did it to one of the least of these who are members of my family, you did it to me" (Matthew 25:31-46).

1. Feed the hungry.

2. Give drink to the thirsty.

3. Clothe the naked.

4. Shelter the homeless.

5. Visit the sick.

6. Visit the imprisoned.

7. Bury the dead.

The Seven Spiritual Works of Mercy

Based on Christ's teachings and Christian practice since the Apostles.

1. Counsel the doubtful.

2. Instruct the ignorant.

3. Admonish sinners.

4. Comfort the afflicted.

5. Forgive offenses.

6. Bear wrongs patiently.

7. Pray for the living and the dead.

VOICES OF TRADITION

Throughout this course you've read about many different people of faith. Below you'll find a prayer, a quote, or a biography of some of them.

Saint Paul (d. A.D. 65)

Saint Paul traveled widely through Asia Minor, Greece, and Rome in the first century. His letters are some of the most influential in Christian thought. According to history, Saint Paul was imprisoned and said to have been beheaded by the Emperor Nero. He was buried in Rome in A.D. 65. In A.D. 390 his body was placed in a sarcophagus and put in a basilica by Emperor Theodosius. Part of the basilica collapsed in A.D. 433 and a marble tombstone covered the sarcophagus. After a fire in 1823, a modern basilica, St. Paul's Outside the Walls, was built on that site. The sarcophagus and tombstone were buried under concrete and the papal altar was placed on top of it.

Since Jubilee 2000 there has been much interest in unearthing the sarcophagus. Excavation began in 2002 and was recently completed. The resting place of Saint Paul is now on public view. The original inscription on the sarcophagus reads: *Paulo Apostolo Mart,* or Paul Apostle Martyr.

Adapted from BBC

Saint Teresa of Ávila (1515–1582)

"I began to think of the soul as if it were a castle made of a single diamond or of very clear crystal, in which there are many rooms, just as in Heaven there are many mansions. Now if we think carefully over this . . . the soul of the righteous man is nothing but a paradise, in which, as God tells us, He takes His delight. For what do you think a room will be like which is the delight of a King so mighty, so wise, so pure and so full of all that is good? I can find nothing with which to compare the great beauty of a soul and its great capacity."

—Saint Teresa of Ávila

Writing in 1577, Saint Teresa of Ávila, a sixteenth-century nun and Doctor of the Church (1970), reveals her image of the soul as a castle made of a single diamond in a book called *Interior Castle.* Her description takes the reader through the various rooms of the castle through which the soul must progress before reaching the innermost chamber, which she calls the place of communion with God.

Adapted from Catholic First

Saint Thomas Aquinas (1225–1274)

Saint Thomas Aquinas is acclaimed as one of the most influential and greatest theologians of the Catholic Church and was named a Doctor of the Church by Pope Pius V. It is hard to imagine that he was once called a "dumb ox." He acquired the nickname because he was, as a young boy, big, slow, and solemn. Saint Albertus Magnus (Albert the Great), who taught him in Cologne, said of Saint Thomas Aquinas, "You call him a Dumb Ox; I tell you that the Dumb Ox will bellow so loud that his bellowing will fill the world." In 1933, the celebrated English author G.K. Chesterton wrote a profile of the saint titled, *Saint Thomas Aquinas: The Dumb Ox.*

Saint Thomas Aquinas was canonized in 1323 and is the patron of Catholic universities, colleges, and schools.

Adapted from *Catholic Treasures*

Father Thomas á Kempis (1379–1471)

Happy is that soul, which heareth the Lord speaking within her, and from His mouth receiveth the word of comfort. Happy ears, which receive the strains of the divine whisper, and take no notice of the whisperings of the world. Happy ears indeed, which hearken to truth itself teaching within, and not to the voice which soundeth without. Happy eyes, which are shut to outward things, but are attentive to things interior. Happy they, who penetrate into internal things, and endeavour to prepare themselves more and more by daily exercises for attaining to heavenly secrets.

—*The Imitation of Christ*

Thomas á Kempis, originally named Thomas Hemerken, was a fifteenth-century German monk who spent his entire monastic life at the monastery of Mount St. Agnes at Zwolle, northeast of Amsterdam. His works stressed using the example of Christ to seek out a spiritual lifestyle. His devotional, *The Imitation of Christ,* based on the life and teachings of Jesus, has been translated into more languages than any other book except the Bible. It was written as an instruction for his fellow monks and much of it is laid out as a conversation between Jesus and the Disciple. Saint Ignatius of Loyola, who read a chapter from this book every day, often gave it as a gift to those he met.

Adapted from *Faith Alone*

Saint Francis of Assisi (1181–1226)

Saint Francis of Assisi, founder of the Franciscan Order, was born at Assisi in Umbria (central Italy). He worked with his father, a wealthy cloth merchant. Despite a life of ease, Francis sought out God and the Church. While praying in the old chapel at Saint Damian's, Francis heard a voice telling him, "Francis, repair my house which is falling into ruin." Francis thought this "house" referred to that particular chapel, so he sold the fabric from his father's shop for money to repair the church. His father renounced him as his heir. After that incident, Francis begged for stones and rebuilt the chapel with his own hands.

But it was the Church that Francis was called to rebuild. His life took a new direction and he started living a simple life directed only by the Gospel. His followers joined him in preaching the Gospel. Francis received approval for his brotherhood from Pope Innocent III. Within ten years his order had increased to five thousand men.

Francis suffered with the stigmata, the visible marks of the five wounds of Christ on the cross. He died at the age of forty-five. He wished to be buried on a hill outside Assisi, where criminals were executed. However his body was placed in the church of St. George, where he had first preached. Pope Gregory IX canonized Francis at St. George's on July 16, 1228. The next day the Pope laid the first stone of the great double church of St. Francis (now known as the Papal Basilica of St. Francis of Assisi). In 1230, Francis' body was buried under the high altar in the lower church. His coffin was discovered in 1818. Francis is considered the patron saint of ecologists and merchants.

Adapted from Eternal Word Television Network

Saint Thomas More (1478–1535)

"I die the king's good servant, and God's first."

—Saint Thomas More (Translation of the Paris Newsletter account, August 4, 1535)

Saint Thomas More was born in London. His family had a long tradition of service to England. His grandfather was a lawyer, alderman, and then sheriff. His father was a lawyer, then a judge. He studied law at Oxford and served in Parliament.

When he was forty-one, Saint Thomas More accepted the invitation to join King Henry VIII's service. He served in many capacities and became Lord Chancellor in 1529. As Lord Chancellor, he refused to sign a letter asking the Pope to annul King Henry VIII's marriage to Catherine of Aragon. He also refused to take an Oath of Supremacy declaring the king the supreme head of the Church of England. For this he was accused of treason and beheaded.

His body of work includes biographies, histories, poems, treatises on religious subjects, instructions and prayers, and even his own epitaph. He was canonized by Pope Pius XI in 1935 and is the patron saint of lawyers.

Adapted from *Catholic Encyclopedia*

Saint Ignatius of Loyola (1491–1556)

Saint Ignatius was born at the Castle of Loyola in Guipúzcoa, Spain. He became a page, and then a soldier in the Spanish Army fighting against the French. After suffering an injury to his leg, he spent a year recuperating. During that time he read the lives of the saints, and decided to become a saint himself.

He lived a life of extreme poverty and self-denial. He devised a system of spiritual exercises, which he hoped would help people encounter Christ on a personal level.

His education included eleven years in various universities. A group of young men gathered around him. Together they traveled to Rome and presented themselves to the Pope. The Pope saw this group as an antidote to the Protestants, who were rejecting Church leadership. In 1540, the Pope designated Ignatius' group to be a new society—the Society of Jesus, or the Jesuits.

Ignatius founded the Gregorian University in Rome and a college in Germany designed to train priests. Within twenty-five years, more than one thousand Jesuits ran one hundred colleges in Europe and the New World. Their rigorous program of study included the Ignatian program of spiritual exercises, and created an educated group of Catholics who could challenge the best Protestant minds of the time.

He was canonized in 1622.

Saint Irenaeus of Lyons (c. A.D. 115–202)

Saint Irenaeus was born in Smyrna, Asia Minor (modern Izmir, Turkey), but little is known of him until A.D. 177. Prior to being named bishop of Lugdunum in Gaul (now Lyons, France), history tells us that he probably had been a presbyter of the church at Lyons for several years. He was a disciple of Polycarp, who was a disciple of John the Evangelist.

His most famous work is *Against Heresies,* which describes and refutes Gnosticism (the conviction that matter is evil). He based his arguments on the works of Saint John, whose Gospel is often cited by the Gnostics.

There is not much information about his later years. Jerome mentions him as a martyr, although there is no evidence of how he died. He was buried under the church of Saint John in Lyons, later named Saint Irenaeus. The Calvinist Huguenots destroyed his tomb in 1562.

Saint Iranaeus is the patron saint of the Archdiocese of Mobile, Alabama.

Adapted from *Religion Facts*

Saint Augustine (A.D. 354–430)

God of life, there are days when the burdens we carry
chafe our shoulders and wear us down;
when the road seems dreary and endless,
the skies gray and threatening;
when our lives have no music in them
and our hearts are lonely,
and our souls have lost their courage.
Flood the path with light, we beseech you;
turn our eyes to where the skies are full of promise.

—Saint Augustine

Prayers of the Saints: An Inspired Collection of Holy Wisdom, ed. Woodeene Koenig Bricker [San Francisco: Harper Collins, 1996]

Saint Jerome (c. A.D. 340–420)

Saint Jerome, one of the four Latin Doctors of the Church, was born in Dalmatia (modern day Croatia), studied in Rome, and traveled to the Holy Land. He spent three years in the Syrian Desert before starting the Latin translations of Hebrew and Greek manuscripts of the Bible.

Many famous painters have depicted Saint Jerome's time in the desert. One of the most famous paintings is "Saint Jerome Praying in the Wilderness" (c. 1480), an unfinished painting by Leonardo da Vinci which is now in the Vatican Museums in Rome. It depicts an elderly, gaunt Saint Jerome kneeling on rocky ground, gazing toward a crucifix. He holds a rock in his right hand with which he is traditionally shown beating his chest in penance. At his feet is a lion, which allegedly became a loyal companion after he extracted a thorn from its paw. The lion, the stone, and a cardinal's hat are the traditional attributes of the saint. To the right of the painting is a faintly sketched church, seen through the opening in the rocks. The church's presence may reflect Saint Jerome's position in Western Christianity as one of the Doctors of the Church.

Adapted from Universal Leonardo

Saint Clare of Assisi (1193–1253)

Look, look on Jesus, poor and crucified, look on this Holy One, who for your love has died, and remember as you contemplate the sacred mysteries, this Jesus whom you gaze upon, loves you most tenderly.

—Saint Clare of Assisi

Saint Clare was born in Assisi, Italy, to a noble family. At a time when most women married, she was determined not to marry. She encountered Saint Francis and often met with him, praying and discussing her spiritual journey.

When Clare told her parents that she wanted to join Saint Francis in his life of poverty, they refused to agree. She and Saint Francis received permission from the local bishop, and on Palm Sunday, 1212, Francis received Clare. Her hair was cut, and she was given a coarse robe and cord to wear. A woolen cloth was placed on her head. She was consecrated into the Second Order of Franciscans and placed under the protection of the Benedictine Sisters of St. Paul until Francis could set up a convent for her.

Francis turned over the grounds of San Damiano to Clare. She attracted many young women to follow the ways of Jesus in a simple life of poverty and prayer. Her best friend, her sister, and even her mother joined the convent. The Order of Poor Clares had Clare as their superior.

Saint Clare lived a life of prayer and fasting. She wrote a rule for the community to follow and presented it to the Pope for approval. She died two days after receiving the approval and was buried at San Damiano Church. Pope Alexander IV canonized her in 1255. In 1260, when the people of Assisi built a larger monastery for Clare's sisters, her body was transferred to the Basilica of Santa Chiara in the town of Assisi. Saint Clare is what is known as an "incorruptible"; that is, her body has not decayed over the years.

Saint Joan of Arc (1412–1431)

The patroness of soldiers and of France, Saint Joan of Arc was born in the village of Domrémy, near the province of Lorraine. She is said to have heard the voices of Saint Michael, Saint Catherine of Alexandria, and Saint Margaret of Antioch, which told her to go to the King of France to help him reconquer his kingdom. At that time the English king was after the French throne.

Saint Joan was only seventeen when she told the King of England to withdraw his troops from French soil. She was given a small army with which she entered Orléans on May 8, 1429. Due to her military successes she assisted Charles VII to enter Rheims on July 17, 1429, and be crowned with her at his side.

In 1430 she was captured by the Burgundians and sold to the English. She was imprisoned, tried by an ecclesiastical court, and condemned to death as a heretic. She was burned at the stake at Rouen on May 30, 1431. At her death, she asked for a crucifix, which she held up until she died. Her body was thrown into the River Seine. She was later exonerated of all guilt, canonized in 1920 by Pope Benedict XV, and called Saint Joan of Arc, the Maid of Orleans and patroness of France.

Saint Anselm

"O God, let me know you and love you
so that I may find joy in you;
and if I cannot do so fully in this life,
let me at least make some progress every day,
until at last that knowledge, love and joy
come to me in all their plenitude.
While I am here on earth let me know you fully;
let my love for you grow deeper here,
so that there I may love you fully.
On earth then I shall have great joy in hope,
and in heaven complete joy in the fulfillment of my hope."

—Saint Anselm

Saint Joseph

All we know about Saint Joseph comes to us from Scripture. Matthew 13:55 tells us that Joseph was a working man, a carpenter. His family was descended from David, the king of Israel (Matthew 1:1-16 and Luke 3:23-38). He was betrothed to Mary and took care of her and Jesus (Luke 2:1-7). He was a man of faith, obedient to God (Matthew 2:13-23), and a loving father to Jesus (Luke 2:48, 4:22).

Because we do not read about Saint Joseph during Jesus' public life, at his death, or Resurrection, many historians believe he probably had died before Jesus entered public ministry.

Saint Joseph is the patron of the dying, the universal Church, fathers, carpenters, social justice, and Belgium, as well as many other cities, countries, and Catholic dioceses around the world.

Adapted from Catholic Encyclopedia

Saint Anne

"Good Saint Anne, I have come to honor you and invoke you with all these pilgrims in the Shrine of Beaupré. Since the beginning of the Church in Canada, many people have experienced the effect of your power and kindness. Extend your kindness to the Church of today. May it renew its fervour to accomplish the Mission that Christ has confided to it and may Redemption become more and more abundant in this world that is so in need of light, justice, and peace."

—Pope John Paul II, September 10, 1984

Although they are not named in the Bible, ancient tradition claims that Saint Anne was the wife of Saint Joachim and mother to Mary. Tradition says that Anne was quite elderly when Mary was born, and that Mary was their only child. Her name first appears in Christian writing around A.D. 150.

Devotion to Saint Anne became very popular in France at the settlement of Quebec. Native Americans (called the First Nations in Canada) called Saint Anne "Grandmother in the Faith." In 1876, Saint Anne was proclaimed the patron saint of Quebec and co-patron of Canada.

One of her most famous shrines is at Sainte-Anne-de-Beaupré in the province of Quebec. The village of Sainte-Anne-de-Beaupré near Quebec City is named for and home of the Basilica of Sainte-Anne-de-Beaupré, a major Catholic shrine and place of healing that attracts pilgrims every year.

The first basilica was destroyed by fire in 1922 and replaced by the present basilica, which was completed in 1926. In 1984, Pope John Paul II visited the shrine, which is the first shrine in North America, and the largest shrine in the world dedicated to Sainte-Anne.

Adapted from Sainte-Anne-de-Beaupré Sanctuaire Shrine

Saint George (c. A.D. 263–303)

Not much is known of Saint George's early years. He was born in Lydia near Jerusalem. At seventeen, he enlisted as a cavalry soldier in the army of the Roman Emperor Diocletian. He became a high-ranking officer, rising through the ranks because he was an able soldier and horseman. When the emperor began persecuting Christians, George, who was a devout Christian, requested an audience with the emperor, at which time he pleaded with him to stop persecuting Christians. The emperor commanded George to recant his religion. When he refused, George was arrested, tortured, and finally put to death on April 23, 303. George was canonized a saint by Pope Gelasius in A.D. 494.

The most famous story attached to Saint George is called the "Golden Legend." It is the story of a dragon that lived in a swamp. No army could defeat it. The monster ate sheep and cattle each day; when these were scarce, lots were drawn and young girls were substituted. According to the story, Saint George blessed himself, rode to battle against the dragon, and killed it in a single blow with his lance. He was awarded money, which he then distributed to the poor before he rode away.

Due to his chivalrous behavior, devotion to Saint George became popular in Europe after the tenth century. His symbol was a red cross on a white background. It became the banner for the knights who fought in the Crusades. He is considered the patron saint of Scouting, England, Canada, and many other cities, countries, and groups

Adapted from Britannia Online

Saint Michael the Archangel

"May prayer strengthen us for the spiritual battle we are told about in the Letter to the Ephesians: 'Draw strength from the Lord and from His mighty power' (Ephesians 6:10). The Book of Revelation refers to this same battle, recalling before our eyes the image of St. Michael the Archangel (Revelation 12:7). Pope Leo XIII certainly had a very vivid recollection of this scene when, at the end of the last century, he introduced a special prayer to St. Michael throughout the Church. Although this prayer is no longer recited at the end of Mass, I ask everyone not to forget it and to recite it to obtain help in the battle against forces of darkness and against the spirit of this world."

—Pope John Paul II, April 24, 1994

Saint Michael the Archangel,

defend us in battle.

Be our protection against the wickedness and snares of the devil.

May God rebuke him, we humbly pray;

and do Thou, O Prince of the Heavenly Host -

by the Divine Power of God -

cast into hell, satan and all the evil spirits,

who roam throughout the world seeking the ruin of souls.

Amen.

There are writings about Saint Michael the Archangel and devotion to him in Jewish, Christian, and Muslim cultures. He is considered the leader of the army of God during the Lucifer uprising, the guardian angel of Israel, and the guardian and protector of the Church.

Saint Michael is mentioned four times in Scripture. Because of these references, Christian tradition gives to Saint Michael four offices: to fight against Satan; to rescue the souls of the faithful from the power of the enemy, especially at the hour of death; to be the champion of God's people; and to call away from earth and bring men's souls to judgment.

Saint Michael is the patron of Germany, police officers and soldiers, as well as many other groups.

Adapted from Catholic Encyclopedia

Saint Rose of Lima (1586–1617)

Apart from the cross, there is no other ladder by which we may get to heaven. When we serve the poor and the sick we serve Jesus. We must not fail to help our neighbors, because in them we serve Jesus.

—Saint Rose of Lima

The patron saint of Latin America and the Philippines, Saint Rose of Lima was born in present-day Lima, Peru, and named Isabel at birth. At her confirmation, she took the name Rose, because as an infant her face had been seen transformed by a mystical rose.

She was troubled with terrible loneliness and sadness at times in her life, and sometimes for her God seemed far away. Yet she cheerfully offered all these troubles to him. In fact, during her last sickness she prayed "Lord, increase my sufferings, and with them increase your love in my heart."

Saint Rose emulated Saint Catherine of Siena and fasted three times a week. She did needlework and sold it so that she could help the sick and infirm in her community. She entered a Dominican convent and took the vow of perpetual virginity. She died at age thirty-one and many miracles followed her death. Pope Clement X canonized her in 1671, the first American to be so honored.

Adapted from Catholic Fire

Saint Olaf (995–1030)

Saint Olaf was the son of King Harald Grenske of Norway. In his early years he traveled as a Viking to England, where he was involved in many battles and became interested in Christianity. He was named king of Norway (1015–1028) and made Christianity the basis of his kingdom. He brought many bishops and priests from England. He is regarded by the Norwegians of our day as the great champion of national independence. He died on the battlefield and many miracles were reported after his death. Saint Olaf was canonized in 1888 and is the patron saint of Norway.

The Royal Norwegian Order of Saint Olaf was founded by King Oscar I in 1847 and is conferred as "a reward for distinguished services rendered to the country and mankind." Recipients of this award have included Charles deGaulle, Lech Walesa, Nelson Mandela, and Winston Churchill.

Adapted from Catholic Encyclopedia

Saint Patrick (A.D. 387–461)

One of the world's most popular saints, Saint Patrick was born in Scotland to Roman parents. At sixteen, he was captured and taken to Ireland as a slave. During his captivity, he turned to God in prayer. He escaped when he was twenty after having a dream in which he was told to leave Ireland by going to the coast. Some sailors there took him back to Britain, where he reunited with his family.

After another dream in which the people of Ireland asked him to return, he began his studies for the priesthood. He was ordained a priest and later a bishop. It was then that he was sent to preach the Gospel in Ireland. He was sent to minister to the Christians already there and to convert the rest of the population who were mostly Druids or pagans. With his disciples, he preached and converted thousands. For forty years he built churches wherever he went and the country converted to Christianity. He is known for using the shamrock to explain the mystery of the Blessed Trinity.

He died on March 17, the day we still celebrate his life. He is the patron saint of Ireland and Nigeria. In the United States there is a parade and celebration every March 17 to celebrate Saint Patrick's life. In the first St. Patrick's Day parade in the United States, Irish soldiers serving in the English military marched through New York City on March 17, 1762.

Adapted from Catholic Encyclopedia

Saint Francis Xavier (1506–1552)

Saint Francis Xavier was born in the family castle of Xavier, near Pamplona, Spain. While studying at the University of Paris, he met Ignatius Loyola. He joined with him and in 1534 became one of the seven who founded the Society of Jesus (the Jesuits).

He was ordained in 1537, went to Rome, and in 1540 was ordered with another Jesuit to minister in the Far East as the first Jesuit missionaries. When he arrived in India in 1542, he discovered that the Indian converts knew very little about Christian beliefs. He wrote basic prayers and the creed in simple rhymes that were easy for the new converts to remember and recite. Indian children would follow him around and recite the Lord's Prayer and other prayers with him. Through him, Catholicism gained a firm foothold in India, Japan, and Southeast Asia.

Pope Pius X declared Francis Xavier patron saint of Christian missions. He is also known as "the Apostle to India" and as "the Apostle to Japan," since he at a later time also traveled to that country. He was canonized with Saint Ignatius of Loyola in 1622 by Pope Gregory XV, and is one of the patron saints of India, Borneo, and Japan.

Saint James the Greater (d. A.D. 44)

Saint James the Greater, older brother to Saint John the Apostle, is called "the greater" because he became an Apostle before Saint James the Lesser. He was a disciple of Saint John the Baptist and a fisherman, and left everything to follow Christ (Matthew 4:22).

It was James who went with Jesus when he raised Jairus' daughter. He was with Jesus when he was transfigured on the mountaintop and in the Garden of Gethsemane. Several incidents scattered through the Gospels suggest that James, along with his brother John, had a particular personality indicated by the name "Boanerges," sons of thunder, given to them by Christ (Mark 3:17); that is, they were burning and impetuous in their evangelical zeal. He preached in Samaria, Judea, and Spain and was the first Apostle to be martyred (Acts 12:1).

His work in Spain probably led to his patronage of the country and all things Spanish. For centuries, the Spanish army rode into battle with the battle cry "Santiago!" ("Saint James!"). He is also the patron saint of Chile, Guatemala, and Nicaragua.

Adapted from Catholic Encyclopedia

Saint Ignatius of Antioch

> "The goals of the earth and the kingdoms of this world shall profit me nothing. It is better for me to die for the sake of Jesus Christ than to reign over the ends of the earth."
>
> —Saint Ignatius of Antioch, letter to the Romans

The second Bishop of Antioch, Syria, Saint Ignatius was made bishop by Peter, the first Pope. He traveled through Asia Minor and Greece and wrote encouraging letters to those communities. It was Bishop Ignatius who first used the term "catholic" to describe the whole Church. His letters connect us to the early Church.

Ignatius was sentenced to death during the reign of Emperor Trajan. He was taken to the Flavian amphitheater where he was killed by wild lions. Of his impending death as a martyr, he wrote to the disciples in Rome: "Permit me to imitate my suffering God . . . I am God's wheat and I shall be ground by the teeth of beasts, that I may become the pure bread of Christ."

Adapted from Catholic Encyclopedia

Saint Thérèse of Lisieux (1873–1897)

Saint Thérèse was born at Alençon, France. After her mother's death the family moved to Lisieux. She wanted to enter the contemplative life, as her sisters had already done, but could not because of her young age. While visiting Italy, she and other pilgrims were granted an audience with Pope Leo XIII. After she asked the Pope if she could enter the convent at the age of fifteen, she was permitted to do so. Her health gradually declined. She accepted her infirmity with patience up to the moment of her death at age twenty-four. She was canonized by Pope Pius XI in 1925 and named universal patron of the missions, along with Saint Francis Xavier.

Pope John Paul II named Saint Thérèse Doctor of the Church in 1997 because of the soundness of her spiritual wisdom and teaching.

Adapted from the Vatican website

GLOSSARY

A

active religious prayerful and devout religious sisters and brothers who usually live in community and work among the people; their practice of spirituality is appropriate for their calling and true to the spirit of their founders (p. 209)

actualization taking something that was once potential and putting it into action or making it actually happen (p. 94)

almsgiving money or goods given to the poor out of love (p. 123)

Assumption the teaching affirming that at the end of her life, Mary was taken up, body and soul, into Heaven (p. 190)

B

beatific vision being completely and totally in the divine presence and seeing the face of God (p. 215)

Beatitudes the teachings of Jesus in the Sermon on the Mount, addressing how to respond to the desire for happiness that God has given each of us (p. 148)

begotten the eternal relationship between Jesus and God the Father, meaning Jesus is the only Son of God and he is God himself. The Father generates, the Son is begotten, and the Holy Spirit proceeds (see CCC, 254). (p. 69)

C

Christ from the Greek translation of the Hebrew "messiah," which means "the anointed one"; name proper to Jesus, who is priest, prophet, and King (p. 35)

Christian anthropology the study and understanding of what it means to be human in relationship to God (p. 126)

Christian disciples those who hear the Gospel message of Jesus, accept it, and live their lives according to it (p. 17)

Christology the branch of theology devoted to the study of Christ (p. 70)

cloistered set apart or shut off from others as in a convent or monastery (p. 209)

communion our calling to share in the life of the Trinity, the inseparable divine Persons who each does what is proper to him (see CCC, 265, 267) (p. 37)

Communion of Saints those united with Christ, both living and dead, on the Earth, in Purgatory, and in Heaven; also refers to the holy things, such as Sacraments (especially the Eucharist), that unite the Church and the community of holy people (p. 181)

Constitution on the Sacred Liturgy first major official document of the Second Vatican Council, which set principles for liturgical reform (p. 17)

consubstantial with the Father, the Son is one and the same God (p. 67)

contemplative religious hermits, monks, and nuns who set themselves apart from the world, living cloistered lives of prayer and devotion (p. 209)

conversion the lifelong process guided by the Holy Spirit involving a fundamental reorientation of life toward God and away from sin (p. 123)

convocation an assembly of people who have been called together from various places (p. 35)

covenant a solemn agreement between human beings or between God and his People involving mutual commitments or guarantees (p. 144)

creation the act by which God alone, from nothing, brought into being all that exists outside of himself freely, directly, and without any help (p. 115)

D

detachment an attitude of spiritual freedom, which allows one to use material goods without becoming enslaved by them (p. 149)

discernment process—through prayer, study, Scripture reflections, and discussions—of determining what God is calling us to do, both in a specific circumstance as well as in the big picture of our lives (p. 143)

disciple someone who studies and follows the teachings of a master (p. 7)

disordered affections the emotions and passions of the heart which are not directed toward their proper objects (p. 118)

domestic church the experience of learning and growing in faith, prayer, and virtues within one's family, particularly through prayer, love, and forgiveness (see CCC 1657) (p. 208)

E

ecumenical dialogue conversations between different Christian denominations, working toward Christian unity (p. 185)

ecumenism the desire to restore the unity of Christians throughout the world, which is a gift from Christ to the Church (p. 185)

the elect God's chosen ones who persevere in faith and enter into glory with Christ in Heaven (p. 216)

Emmanuel a name given to Jesus, which means "God is with us" (p. 35)

eschatology literally means the study of "last," and refers to the part of theology that studies topics related to the end of time: death, judgment, resurrection of the body, Heaven, Purgatory, and Hell, the coming of Jesus on the last day, etc. (p. 215)

evangelize to share the Good News of Christ and the experience of Christ and his Gospel in the things we say and do (p. 169)

F

faith a theological virtue through which we believe in God and all that he has revealed (p. 5)

final judgment the judgment of the hearts and works of all people and the definitive triumph of good over evil at the end of time. At the time, the material world will be transformed and Christ's Kingdom of justice and peace will be fully established (p. 216)

the fullness of time a time fixed by God in which divine prophecies about the Messiah's coming on Earth are fulfilled (p. 70)

G

Gentiles members of "the nations," that is, anyone not belonging to the Jewish community (p. 104)

Golden Rule in everything, do to others what you would have them do to you (p. 146)

grace our participation in the life of God and his free help that allows us to respond to his call to become his children (p. 118)

Great Commission the final command Jesus gave to all of his followers, to spread the Good News of God's plan for salvation to the whole world (p. 169)

H

Heaven the state of supreme happiness for those who have died in God's grace and friendship; being united forever with God the Father, Son, and Holy Spirit, the Virgin Mary, the angels, and the just after death (p. 215)

Hell the state of eternal separation from God after death, through the free choice to reject God's offer of forgiveness and Redemption (p. 215)

hierarchy the Apostles and their successors, the bishops, to whom Christ gave the authority to teach, sanctify, and govern the Church (p. 174)

holiness the perfection of charity (p. 125)

human dignity because we are created by God, in the image and likeness of God, each person has a specialness or integrity (p. 24)

hypocrite person who says one thing, but does another; person guilty of spiritual pride, particularly a person who does the right thing for the wrong reasons (p. 202)

hypostatic union in Christology, the union of the divine and human natures in the one divine Person of the Son of God, Jesus Christ (p. 99)

I

"I am" statements direct statements by Jesus in the Gospel according to John concerning who he is (p. 200)

Immaculate Conception from the moment of her own conception and by grace from God and the virtue of the merits of Jesus Christ, Mary was preserved from Original Sin (p. 188)

Incarnation the fact that the Son of God assumed human nature and became man in order to accomplish our salvation in that same human nature (see CCC, 461) (p. 39)

intercession or **intercessory prayer** praying to God on behalf of or for the needs of someone else (p. 183)

J

justification God's gracious action that "[cleanses] us from our sins and communicates to us 'the righteousness of God through faith in Jesus Christ' (Romans 3:22)" (CCC, 1987) (p. 122)

K

Kingdom of God also called the reign or rule of God, or the Kingdom of Heaven, it is the state of righteousness and joy in the Holy Spirit that the ministry of Jesus announced and inaugurated and which is mysteriously present in the Church today, most especially in the Eucharist (p. 148)

L

laity or **lay persons** refers to all members of the Church who are not ordained as bishops, priests, or deacons (p. 174)

Law of the Gospel also called the New Law, it is summarized in Jesus' New Commandment to "love one another as I have loved you" (John 15:12) (p. 146)

logos a Greek term meaning "word"; in Christian theology, it refers to the Second Person of the Blessed Trinity (p. 33)

the Lord's Prayer the quintessential prayer of Christians given by Jesus to his followers (also called the "Our Father") (p. 204)

M

mediator one who serves as intermediary, to intercede and/or reconcile differences (p. 7)

merit the reward which God promises and gives to those who love him, and who by his grace perform good works (see CCC, 2008) (p. 181)

messiah a Hebrew word meaning "anointed" (p. 34)

missionary mandate the command to the whole Church to further the mission of Jesus Christ, including spreading the Good News in word and deed, loving one another, and working for peace and justice as we participate in bringing about the Kingdom of God (p. 170)

Mosaic Law the Law, most importantly the Ten Commandments, that God gave to Moses on Mount Sinai to guide the lives of the Israelites (p. 144)

mystical Body of Christ the Church, united with Christ (p. 172)

N

natural law God's fatherly instruction that is written on the human heart and accessed by human reason (p. 145)

O

obedience Jesus' compliance with God the Father's plan for salvation (p. 90)

original justice the harmony inside the human person, between a man and woman and between the first humans and all creation (p. 34)

P

parables allegorical stories with hidden truths or meanings that question commonly held perspectives and were used by Jesus to provide insights into the Kingdom of God (p. 89)

particular judgment the judgment of each individual at the moment of death by Christ that determines the immediate entrance of the soul into Heaven, Purgatory, or Hell (p. 128)

Paschal Mystery Christ's work of Redemption accomplished through his Passion, death, Resurrection, and Ascension (p. 133)

perseverance steadfastness, holding to a course of action without giving way (p. 202)

Pharisees leaders and teachers of Jewish faithful who held on to the Torah as the source of their understanding of faith (p. 213)

pneumatology the branch of theology devoted to the study of the Holy Spirit (p. 73)

prayer the raising of one's mind and heart to God, in which we enter into a conscious, loving communion (p. 199)

procession a theological term for how the Spirit proceeds from the Father and the Son as from a single principle (p. 72)

public ministry the approximately three years following his baptism in which Jesus publicly preached the Good News of salvation (p. 89)

Purgatory a purification after death that prepares the soul to enter into Heaven (p. 215)

R

Redemption Christ's work in freeing us from the domination of evil and sin (p. 118)

religion a set of beliefs and practices followed by those who serve and worship God (p. 24)

S

Sacrament of Holy Orders the Sacrament in which only a baptized man, found by the Church to be suitable for the ministry is ordained as a deacon, priest, or bishop who continues the mission that Christ gave to the Apostles (p. 178)

Sadducees the priestly class/aristocracy; closely linked to leadership of the Temple; known for being conservative and taking a strict, literal interpretation of Scripture (p. 213)

salvation God's gift of forgiveness of sins and the restoration of friendship with God (p. 119)

salvation history the scriptural account of how God over many centuries prepared to heal the separation between God and his People (p. 34)

sanctification the work of the Holy Spirit to make human individuals holy with our cooperation (p. 122)

sanctify to bring people to holiness through the Sacraments; this begins with Christ sending the sanctifying Holy Spirit to Church members who respond to God's grace (p. 174)

Sermon on the Mount the summary of key teachings of Jesus found in the Gospel according to Matthew (p. 146)

signs in a broad sense, actions or events that convey meaning by pointing to something other than themselves (p. 94)

solidarity union of interests, sympathies, and responsibilities (p. 40)

solitude the condition of being alone; in the spiritual life, separation from human company or being busy in order to be wholly present to and attentive to the mystery of God (p. 202)

Son of God In the Gospel, the term signifies the unique relationship of Jesus to the Father (p. 33)

Son of Man a title recorded in Scripture that Jesus uses to describe himself (p. 35)

soul the spiritual principle of a human person; each human soul is individual and immortal, and created by God immediately (p. 128)

steward someone who takes on the responsibility God gave humans to take care of the Earth and everything in it (p. 128)

T

theology the study of God, based on divine Revelation (p. 64)

Trinity the mystery of one God in three divine Persons: Father, Son, and Holy Spirit; this is the central mystery of the Christian faith and life (p. 37)

Triune God One God in three Persons with God the Father, Jesus the Son, and the Holy Spirit (p. 53)

U

unity the members of the Church are united under the Pope and bishops, profess the same faith, and join in common worship (p. 183)

W

witnesses sharers of the truth that we have come to know about Christ, and offer evidence of this truth in our own lives (p. 169)

INDEX

Page numbers in boldface indicate where the term is first defined in the text.

A

Abba 64
Abraham 6, 34, 76, 148, 200
actualization **94**, 244
Adam and Eve 34
almsgiving **123**, 244
Alpha and Omega 38, 135, 150
Annunciation 51, 191
Apocalypse Tapestry 218
Apostle Paul 104
Apostle Philip 107
Apostles 16, 44, 89, 169, 174, 178, 180
   proclaim faith 170
Arians 69
Ascension 99, 119, 133, 170, 178, 191
Assumption **190**, 191, 244

B

Baptism
   candle 133
   Sacrament of 133
   symbols 133
Bartimaeus 14
beatific vision **215**, 216, 244
Beatitudes 6, 145, 146, **148**, 149, 244
begotten 67, **69**, 244
beliefs 7, 9, 107, 126, 215
Boulding, Maria 39
boy with a spirit 14

C

Câmara, Dom Hélder Pessoa 176, 177
Cantalamessa, Father Raniero 90
Catholic Charities 105
Catholic Tradition 33, 115, 116, 122, 178, 183, 215, 216
Catholic Volunteers in Florida 158
Cavalletti, Sofia 160, 161
Christ **35**, 37, 40, 50, 67, 89, 107, 133, 180, 185, 190, 218, 219, 244
   believing in 7, 169
   Communion of Saints **181**, 209
   disciple of 125
   divine nature 40
   example of 123
   final judgment 215
   Holy Spirit 37, 174
   human nature 40, 90, 99, 102
   judge living and dead 216
   Kingdom 217
   light of 133
   Lord's Prayer 206
   message 174
   mission 174
   missionary mandate 170
   Mystical Body of 172
   One in 183
   people of 35
   prayer directed to 212
   redeemed in 122
   relationship with God 126
   relationship with us 126
   Resurrection 16, 37, 72, 80, 96, 115, 119, 125, 133, 134, 169, 178, 190, 191, 213, 215
   reveals our faith 75
   Sacraments 73
   study of 70
   transformed death 213
   Trinity 53
   united in 183
Christian anthropology **126**, 244
Christian disciples **17**, 244
Christology **70**, 244
Ciszek, Father Walter, SJ 22, 23
cloistered **209**, 244
communion **37**, 52, 181, 206, 216, 244
Communion of Saints **181**, 188, 209, 244
Constitution on the Sacred Liturgy **17**, 244
consubstantial **67**, 71, 244
conversion 89, **123**, 149, 244
convocation **35**, 37, 172, 244
Corinth 116
covenant 7, 34, **144**, 244
creation 34, 61, 62, 71, 76, **115**, 116, 118, 128, 133, 157, 244

D

Day, Dorothy 8
detachment **149**, 155, 244
Diego, Juan 189
discernment **143**, 144, 244
disciple(s) **7**, 17, 20, 244
   community of 35, 40, 128, 159, 172
   Mary 190
   respond to Jesus' call 104
Discipleship 7, 20
   and faith 17
disordered affections **118**, 244
divine nature 40, 69, 70, 99, 148
   of Christ 40
dogma 67

domestic church **208**, 244

Donne, John 126

E

ecumenism **183**, 244

elect, the **216**, 244

Emmanuel **35**, 244

eschatology **216**, 244

eternal life 7, 70, 76, 122, 123, 134, 148, 152, 153, 207

Eucharist 16, 35, 38, 156, 172, 174, 181

evangelization 18, 174

evangelize **169**, 244

F

faith **5**, 6, 10, 13, 14, 40, 51, 99, 118, 122, 133, 172, 178, 183, 209, 244

 and deeds 215, 216

 and discipleship 17, 20

 and freedom 24

 and religion 25

 Catholic 191

 challenges 20

 Christian 73

 growing in 7

 head, heart, and hands 9

 Jewish 188, 215

 Job 77

 Mary 190

 relationship with Jesus 16, 17

 religious 7

 response to evil 76

final judgment 128, 206, 207, **216**, 244

Frank, Anne 126

fullness of time **70**, 245

G

Genocide 77

Gentile 107, 245

Gnostics 69

God

 attributes of 51

 creator of Heaven and Earth 62

 face of 216

 revealed in Christ 201

 Spirit of 71

 the Father 62, 64, 66, 67, 69, 150, 204

 the Son 67, 69

Golden Rule **146**, 152, 245

Grace **118**, 245

Great Commission **169**, 245

H

Health Care 11

Heaven 128, 181, 190, **215**, 216, 217, 218, 245

 and Earth 118

 ascend 169

 Ascension 99, 170, 191

 saints 181

Hell 128, **215**, 216, 245

hierarchy **174**, 178, 245

holiness **125**, 245

Holy Spirit 6, 7, 9, 17, 19, 24, 33, 37, 38, 50, 51, 61, 62, 64, 67, 69, 70, 71, 72, 73, 107, 118, 122, 123, 129, 133, 146, 147, 150, 169, 170, 172, 174, 178, 180, 183, 190, 208, 209, 210, 211, 213

 Divine Person 50

 guides us 180

 ministry of Jesus 72

 mission 72

 Nicene Creed 72

 theology 72

human condition 118

human dignity **24**, 40, 128, 150, 245

human nature

 desire for happiness 157

human solidarity 126

hypocrite **203**, 245

hypostatic union **99**, 245

I

"I am" statements 200, **201**, 245

Immaculate Conception **188**, 190, 245

Immersion 133

Incarnation **39**, 40, 69, 245

 mystery of 39, 98

Infancy Narratives 188

intercessory prayer **183**, 245

J

Jesus

 and Mary 191, 192

 believing in 7

 disciple of 17, 19, 107

 face of 92, 157

 followers of 20, 24, 169, 170, 181

 gestures 94

 Good Shepherd 157

 human nature 90

 miracles 94

 New Commandment 145, 146, 147

 of Nazareth 87, 94

 silences 94

 Son of Mary 39, 40, 70

story of 33
Job 77, 80
John the Baptist 39, 92, 200, 204
Jordan River 39
justification **122**, 123, 245

K

Kempis, Thomas á, Father 87, 95, 237
Kingdom of God 17, 38, 73, 88, 89, 92, 143, **148**, 149, 150, 155, 159, 169, 170, 204, 206, 213, 217, 245
        how to enter 153, 155, 156

L

laity **174**, 245
Law in the Old Testament *See* Moses, Law of
Law of the Gospel **146**, 147, 159, 245
laying on of hands 178
Lazarus 90
Lent 122, 123
Lenten disciplines 123
Lewis, C.S. 73, 76, 80, 206
Litany of the Saints 182
logos **33**, 245
Lord's Prayer 64, **204**, 206, 207, 217, 245
Lydia 107

M

Martha 90
Mary 7, 90
        and Jesus 191, 192
        and Joseph 39
        Assumption 190
        disciple 190, 191, 192
        intercedes with God 181, 190
        life of 191
        Magnificat 191
        Mother of God 188, 190, 191
        Mother of Jesus 89, 188
        Mother of the Church 190
        seven characteristics of 190
        Virgin 33, 35, 39, 51, 69, 188
McBride, Alfred 48
McGinnis, James 46, 47
Mead, Sister Janet 204
mediator **7**, 64, 70, 245
merit **181**, 245
Merton, Thomas 119
Messiah **34**, 35, 37, 40, 72, 98, 170, 200
missionary mandate **170**, 245
Monophysites 69
Mosaic Law **144**, 245

Moses 6, 34, 133, 144, 145, 199, 200, 201
        Law of 144, 145, 146, 147, 149, 153
Muglia, Chris 61
mystery of faith 50, 199
mystical Body of Christ **172**, 245

N

National Migration Week 65
Nazareth 88
Nestorians 69
Nicene Creed 67, 72
Noah 6, 34, 76, 133
Nouwen, Henri J. M. 202
Novena 210

O

O'Connor, Flannery 130, 131
original justice **34**, 245
Original Sin 34, 77, 118, 122, 187, 191
Our Father *See* Lord's Prayer
Our Lady of Guadalupe 189

P

parable 19, **89**, 90, 155, 245
Paraclete 51
particular judgment **128**, 215, 216, 218, 245
Pascal, Blaise 129
Paschal Candle 133, 135
Paschal Mystery **133**, 246
patron saints 184
Pentecost 37, 190
perseverance **202**, 203, 246
Pharisees 90, **213**, 215, 246
pneumatology **73**, 246
Pope Benedict XVI 21, 65, 127, 170
Pope John XXIII 11
Pope John Paul II 52, 126, 128, 174, 189, 206
Pope Leo XIII 210
Pope Paul VI 18
Pope Pius IX 188
poverty 45, 179
prayer 9, 16, 123, 183, 190, **199**, 202, 203, 204, 209, 212, 246
        commitment 181
        consecratory 178
        Job 80
        Mary 190
        Mass 208, 209
        sincere 211
procession **72**, 246
public ministry **89**, 246
Purgatory 128, 181, **215**, 216, 246

Q

quintessential prayer *See* Lord's Prayer

R

Racism 68
Redemption 40, **118**, 122, 123, 133, 134, 190, 246
religion and faith 24, 25
Revelation 7, 72, 96, 128, 178
Ritger, Kate E. 213
Rose, Danielle 50
Ruah 71
Rubleu, Andrei 63

S

Sacrament of Baptism 133
Sacrament of Holy Orders **178**, 246
Sacrament of Penance 123
Sacrament of the Eucharist 181
Sacraments 9, 16, 64, 73, 122, 133, 174, 181
Sacraments of Initiation 133
Sadducees **213**, 215, 246
Saint Anne 240
Saint Anselm 188, 240
Saint Augustine 119, 211, 239
Saint Clare of Assisi 239
Saint Francis of Assisi 91, 155, 238
Saint Francis Xavier 242
Saint George 241
Saint Ignatius of Antioch 214, 243
Saint Ignatius of Loyola 238
Saint Irenaeus of Lyons 115, 238
Saint James the Greater 242
Saint Jerome 239
Saint Joan of Arc 178, 239, 240
Saint Joseph 240
Saint Michael the Archangel 241
Saint Olaf 242
Saint Patrick 242
Saint Paul 7, 80, 155, 216, 237
Saint Rose of Lima 241, 242
Saint Teresa of Ávila 144, 237
Saint Thérèse of Lisieux 208, 243
Saint Thomas Aquinas 51, 237
Saint Thomas More 95, 238
salvation 37, 50, 51, 92, **119**, 133, 169, 170, 246
salvation history **34**, 35, 38, 76, 200, 246
sanctification **122**, 123, 246

sanctify **174**, 246
Septuagint 215
Sermon on the Mount **146**, 147, 246
sign 37, **94**, 98, 181, 246
sin result of evil 76, 77
solidarity **40**, 97, 246
solitude **202**, 209, 246
Son of God **33**, 37, 51, 67, 69, 70, 99, 102, 188, 192, 246
Son of Man **35**, 246
soul 104, 128, 129, 145, 190, 219, 246
        judgment 216
stained glass 36
steward **128**, 246
Synoptic Gospels 153

T

Ten Commandments 144, 145, 146
theology **64**, 246
        Holy Spirit 72
Torah 213
Tradition *See* Catholic Tradition
        apostolic 178
        of the Church 53
Transfiguration 51
Trinity **37**, 51, 58, 59, 62, 64, 69, 70, 71, 118, 180, 246
        Baptism 133
        Blessed 183
        Divine Person 72
        mystery 33
        prayer directed to 212
        revealed 50
        Second Person 99, 190
        three Persons 50, 53, 61, 67, 74, 181, 183, 211
Trinity Monastery 78, 79
Triune God 51, **53**, 61, 62, 133, 212, 214, 216, 246

U

unity 53, 170, 181, **183**, 185

V

Vulgate 215

W

Walker, J. Michael 100, 101
witness 15, 16, 157, **169**, 185, 246
woman with a hemorrhage 10, 13
World Youth Day 21

ENDNOTES

[1] USCCB *Health Care for All*

[2] (CCC, 2840) Cf. I Jn 4:20.

[3] (CCC, 292) St. Irenaeus, Adv. haeres. 2, 30, 9; 4, 20, I: PG 7/1, 822, 1032.

[4] John 8:12.

[5] John xi. 28.

[6] (CCC, 1703) GS 14 § 2.

[7] (CCC, 1703) GS 24 § 3.

[8] (CCC, 491) Pius IX, Ineffabilis Deus (1854): DS 2803.

cover Michael Melford/Getty Images; **title page** Michael Melford/ Getty Images; **iv** Chuck Savage/CORBIS; **v** Marc Dozier/Hemis/ CORBIS; **vii** Barbara Davidson/Dallas Morning News/CORBIS; **viii** Bettmann/CORBIS; **ix** Elizabeth Barakah Hodges/Getty Images; **2-3** Bkgr DAJ/Getty Images; **4 t** Galina Barskaya/Big Stock Photo; **b** John Spink, © 2005 NFCYM; **5** Auslöser/Corbis; **7** Philadelphia Museum of Art/CORBIS; **8** David Young-Wolff/ PhotoEdit; **10** Kristy-Anne Glubish/Design Pics Inc.; **11** Index Stock/FotoSearch; **12** Allen, Willie J. Jr/ZUMA Press/CORBIS; **14** Rubberball Photos/FotoSearch; **16** Richard T. Nowitz/ National Geographic/Getty Images; **17** Pascal Deloche/Godong/ Corbis; **18** Jack Kurtz/The Image Works; **20** James Hardy/ PhotoAlto/Corbis; **21** Getty Images; **22-23 Bkgr** Art Directors & TRIP/Alamy; **23 inset** Bettmann/CORBIS; **26** Image Source/ CORBIS; **27** Ocean/CORBIS; **29** Art Resource, NY; **30-31 Bkgr** John Spink, © 2005 NFCYM; **32 t** Sean White/ DesignPics, **l** Lukasz Kulicki/iStockPhoto; **34 l** DeA Picture Library/Art Resource, NY, **m** The Granger Collection, New York, **r** Atlantide Phototravel/CORBIS; **35 l** Striding lion, Babylon, Neo-Babylonian Period (glazed bricks), Mesopotamian/Museum of Fine Arts, Boston, Massachusetts, USA/Maria Antoinette Evans Fund/The Bridgeman Art Library International, **r** Scala/Art Resource, NY; **36** Jim DeLillo/iStock Photo; **37** Sketch for an Annunciation (oil), Giordano, Luca (1634-1705)/Private Collection/© Agnew's, London, UK/The Bridgeman Art Library; **39** Dave G. Houser/Corbis; **41** David Young-Wolff/PhotoEdit; **46-47 Bkgr** Richard Cummins/CORBIS; **46 inset** The Institute for Peace and Justice; **48** Ocean/CORBIS; **50** Tatyana Chernyak/Big Stock Photo; **51** Novgorod School/The Bridgeman Art Library/Getty Images; **52** David H. Lewis/iStockphoto; **53** NASA/JPL; **55** Ocean/CORBIS; **57** Brooklyn Museum/Corbis; **58-59 Bkgr** Paul Hutley; Eye Ubiquitous/CORBIS; **60** John Wilkes Studio/Corbis; **61** Frans Lemmens/Corbis; **63** The Holy Trinity, 1420s (tempera on panel) (for copy see 40956), Rublev, Andrei (c.1370-1430)/Tretyakov Gallery, Moscow, Russia/The Bridgeman Art Library; **65** AFP/Getty Images; **67** Smithsonian American Art Museum, Washington, DC/Art Resource, NY; **68** Ron Haviv/VII/AP Images; **71** John and Lisa Merrill/Corbis; **72** James Shaffer/PhotoEdit; **73** Scott Gilbert/ Getty Images; **77** JASON REED/Reuters/CORBIS; **78-79 Bkgr** Jon Burbank/The Image Works; **79 inset** Jon Burbank/The Image Works; **81** Ocean/CORBIS; **83** Altar frontal depicting the Trinity between St. Sebald and Archangel Michael, from Nuremberg, c.1410-20 (textile), German School, (15th century)/Germanisches Nationalmuseum, Nuremberg (Nuernberg), Germany/The Bridgeman Art Library; **84-85 Bkgr** Chuck Savage/CORBIS; **86 l** John Spink, © 2005 NFCYM, **r** Getty Images; **87** Getty Images; **88** © NASA/courtesy of nasaimages.org, **91** Bob Daemmrich/PhotoEdit; **97** Angela Hampton Picture Library/Alamy; **98** Burke/Triolo Productions/ Brand X/Corbis; **99** Blend Images/FotoSearch; **100-101 Bkgr** courtesy of J. Michael Walker; **100 inset** Annie Wells; **104** Pete Leonard/Corbis; **105** Getty Images; **106** iChip/ BigStock; **109** Ocean/CORBIS; **112-113 Bkgr** Patrik Giardino/ CORBIS; **114 l** Design Pics/FotoSearch, **r** Chris Bernard Photography/iStockphoto; **115** Sébastien Désarmaux/Godong/ Corbis; **116** © NASA/courtesy of nasaimages.org; **117** Jed Share and Kaoru/Corbis; **120** Robert Michael/Corbis; **123 l and r** Bildarchiv Preussischer Kulturbesitz/Art Resource, NY; **124** MUSA AL-SHAER/AFP/Getty Images; **127** Marco Simoni/Getty Images; **130-131 Bkgr** G2019/shutterstock; **131 inset** AP Images; **133** Exodus, 1999 (oil on canvas), Mcbee, Richard (b.1947) (Contemporary Artist)/Private Collection/The Bridgeman Art Library; **134** John Spink, © 2005 NFCYM; **135** MUSA AL-SHAER/AFP/Getty Images; **137** Ocean/ CORBIS; **139** Judy McPhail/Big Stock Photo; **140-141 Bkgr** SHOGORO/Getty Images; **142 l** Eric Audras/ PhotoAlto/Corbis, **r** Patrik Giardino/Corbis; **143** Bettmann/ CORBIS; **147** Annie Griffiths Belt/CORBIS; **148** Blair Kasfeldt/ Big Stock Photo; **149** Jupiterimages/Getty Images; **151** Bill Wittman; **155 t** Terry Wilson/iStockphoto, **b** Ronald Wittek/Getty Images; **157** Stock Connection Photos/fotosearch; **158** Catholic Volunteers in Florida; **160-161 Bkgr** John Giustina/CORBIS; **161** inset Douglas R. Gilbert; **163** Ocean/CORBIS; **165** Michael McGrath; **166–167** Barbara Davidson/Dallas Morning News/ CORBIS; **168 t** James Steidl/shutterstock; **168 b** Fred de Noyelle/Godong/Corbis; **170** Bill Wittman; **171** Bill Wittman; **172** Neustockimages/iStockphoto; **174** Oscar C. Williams/ shutterstock; **176–177 bkgr** Hervé Collart/Sygma/Corbis; **176 inset** Gianni Giansanti/Sygma/Corbis; **179** Sean Warren/ iStockphoto; **180** Bill Wittman; **181** FotoSearch; **182** Elizabeth Barakah Hodges/Getty Images; **184** Alan Oddie/PhotoEdit; **188** memo/fotolia; **189** Bill Wittman; **191** JOHN SPINK/AJC staff; **193** Ocean/CORBIS; **195** Purestock/Getty Images; **196–197** Adam Gryko/shutterstock; **198 t** Steve Crise/CORBIS; **198 b** Bill Wittman; **199** Friberg Fine Art; **203** AP Images; **204** Dave Bradley Photography/Getty Images; **205** Vladimir Godnik/moodboard/CORBIS; **208** Tim Pannell/Corbis; **210** AP Images; **212** Bill Wittman; **217** Richard Klotz/Big Stock Photo; **218–219** Marc Dozier/Hemis/Corbis; **220** Alexey Stiop/Big Stock Photo; **221** Ocean/CORBIS; **223** The Ascent of the Blessed, detail from a panel of an altarpiece thought to be of the Last Judgement (oil on panel), Bosch, Hieronymus (c.1450–1516)/Palazzo Ducale, Venice, Italy/Giraudon/The Bridgeman Art Library